Under Protest

April 26, 2010

Dear Steve,

Thanks so much for
all of your support. I
know South Africa is
important to you and hope
you enjoy the book.

Warm regards,

hidden histories series

Under Protest
The Rise of Student Resistance at the University of Fort Hare

Daniel Massey

Series editors:
Johannes du Bruyn,
Nicholas Southey,
Russel Viljoen

hidden histories series

Unisa Press
Pretoria

© 2010 University of South Africa
First edition, first impression

ISBN 978-1-86888-542-8

Published by Unisa Press,
PO BOX 392, Muckleneuk Pretoria,
South Africa

Cover design: Dawid Kahts
Copy-editor: Liz Stewart
Typesetter: Pamset, Johannesburg
Indexer: Tanya Barben
Printed by: Harry's Printers, Pretoria

Contents

Abbreviations and Acronyms

AAC	All African Convention
ANC	African National Congress
APDUSA	African People's Democratic Union of South Africa
ASA	African Students' Association
ASUSA	African Students' Union of South Africa
BPC	Black People's Convention
Fedsem	Federal Theological Seminary
ICU	Industrial and Commercial Workers' Union
IFP	Inkatha Freedom Party
MK	*Umkhonto we Sizwe*
NAD	Native Affairs Department
NEUM	Non-European Unity Movement
NRC	Natives' Representative Council
NUSAS	National Union of South African Students
PAC	Pan Africanist Congress
QVM	Queen Victoria Memorial
Rhodes	Rhodes University
SABC	South African Broadcasting Corporation
SABRA	Suid-Afrikaanse Buro vir Rasse-Aangeleenthede/South African Bureau for Racial Affairs
SACP	South African Communist Party
SANAC	South African Native Affairs Commission
SANC	South African Native College
SANNC	South African Native National Congress
SASO	South African Students' Organisation
SOYA	Society of Young Africans
SRC	Students' Representative Council
TLSA	Teachers' League of South Africa
UCM	University Christian Movement
UCT	University of Cape Town
UDF	United Democratic Front
UDI	Unilateral Declaration of Independence
UNISA	University of South Africa
Wits	University of the Witwatersrand
YL	(African National Congress) Youth League

Illustrations

All illustrations are reproduced with permission of the stated holding institutions or copyright holders.

Chapter 2

Chapter 3

Chapter 4

Interviewees

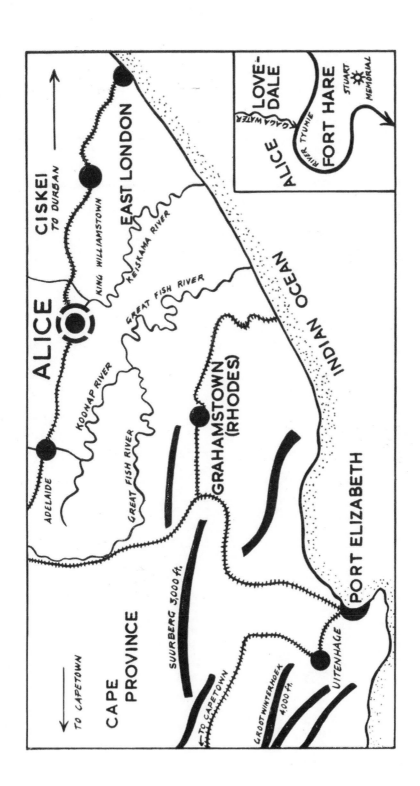

A map from the 1959 Fort Hare calendar

Foreword

During early 1959 I travelled overnight from Durban by the Southampton bound *Edinburgh Castle*, one of the ships that were operated by the Union-Castle Line. I disembarked at its next port of call, East London, in the Eastern Cape. My final destination was Fort Hare, where I would commence studies towards a Bachelor of Science degree. From East London I boarded a train and alighted at a small railway siding called Blaney. From there I took another train bound for Port Elizabeth and got off at Alice railway station. A few kilometres from that railway station was Fort Hare – 'the most historically significant institution for higher education in sub-equatorial Africa'. This was the beginning of a roller-coaster period of three years in my life.

Although I had become politically conscious at the tender age of six, when, with my father, I followed the 1948 surge to power of the National Party (NP) of Dr Malan and the demise of the United Party of General Smuts, and the following year, the tragedy of the anti-Indian riots in Durban and, in 1952, the Defiance Campaign, I had spent the four years, 1955–1958, in the relatively cloistered environment of a Roman Catholic boarding High School at Inkamana in Northern Natal run by German nuns and monks of the Benedictine Order, largely shielded from the debilitating effects of Bantu education and the tumultuous events of the mid-fifties. Fort Hare was an eye opener. The year 1959 was a hectic year in the history of South Africa, in general, and Fort Hare, in particular. Political activity in the country was at fever pitch. The Pan Africanist Congress (PAC) had exploded onto the political scene after Robert Sobukwe and others had broken off from the African National Congress (ANC). The racist regime headed by the National Party had entrenched itself in power with a battery of oppressive measures that found themselves on the statute book masquerading under the guise of laws. The subjugation of, especially the indigenous people of the country was becoming more severe, particularly after the introduction of the devastating Bantu Education in the mid-fifties. Many educators, including my father and my uncle Michael, the musicologist, both of whom, together with their sister Renee, were ex-Fort Harians, had resigned from teaching in protest against Bantu education. Fort Hare became a hive of protest activity as the students and members of faculty tried to avert the inevitable – the impending takeover of the University College by the apartheid regime and its transformation into a tribal ethnic university. Towards the end of the year most of the members of staff had either resigned or been fired. 1960 was the year of Sharpeville and the banning of the ANC and the PAC. It was also the first year of the apartheid Fort Hare when the students became the guinea pigs of lecturers that had recently qualified at Afrikaans universities, some of whom could hardly express themselves in English. 1961 marked the adoption of the armed struggle by *Umkhonto we Sizwe*, the declaration of South Africa as a republic and the knocking of the final nail into the coffin of the old Fort Hare.

Fast-forward to 1999 when I met Daniel Massey, the author of this book. This was forty years after I had first set my foot at Fort Hare. He interviewed my about my recollections of the place and the times. I had been back to Fort Hare only about twice or thrice since I left at the end of 1961. The memories started flooding back – the hostels: Anglican Beda, Methodist Wesley, Presbyterian Iona, with its Philistines, Barbarians and Porcupines, respectively, the Annexe and Elukhanyisweni; the mass meetings at the Christian Union (CU) hall; the evening dance practices (*maswayiswayi*) at the CU with the 'Blue Bottles'; the students – Seretse Choabi, Chris Hani, Stanley Mabizela, Krish Mackerdhuj, Edmie Mali (Manto Tshabalala-Msimang), Klaas Mashishi, Ivy Matsepe (Matsepe-Casaburri), Thami Mhlambiso, Sobhizana Mngqikana, Billy Modise, Peter Mopp, Abie Nkomo, Aubrey 'Madzunya' Nkomo, Zola Ngcakani, Asher Ntanga, Stella Sigcau, 'Doc' Somyalo, Leslie S'khalangaye Xinwa, and faculty, Professors Beard, Davidson, Galloway, Guma, Matthews, Ngcobo and Nyembezi; lecturers, Ms Darroll, Masondo, Phahla, Seretlo and others; the Fort Hare parlance, such as, '*magile*', 'crouching for jaguars at Ntwana Street', being 'hoofed by an Elukanite'. The author promised to write a book covering, *inter alia*, the period 1959–1961, when I studied there.

In October 2008 I again met the author who informed me that he had almost completed writing the book and wished that I write the foreword. He promised to send me the final draft. On reading the proofs of this book I realise that the author has done a masterful job of capturing the essence of the *esprit de corps* of the Fort Hare I knew during those trying times. Fort Hare was not insulated from what was happening in the rest of South Africa at the time. The battles that Mr Massey so ably describes in this book were being fought not only in the little town of Alice but everywhere else in South Africa. The apartheid regime had decided that, in the execution of its grand design of racial separation based on white racial superiority, it would control the education of Africans at primary, secondary and tertiary level in order to equip them for their 'proper role and place' in South African society. The education that they were receiving at missionary schools, in general, and at Fort Hare, in particular, did not adequately prepare them for this role, but fed them with false and dangerous notions of equality with Whites and turned them into Black Englishmen. Fort Hare, which had become a 'microcosm of non-racial society in the heart of apartheid South Africa' over a period spanning more than forty years, had to fit into the Bantustan scheme and become an ethnic university – a contradiction in terms!

Mr Massey has done an excellent job in chronicling the birth, life and death of Fort Hare. I believe that *Under Protest* should be compulsory reading for anyone wishing to understand the history, during the first half of the twentieth century, of the premiere educational institution south of the Equator, in the context of the South African struggle for political liberation and economic emancipation. Fort Hare was not only the womb that incubated the giants of the South African liberation struggle, such as Govan Mbeki, Oliver Tambo, Nelson Mandela and Robert Sobukwe, but was also the crucible that fashioned leaders in all fields of human endeavour in South Africa itself and other Southern African Development Community countries and Kenya and Uganda. Mr Massey has made a valuable contribution to the ever-burgeoning output of literature dealing with a crucial era in the history of South Africa. He has skilfully made use of the oral tradition to which many Africans are accustomed to accumulate and assemble his material in an easily readable format. The use of contemporaneous photographs enhances the narration and, for one who lived through the destruction of Fort Hare, it is difficult not to succumb to a feeling of nostalgia. The 'kid from the Bronx, New York' deserves a pat on his back for a job well done.

Adv Marumo Moerane SC
Durban
South Africa
4th May 2009

Acknowledgements

The recollections of 34 Fort Harians form the heart of this book, and I am indebted to all of my interviewees for their time, hospitality and, most of all, their memories. Many of the interviewees would often ask how a kid from the Bronx, New York, ended up studying the history of Fort Hare; the answer is complicated and involves a long list of people and organisations.

InterStudy first encouraged me to attend Fort Hare in 1997. Brown University's Arnold Fellowship funded my return trip, giving me the opportunity to spend a year steeping myself in the history of Fort Hare. Anani Dzidzieyno would not allow me to consider a job offer at the National Broadcasting Company when South Africa beckoned. Michael Harper taught me to keep score. Newell Stultz introduced me to Tom Karis, whose enthusiasm about the project got me started, and kept me going when doubts crept in. Tom introduced me to Gail Gerhart, who, with similar eagerness, edited the entire manuscript and pushed me towards finishing.

At Fort Hare, a host of individuals helped in many ways. They include: Noel Knickelbein, Bavusile Maaba, Sandisiwe Majikija, Mosoabuli Maamoe, Mncedi Mgwigwi, Wabsie Mntambo, Nothemba Mrwetyana, Mbulelo Mzamane, Alan Shaw, Mark Snyder and Dr Mvuyo Tom. Courses taught by Tim Stapleton and John Hendricks provided me with the background in South African history crucial to the execution of this project. At Rhodes University's Cory Library, Victor Gacula, Shirley Kabwato and Sally Schramm helped facilitate photo research.

A special thanks to Herby Govinden, Rama Thumbadoo, Isaac Mabindisa, Jiyana Maqubela, Pulane Ngcakani, Yolisa Soul, Makhenkesi and Nambita Stofile and Terence Beard, who shared personal photographs. Lulu Callinicos graciously provided photos of Oliver Tambo and information on his time at Fort Hare. I'm grateful to Raymond Suttner and to UNISA Press for recognising the importance of bringing Fort Hare's hidden history to light. Thanks especially to my editor, Nicholas Southey; to Elizabeth le Roux, Hetta Pieterse, Charl Schutte, Elna Harmse, Lindsey Morton, Arnika Ejsmund and Dawid Kahts; and also to Elizabeth Stewart for her thoughtful and precise copy editing. I am also very grateful to Marumo Moerane for writing the preface to this book, and to Dr Mvuyo Tom for his afterword.

Seán Morrow first gave me the idea of converting my research into an MA thesis. His friendship, patience, insight and passion have been invaluable. Thanks also to Barbara Morrow for her friendship and interest in my project. Sadie Forman was a most unlikely 'classmate', but how lucky I was to learn both with and from her. Yolisa Soul welcomed me into her family and home. She never complained when I came knocking on her door at three in the morning to watch my beloved Knicks fight for a National Basketball Association championship. Her daughter Thabi and nieces Dindi and Natalia treated me like a brother.

Other friends helped make South Africa a place to which I will always return. Amanda Giyose gave me unconditional friendship and a god-daughter, Dinilethu. Soccer matches, political chats and *tsotsitaal* lessons with Mzuphela Maseti will always be cherished. The Taus – Motena, Mosa and Mathe – made their homes in Lesotho and King William's Town my homes. Terri Barnes and John Pape cared for me during Cape Town research trips. Their sons, Lewis and Lonnie, provided me with welcome breaks from work in the form of backyard cricket matches. Tembinkosi Bonakele taught me the ins and outs of South African politics and how to *toyi toyi*. Siphiwo Mahala kept me company on long road trips to Durban and the Transkei, and treated my project as if it were his. His sisters Noncgi and Nompiwo welcomed me into their home and hearts.

Special thanks to the Fachers, the Gribbens, the Nelsons, the Rubens, Colin Bundy, Malinda Campbell, Simbarashe Chanduru and family, John D'Aponte, Lisa Giaffo, Grannie, Lili Grossman, Nomsa Hani, Moira Herbst, Adrianna Hernandez-Stewart, Sean Jacobs, Peter Kallaway, Chikako Kobayashi, Lewis Manthata, Liana Maris, Ellen Massey, Jen Mazer, Sierra Stoneman-Bell and Bob Windrem.

But all that does not explain how I got to South Africa in the first place. I owe that to my family, who instilled in me a sense of humanity that made South Africa a place I simply had to visit. Thanks, Mom, Dad, Billy, Alicia, Bessie, Bonnie and Javi for being my biggest supporters.

Introduction

Can you separate the history of South Africa
from what took place around Fort Hare?
Govan Mbeki

In May 2002, Minister of Education Kader Asmal announced a restructuring of South Africa's higher education system. The sweeping changes – which involved streamlining a bloated university system created by the architects of apartheid to promote separate development – were designed to redress past inequality, promote growth in student numbers and establish institutions better able to meet job market demands. Asmal's plan followed years of extensive debate over the future of Fort Hare and other historically disadvantaged universities. With apartheid dead, was it time to dismantle the institutions the government had concocted to entrench its power?

The future of the University of Fort Hare appeared bleak. Rumours circulated that nearby Rhodes University would swallow it up. Yet in the end, while Asmal called for many of the historically disadvantaged universities to merge with other institutions, he left Fort Hare alone. 'The University of Fort Hare, which has come to symbolise our history of struggle, will be retained,' said Asmal in an Education Ministry release.[1] Fort Hare's own website attributed the university's continued existence to the vital role it had played in educating leaders of the fight for majority rule in South Africa.[2]

In 1997, while a junior at Brown University in Providence, Rhode Island, I spent a semester at the University of Fort Hare, in the Eastern Cape town of Alice, and quickly became aware of this history for myself.[3] A university driver fetched me from the airport in nearby East London, and we made the one and a half hour drive inland. After dodging goats and cows on the narrow road between King William's Town and Alice, and trying unsuccessfully to

1

acclimate myself to driving on the 'wrong side' of the road, we neared the university. A hill with a stone tower perched on top appeared on our right. The tower, I'd find out, was a memorial to James Stewart, a former principal of Lovedale and one of the missionaries who influenced the founding of Fort Hare.[4] I'd learn that the hill – Sandile's Kop – gained notoriety among students as a place to hold political meetings out of earshot of university authorities.

The historical reference points continued to turn up as we drove beneath a canopy of tree branches and turned onto the campus, where posters of Chris Hani (1959–1961), the former *Umkhonto we Sizwe* (MK) chief of staff and general secretary of the South African Communist Party (SACP), and Oliver Tambo (1940–1943), African National Congress president from 1967–1991, adorned the walls of my Beda hostel room.[5] Over my first few months, I was asked countless times whether I knew of the roles the two Fort Harians had played in the country's history.[6] Scores of students told me that my new home – a modest two-storey red and white building with small single rooms on either side of a railroad hallway – once housed Tambo. Wesley House, which was where Nelson Mandela (1939–1940) once slept, was just down the road, as was a hostel named for Z.K. Matthews, the university's first graduate and a former president of the ANC in the Cape. The library, which housed the ANC archives, was a two-minute walk away. The cultural centre that held the historical documents of the Pan Africanist Congress (PAC) was just down the road.

It did not take long for me to become acutely aware of the prominent role the university had played in the history of the South African liberation movement. Through both formal classroom study and informal social contact with my schoolmates, I began to realise the extent of Fort Hare's impact on the extra-parliamentary political history of South Africa. Eager to understand the Fort Hare experience, I spent parts of 1998 and 1999 travelling through South Africa, interviewing former students. I drove with my friend and research assistant, Siphiwo Mahala, in a battered white Ford Meteor to the rural Transkei to find Ambrose Makiwane (1955–1958), a once-fearsome student leader who went on to become an influential figure in exile. I lost control of the car on a muddy dirt road outside Cala. We spun 360 degrees and severed the tailpipe, but the ensuing fumes didn't prevent us from searching for former Transkei leader Kaiser Matanzima (1935–1939) and his brother George (1942–1945) on the way home. When we finally met them, they were wearing matching black Fort Hare blazers with yellow pinstripes, eager to reminisce, despite their advancing age and deteriorating health. We found Govan Mbeki (1931–1936) in his ANC headquarters office in Port Elizabeth, Mangosuthu

Buthelezi in his Ministry of Home Affairs suite in Cape Town, and in the suburbs of Durban were passed from one Indian student to the next, eager to recall their days at the Fort. I also examined the archives of the university extensively, a significant, previously untapped source of information on Fort Hare.

'There's no way you could have passed through Fort Hare completely unpoliticised,' says Ivy Matsepe-Casaburri (1958–1961).[7] Each year, beginning in 1916, students brought common experiences of growing up in South Africa to a small, tight-knit community in Alice. The town itself, a one-time military outpost on the Tyumie River, did not offer students much in the way of entertainment. Surrounded by hills, in the 1950s it was the epicentre of African education, with at least 80 schools lying within 65 kilometres.[8] When I arrived in 1997, Alice consisted mostly of dirt roads sprouting from an ever-bustling taxi rank, with women sitting under umbrellas, selling bananas, oranges and pears and men barking out destinations in Xhosa. Some of the shops, including the general merchandise store Coopers, had been around during the days of many of my interviewees. Since my first arrival, the roads have been paved and small homes have been built on an abandoned golf course on the outskirts of town, courtesy of the government's Reconstruction and Development Programme (RDP). Alice has grown, but the university, located just over a bridge that spans the Tyumie, with the majestic Amatola mountains as a northern backdrop, remains its core.

Over the years, students arrived in this small town and began to develop a deeper understanding of how the political situation in South Africa affected their lives. As the political consciousness of students crystallised, activism ensued. Joe Matthews (1948–1950), who went on to become the president of the ANC Youth League (YL) shortly after leaving Fort Hare, says,

> It's not just a subjective thing that each individual became political at Fort Hare. The question is why? Why did he become political? And he became political because of what was happening in the country and the world.[9]

Only one choice

Although Thenjiwe Mtintso (1972–1973) arrived during the era of university apartheid in 1972, her story is not unlike those of students who arrived at Fort Hare from the 1930s onwards. She joined the South African Students' Organisation (SASO) while at Fort Hare, the ANC in 1979 and the SACP in 1990. While Mtintso's story is unique, it is symbolic of the Fort Hare experience, as time spent at the university helped the future ANC deputy secretary general better understand her experience of growing up black in South Africa.

Mtintso was born in 1950 in the informal settlement of Shantytown, near Johannesburg. Her mother, Hannah, worked as a nurses' aide, patching uniforms in Baragwanath Hospital. She recalls the abject poverty in which her family lived:

> My earliest memory is just this shack that is full of [17] people. My memory of family is actually asking my mother who exactly is my brother or my sister of the whole lot. There was never enough food. There was never enough sleeping place.

At the age of five, Mtintso's family moved to a one-bedroom apartment in Orlando East, 'an improvement,' she says, 'over the previous [shack] because in the other one there was no bedroom'. Around the age of six or seven, Mtintso's mother sent her to the tiny Transkei town of Mpozolo to live with an aunt. There her aunt was accused of being a witch, and rural poverty and gender oppression added to the urban poverty and racial oppression Mtintso had experienced in Johannesburg. She watched as the family's hut was burnt down when her aunt rejected marriage. 'I thought my mother must have thrown me away,' she says. 'Transkei was worse than anything I had ever experienced.'[10]

Back in Orlando East, Mtintso remembers stealing a shirt from her older sister, Lizzie, to take to boarding school at Clarkebury, in the Transkei. When she returned home, her sister burned the shirt, without saying a word. Months later, after Mtintso told her sister she was embarrassed to bring friends to the house because of the crowded conditions, Lizzie decided it was time to begin her sister's political education.[11] 'She put me down and addressed me on poverty and pride, that as an individual you've got to be proud of what you are,' says Mtintso. 'It does not matter that you are poor. You did not make yourself poor. It's not because of lack of intelligence. And then she started giving me a fuller picture.'[12]

Mtintso began to understand why her aunt's employer, a white woman, lived alone in a house with 12 rooms, while she and her 16 relatives crowded into a single room. She remembers a man named Butshumi, who lived in Orlando when she was a child. He once gave her a copy of Nelson Mandela's *No Easy Walk to Freedom*. As she grew older, memories of Butshumi remained stuck in her mind, especially the time he was arrested for his political activity. She began to understand the forces that conspired to result in his arrest. As a child, Mtintso remembers singing songs in the street during bus strikes: 'We didn't know what they meant, but there was this signal, this sign you had to make with your thumbs up. And I would be amongst the kids who were singing these songs.' Gradually, through her sister's prodding, she began to come to terms with her experiences. 'My sister explained this whole question of race, the relationship between race in South Africa and poverty ... so vividly that I understood.'[13]

At Clarkebury, Mtintso led protests against the poor quality of food and uncomfortable hostel conditions. Eventually, activism prompted her expulsion from the school: 'I went as far as Form 2 and I got kicked out.' Administrators expelled Mtintso in 1966 because they thought she was an agitator. But even though she had assumed a position of leadership among the students, she had yet to mature politically. Mtintso then went on to Morris Isaacson High School, where she again received a lesson because of her poverty.[14] Her sister died and Mtintso was forced to leave school because she could not pay her fees.

She found work in a Johannesburg factory that printed words and designs on ashtrays, glasses and pens. She wanted to save enough money to continue her education. While working, Mtintso took courses at Damelin College and received her matriculation certificate. In 1972, with the aid of two bursaries, she entered Fort Hare. At 23, she was older than most students. She had already begun to understand that being born a black woman in poverty in South Africa meant she 'had no choice in becoming a political activist or not'.[15] Mtintso describes her state of mind on entering Fort Hare:

> Politically there was some relative awareness caused by the environment and the teachings of my sister and the reality of my life ... To me it looked like there was only one choice, to be in some kind of struggle, to change not only my life, but the lives of those around me.[16]

Her arrival coincided with a fierce struggle between the students and the administration over the position of the Students' Representative Council (SRC) on campus. At the same time, Onkgopotse Ramothibi Abraham Tiro, a member of SASO, was expelled from the University of the North at Turfloop for delivering a fiery graduation speech that attacked the system of separate universities. Combining their grievances against the rigid university administration and solidarity with the Turfloop students, the Fort Hare students walked out.

Rec. 6275

Admitted 2/2

THE UNIVERSITY OF FORT HARE
DIE UNIVERSITEIT VAN FORT HARE

APPLICATION FOR ADMISSION TO REPORT FOR REGISTRATION
AANSOEK OM TOELATING OM VIR REGISTRASIE AAN TE MELD

(N.B. This form must be completed by all students who desire to qualify for registration, irrespective of whether a previous application has been made, and irrespective of whether previously registered as a student at Fort Hare.)
(L.W. Hierdie vorm moet voltooi word deur alle studente wat begerig is om vir registrasie te kwalifiseer afgesien daarvan of 'n vorige aansoek ingedien is en afgesien van vorige registrasie as student by Fort Hare.)

THIS FORM MUST BE RETURNED TO THE REGISTRAR NOT LATER THAN 15th JANUARY.
HIERDIE VORM MOET GESTUUR WORD AAN DIE REGISTRATEUR NIE LATER AS 15 JANUARIE NIE.

1. Full name of applicant (in capital letters) ETHEL MTINTSO
   Volle naam van applikant (in hoofletters)
2. Residential address 527 ORLANDO EAST, J.H.B
   Woonadres
3. Date of Birth JOHANNESBURG 7th NOV, 1949
   Geboortedatum
4. Ethnic group to which applicant belongs XHOSA
   Etniese groep waaraan applikant behoort
5. Reference Book Number 4H21216
   Bewysboeknommer
6. Name and address of parent or guardian 527 ORLANDO EAST
   Naam en adres van ouer of voog JOHANNESBURG

7. Station from which journey to University will begin: Railway Station JOHANNESBURG
   Naam van spoorwegstasie waarvan reis na Universiteit onderneem word: Spoorwegstasie:

   Bus Station ORLANDO
   Bushalte
8. Schools attended with dates (new students only) CLARKEBURY HIGH SCHOOL
   Skole bygewoon met datums (alleenlik nuwe studente)

   (1963 — 1967) MORRIS ISAACSON HIGH SCHOOL 1968

9. Religious affiliation ANGLICAN CHURCH
   Kerkverband
10. If not previously registered at a University:
    Indien nie tevore geregistreer nie:
    (i) Name and address of Principal of last school attended MR MATHABATHE
    Naam en adres van Hoof van laaste skool bygewoon

    P.P. MOKWELE, BOX 10, JABAVU.

    (ii) Examination passed (indicate class) NATIONAL SENIOR CERTIFICATE (SECOND)
    Eksamen geslaag (dui aan in watter klas)
    (iii) Whether exempted from Matriculation YES
    Of matrikulasievrystelling behaal is
    (iv) Subjects taken (indicate any distinctions obtained) MATHEMATICS, ENGLISH A,
    Vakke geneem (dui enige onderskeidings aan)

    XHOSA A, AFRIKAANS B, PHYSICAL SCIENCE, HISTORY

11. If previously registered at a University or a College.
    Indien tevore geregistreer aan 'n Universiteit of Kollege
    A.   At what Institution
         By welke inrigting
    B.   (i) Course followed (B.A., B.Sc., etc.)
         Kursus gevolg (B.A., B.Sc., ens.)
         (ii) Subjects passed :
              Vakke geslaag:
              (a) First Year, 19
                  Eerste Jaar, 19

              (b) Second Year, 19
                  Tweede Jaar, 19

              (c) Third Year, 19
                  Derde Jaar, 19

Thenjiwe Mtintso's Fort Hare application

Mtintso explains how she became involved: 'Before I knew what was happening, I was talking. I was asking questions and talking. And for some reason, people were clapping. People were asking, "Who is she?"' Classmates recruited Mtintso to a committee that drafted a memorandum to be presented to the rector, Johannes Marthinus de Wet. When he refused to respond, the students walked out. And gradually, with the maturation of SASO, the students began to realise that there were broader issues to be dealt with. During a strike the following year, which Mtintso says 'completely politicised her', a student got up and said,

> Man, the issue is Bantu Education here. We are busy dealing with somebody who gets expelled, this little bit there, or whether we should have an SRC, but the bigger problem is Bantu Education. Let's address Bantu Education.[17]

Her sister's political lessons nearly 10 years earlier made more sense now. By this time, Mtintso was part of the core of SASO, playing the role of political educator to students around the country that her sister had so expertly assumed towards her years earlier.

Like her stays at Clarkebury and Morris Isaacson, Mtintso's tenure at Fort Hare was brief. She was forced out after the 1973 strike. Yet, although she spent only a year in Alice, it marked the beginning of her political maturation. She says,

> I think the conscientising of myself started with those discussions amongst us SASO activists, just talking about sharing our day-to-day experiences, sharing our lives, who we were, where you come from ... knowing who we are ... I'm saying that my conscientising was mainly from the stories that I was getting from other people, their lives.[18]

Mtintso's path towards political consciousness mirrored that of many Fort Harians. Arrival at Fort Hare, coupled with national political tension, led students to begin to place their personal struggles in context. At various points, the administration, unwittingly, became a goad that spurred action. Though part of an elite few to receive a university education, Fort Hare students were members of a population that bore the brunt of the country's racial policies. The words of Wycliffe Tsotsi (1933–1936), a foundation member of the All African Convention (AAC), who went on to become president of the Non-European Unity Movement (NEUM), are still relevant in discussing Mtintso's time at Fort Hare: 'There was a ferment in the country and the students were part of the population in the country so they were also susceptible to what was going on.'[19] In his article on student politics, Terence Beard, head of the Philosophy and Politics Department at Fort Hare from 1957–1959, writes:

> The community which brought them together … stimulated the articulation of attitudes which had been internalised before coming to Fort Hare and the Fort became a centre for the political socialisation, and in the later years the political mobilisation, of the student body.[20]

As Tsotsi and generations of Fort Hare students to follow came together in Alice, they began to discuss their experiences of growing up black in South Africa, leading to greater understanding and a commitment to fight against the injustices in their everyday lives. And although Fort Hare, under apartheid government control during Mtintso's stay, was far less welcoming to students than it had been in Tsotsi's time, parallel models of political development can be seen through the eyes of other Fort Harians.

Govan Mbeki, the Eastern Cape ANC leader, Nelson Mandela, Oliver Tambo and Chris Hani all cut their political teeth at the Fort. Its former students span a wide spectrum of South African political history, including ex-Labour Party leader Allan Hendrickse (1946–1950), Kaiser and George Matanzima, and Inkatha Freedom Party (IFP) leader Mangosuthu Buthelezi. Former PAC president Robert Mangaliso Sobukwe (1947–1949) also studied at Fort Hare.[21] They each arrived in Alice with varying degrees of political awareness, but their understanding grew during their time at Fort Hare. Beard shows that students were 'united by the single fact of their common identity as members of the dominated groups of the population'.[22] In the case of Mtintso, her experiences with poverty, racism and sexism while growing up prepared her for political development at Fort Hare. She had grown up singing protest songs; when she got to Fort Hare, she learned why.

Christian in spirit, aims and teaching

Yet officials did not create Fort Hare to breed activists. Their motivation was just the opposite. By the 1880s and 1890s, the work of European missionaries was beginning to create a recognisable class of westernised elite Africans. Increasing numbers of Africans were trained as teachers, law agents, magistrates, clerks and missionaries. And many of them could vote because of a non-racial Cape franchise, based on educational qualification and property ownership. Threatened by the burgeoning African voting rolls, the Cape government responded with a series of legal attacks aimed at limiting

Telegramme:
Telegrams :

Spoor:
Rail: Alice.

Verw./Ref.:

Tel. 231.

UNIVERSITEIT VAN FORT HARE,
UNIVERSITY OF FORT HARE,

Privaatsak:
Private Bag: 314,

ALICE, K.P./C.P.

21st September, 1973.

TO ALL STUDENTS OWING FEES *E. T. Mtintso R89,40*

When disturbances began at the University of Fort Hare in August, 1973 all students were warned that failure to attend lectures would render them liable to immediate dismissal from the campus and cancellation of their registration for the year.

No arrangements will be made to enable these students who have been sent down for the rest of the year to write their examinations.

Remission of fees may be granted only in the case of a student who is prevented by illness, or any other reason approved by Council from completing his studies. Council does not approve absence due to the unrest as a valid reason for remission of fees. Students who have been sent down or students whose registration have been cancelled for the year will be responsible for payment of the full outstanding balance for 1973.

Application for admission for 1974 by students who still owe fees for the previous year, will not be considered unless the outstanding amount has been paid in full by 30th November, 1973.

J.M. De WET.

RECTOR.

DJ/ESF

A letter to Thenjiwe Mtintso shows students were expected to pay their fees after the 1973 unrest the number of Africans who could vote. Odendaal writes: 'In theory Africans in the Cape were equal to all others, but in practice white colonialists were "more equal" than they were.'[23]

In 1884, the Registration of Voters Act cut off about 20 000 voters in the Cape by tightening property qualifications. With the incorporation into the Cape in 1894 of the Transkei, which had been home to a large number of mission stations, the government again sought to prevent the formation of a large African voting bloc. In 1892, the Franchise and Ballot Act was passed, raising the property qualifications and introducing a literacy test to determine franchise eligibility. Because of the attack on the non-racial franchise, educated Africans in the Eastern Cape and Transkei adopted a more assertive and radical stance towards the government.[24]

Though they were not overtly militant or anti-colonial, the mission-educated elite began to recognise that they could organise themselves to address their grievances. But missionary leaders viewed any inkling of opposition, even if grounded in a liberal Christian vision of society, with trepidation. Also, greatly influenced by the presence of African American missionaries in the Cape, African independent churches sprang up at a rapid pace, revealing a sense of disillusionment at what had purported to be a Christian society. These churches 'represented an urge for withdrawal from the reality of European conquest and racial discrimination'.[25]

Founded by African Christians seeking freedom from missionary control, the churches began to gain a wide following in the 1890s, marking the beginning of a new political philosophy that ran counter to the traditional Cape liberalism. Eschewing cooperation with sympathetic whites, the African independent churches were forerunners to later Africanist calls for advancement through black unity. The Ethiopian Church was founded in 1892 and the African Methodist Episcopal Church, a black American church that evangelised in South Africa, started up in 1898. Though grounded in religion, the Ethiopian movement had clear political motivations, emphasising that white power should be opposed by black unity.[26]

The missionaries grew fearful that their control over African education would be weakened if a university for blacks were not established in the Cape. In particular they wanted to stem the tide of Africans who were sent by the independent churches to study abroad, worried that they were returning with 'visions of social, economic and political progress for their people, ideals of racial toleration, and expectations of gradual but steadily increasing participation by educated tribesmen in a wider, multi-racial South Africa'.[27]

Similar situations arose elsewhere in colonial Africa later in the century when British support for African universities, previously non-existent, began to grow. It became evident to colonial authorities that it was far more dangerous to British imperial prestige, politically and socially, to deny Africans access to university education than to satisfy their urge to be educated.[28]

The fear of black American notions of equality spreading among educated Africans led to plans to establish an institution of higher learning for blacks in South Africa. In 1878, Principal James Stewart of Lovedale spoke of a 'Native University – Christian in spirit, aims and teaching' evolving from Lovedale, but the idea really gained credence in the peak years of the African exodus to the United States, when it was raised as an issue before the South African Native Affairs Commission (SANAC) of 1903–1905.[29] White anxieties over the growing educational exodus of Africans to America were clearly articulated at the 1903–1905 commission hearings, where missionaries and government authorities testified that American-educated Africans returned to South Africa with 'inappropriate' ideas of equality and freedom.[30] James Henderson, Stewart's successor at Lovedale, testified that Africans who had been sent by separatist churches to colleges in the southern United States would 'bring back with them the attitude of mind towards the Europeans which the former slavery of the States, and the present hostility towards the black race and the lynchings have inculcated'.[31]

It is not surprising that SANAC enthusiastically supported the notion of a college for Africans in the Cape. The commission viewed the college as a means of placating the emerging elite and thus curbing their political aspirations. SANAC generally supported a segregationist policy and was alarmed by the growing political power of the mission-educated elite.

Following SANAC's decision to back an African college, protracted negotiations over the funding, location, and curriculum of the proposed institution began. The plan, known as the Inter-State Native College Scheme, quickly and powerfully overshadowed a more radical programme set forth by the South African Native National Congress (SANNC), which had itself been planning to establish an African college. The SANNC, founded by rivals to John Tengo Jabavu in 1891 in King William's Town, was an outspoken critic of SANAC. H. Isaiah Bud-Mbelle, a leader of Kimberley's Mfengu community and a member of the SANNC, had initially proposed a fund-raising campaign to establish a university for Africans in 1901. The Queen Victoria Memorial (QVM), as it was called, became a major project of the SANNC in the early 1900s, with the ultimate goal of establishing a university for Africans in the Eastern Cape.[32]

The QVM proposal stood in stark contrast to the Inter-State Native College Scheme. While the latter was largely a conservative reaction to the flight of African students to the United States, the QVM plan, like the African independent churches, was a proactive attempt to establish institutions completely independent of white control. Though named in honour of Queen Victoria, the SANNC project represented a break from the previous missionary-dominated educational control. Walter Rubusana, a SANNC leader and proponent of the QVM scheme said:

> I am not an Ethiopian, but I could just as well be one, because the Ethiopian says our nation must help itself, since no white man will lift up the black nation … every nation is uplifted by its educated members. Africa will also be helped by educated Africans who will work hard and give themselves, with their little education, to the nation.[33]

The SANNC was urged to amalgamate its QVM scheme with the new inter-state plan, but refused to abandon the vision of an African university free from white control. While the inter-state plan received support from influential whites and Africans in all the colonies, QVM support was confined mainly to SANNC supporters. Ultimately, the QVM scheme could not keep up with its opponents' organisational skills and resources.[34] The inter-state plan was directed mainly by whites and backed by the Cape government. In contrast to the exclusively black QVM proposal, J. T. Jabavu and Simon P. Gasa were the only Africans on the executive committee board of the scheme.

Delegates to the first Inter-State Native College Convention, December 1905

The inaugural Inter-State Native College Committee, including John Tengu Jabavu (fifth from left) and John Knox Bokwe (kneeling on ground), 1905

Although the QVM scheme never really got off the ground, the debate over the direction of African education delineates the various factions that had begun to emerge in African politics and that would continue to splinter over the years. There were those who sought an integrated society, albeit on colonial terms, and those who preferred to proceed solely on African terms.[35] Led by J. T. Jabavu, the former group opposed the idea of a strong African political organisation. Jabavu envisioned Africans participating with whites, not separate from them, in a single non-racial party, as the ultimate goal. He felt that a strong African group would be seen as a threat to whites and articulate racial distinctions rather than promote non-racialism.[36] Liberal Christian ideas of progress would clash with the Africanist views again in the 1950s, resulting in the formation of the PAC.

Fort Hare was born from the conflict between these divergent views. With a gift of land from the Free Church of Scotland, a grant of 10 000 pounds from the Transkeian Territories General Council and other contributions, the South African Native College opened in Alice on 8 February 1916, after 10 years of planning. Twenty students – 16 African men, two African women and two white men (sons of Lovedale staff members) – arrived in Alice, launching a university that would alter the future of South Africa.

Delegates to the Native College Convention, 1908

Promoters of the Inter-State Native College Scheme, 1908
First row: Rev James Henderson, J.W. Sauer, J.T. Jabavu, A. Cowan
Second row: Rev John Lennox, Sir Philipson Stow, K.A. Hobart Houghton
Third row: Dr Neil MacVicar

Thus, Fort Hare's history is paradoxical and must be viewed in two ways. First, there is a Fort Hare whose roots can be traced to the emergence of a politicised, mission-educated elite in the Cape. The availability of higher education for Africans at Fort Hare was a result of the strides made by the nascent elite in challenging the establishment for equal rights and non-racialism. At the same time, although the fight for Fort Hare represented a triumph for equal access and was a crowning achievement for the emerging elite, its founding must be looked at more critically. What ended up as a missionary school, with the inherent paternalism that comes with such an institution, could have been a revolutionary experiment in African self-development as exemplified by the African independent churches that sprang up in the latter part of the 19th century.

The university provided Africans with prospects for an advanced education, while simultaneously working to control the nature of that education. The approach centred on promoting the status quo by placating the emerging elite and keeping African students in South Africa, where they would be at a safe distance from black American notions of equality. Yet South African history is full of unanticipated consequences and the school created to entrench the

The First Fort Hare Council, including J.T. Jabavu (top, second from left), 1915

power of the ruling class ultimately educated students who threatened the status quo.

But the importance of Fort Hare goes well beyond that of the production of individuals who fought for South Africa's liberation. 'Can you separate the history of South Africa from what took place around Fort Hare?' asked Govan Mbeki in 1996 at the eightieth anniversary celebrations of the university.[37] The university itself has an intricate history that parallels much of what has taken place in the liberation struggle in South Africa. The foundation of this book is former SASO leader Selby Baqwa's (1969–1973) admonition that one cannot possibly understand the history of South Africa without examining the history of Fort Hare.[38] Fort Hare's story is indeed vital in gaining a comprehensive picture of modern South African history. From its inception, Fort Hare was a microcosm of political life in South Africa. Not only have countless leaders of the liberation struggle matured politically at Fort Hare, but exploration of the institutional history of the university is vital for gaining an understanding of 20th and 21st century African elite, of the emergence of African nationalism in its various organised forms, and of the policies of the apartheid government.

Before delving into the history of Fort Hare, some housekeeping is in order. The organisational status of Fort Hare changed through the years. Prime Minister General Louis Botha opened the school in 1916 as the South African Native College, with Alexander Kerr, a 30-year-old Scottish missionary, serving

Officials, including J.T. Jabavu (top, third from left), General Louis Botha (seated, second from left) and Alexander Kerr (seated, far right) celebrate the opening of the South African Native College, 1916

as the first principal. The Anglican, Methodist and Presbyterian churches provided financial support for residences, and the government made annual grants-in-aid to the college, which was the first for blacks in South Africa and one of the first in sub-Saharan Africa. From 1916–1923 it was a secondary school, preparing students for the South African matriculation examination, a prerequisite to university entrance. Two teachers – Kerr and Davidson Don Tengo Jabavu – taught six subjects: English, Bantu languages, Latin, South African and European history, mathematics and physical science. In 1923 Fort Hare was incorporated under the Higher Education Act, thus adding to its curriculum study towards the award of degrees, which were those of the University of South Africa (UNISA). Importantly, it also began to receive the same government subsidies offered to other universities. That year, Z.K. Matthews and Edwin Ncwana became the university's first graduates. By 1925, the student body had grown to 99.

For the next dozen years, the college taught three groups of students: a small number taking courses in agriculture, business procedure, teaching and minis-try, all below matriculation level; a larger group preparing for matric-ulation; and a steadily increasing segment of the student body that were being prepared for arts and science degrees as external students of UNISA. By 1935, the student body had swelled to 156 and the university was on its way to dispensing with matriculation work.

In 1937, Fort Hare abandoned mat-riculation studies and focused sol-ely on degrees and diplomas. Then, in 1951, Fort Hare was granted relative autonomy from UNISA, affiliating itself with nearby Rhodes University. In 1952, its name was changed to the Uni-versity College of Fort Hare and

Fort Hare's first graduates, Z.K. Matthews and Edwin Ncwana, 1924

Zachariah Keodirelang Matthews and Frieda Bokwe in Alice
some time before their 1928 wedding

its students began to receive Rhodes degrees. The goal was for Fort Hare to one day become completely autonomous, but that status was dealt a blow by the apartheid government's separate university legislation of the late 1950s. In 1960 – following five years of protest by Fort Hare Senate, staff and students – the college was transferred to the Department of Bantu Education by Act No 64 of 1959.

The years 1955–1960 thrust Fort Hare into a state of turmoil from which it has yet fully to emerge. What made the establishment of separate universities particularly grave in the case of Fort Hare was that, unlike the other proposed universities, Fort Hare had been in existence since 1916, and had grown into a thriving home for black intellectuals. Fort Hare had produced politicians, lawyers, clergy, and many other professionals. The universities to be formed under the Extension of University Education Act were to be created. Fort Hare, as it had been, was to be destroyed. Although Bantu education ended officially at Fort Hare in 1990, scars of the post-1960 era remain in the financial, organisational and academic spheres.

Thus, the purpose of this book will be twofold. It will examine patterns of political development among students at Fort Hare, looking for example at why most Fort Harians rejected all forms of collaboration with apartheid, while others, like Kaiser Matanzima and Mangosuthu Buthelezi, ultimately participated in government structures. Why did some Fort Harians embrace multi-racialism, while others opted for a more assertive black nationalism that rejected cooperation with non-Africans? Did the Fort Hare experience lead students in a certain direction or were outside factors more significant?

The book also uses the perspective of student experiences to illustrate the place of the University of Fort Hare in South African history. It explores the political history of the university and its role in the proliferation of extra-parliamentary activity in South Africa from the 1930s onwards, focusing on the 1960 government takeover and the effects of university apartheid thereafter. While these two themes will inevitably overlap, there is an important distinction to be made: Fort Hare is not just an important place because it produced the likes of Mandela and Tambo. Others who went on to lead far less high profile lives were also shaped by time spent at Fort Hare and thus an examination of what it was like to be a student there can contribute to a broader understanding of the university's role in South African history. In short, the influence of Fort Hare in shaping the political, social and cultural identity of black South Africans has been wide and deep.

A cause to celebrate?

Oral sources are the backbone of this study, although published secondary sources were consulted and are listed in the bibliography. Biographies and autobiographies were important in placing student lives in a wider context. Lastly, the university archives proved invaluable.

In 1969, Fort Hare was granted autonomy by the Fort Hare Act, passed by the apartheid government. Long a constituent college of various other 'white' institutions, Fort Hare was finally given the chance to issue its own degrees and move along its own path of development. However, in 1970, in the era of university apartheid, autonomy – a long-sought-after goal for the entire university community – was not a cause for celebration for the students. While the administration planned a gala braai complete with fireworks, the students were not in a mood to rejoice. They saw the granting of autonomy as the cheapening of their degrees and the 'ghettoisation' of their education. They viewed the act as the continuation of the apartheid policy of curbing the critical and independent thinking for which Fort Hare had become known, and replacing it with a curriculum designed to promote the policy of separate development.

Yet there is no hint of the students' sentiments towards autonomy in the administrative records of the university. The minutes of Senate meetings show excitement on the part of the management of the university over the prospect of autonomy and a feeling of accomplishment once it was granted. Details of a festival planned to celebrate the university's independence and a commemorative book to mark the occasion are mentioned. Tellingly, however, there is no record of the students' boycott of the festivities.

The case of Stanley Mabizela involves a similar lacuna. According to university records, he was expelled for calling Kaiser Matanzima, a member of the Advisory Senate of the university after the government takeover, a dog and a sell-out. Mabizela at the time was the president of the Youth League (YL) at Fort Hare and a thorn in the side of the administration. The documents fail to mention that Mabizela was not the student who made the comments about Matanzima. Griffiths Mxenge (1957–1961), a less politically active student, was the guilty party.[39] Mabizela refused to sell out this younger comrade, all the while aware that his academic career was at stake.

As these examples illustrate, there is considerable dissonance between the administrative records of Fort Hare and the recollections of its students. When the government took over the university in 1960, the Fort Hare administration was transformed into an extension of the apartheid regime. Oral sources give us information about social groups whose written history is either missing or distorted.[40] The history of the students of Fort Hare, where documented, is largely misrepresented.

Oral history is a valuable technique for recording the experiences of those people the noted American writer and cultural critic Ralph Ellison would call the invisible. Documents on the history of Fort Hare from a student perspective are difficult to find. While some minutes from SRC meetings were uncovered in the archive at Fort Hare and others are available in the Cory Library at Rhodes, most of the documentary sources, as in the cases noted above, are written from an administrative point of view. And, since Fort Hare was first a missionary and then an apartheid government institution, using these materials to find out what it was like to be a student at Fort Hare is inherently problematic. Inevitably, these sources fall into Ellison's category of 'those lies his keepers keep their power by'.

Though interviews with Fort Harians often revealed unknown events or unknown aspects of known events, oral history is less about exact events and more about their meaning in a bigger picture. While written sources tell us that Fort Harians supported a nurses' strike at Lovedale in 1949, oral accounts relate just how that strike thrust many of those involved onto a course of political action from which they would never turn back. Oral histories tell us about the boycott of the governor-general's visit in 1950, but not what that boycott meant to those involved. Portelli writes that oral sources are unique because they

> ... tell us not just what people did, but what they wanted to do, what they believed they were doing, and what they now think they did. Oral sources may not add much to what we know, for instance, of the material cost of a strike to the workers involved; but they tell us a good deal about its psychological costs.[41]

In the case of Fort Hare, oral sources do add to our knowledge of specific events; more importantly, however, they help us gain an overall picture of how specific events and people worked to create a spirit of nationalism on a campus administered to curb just that.

To be sure, oral history is not perfect. Years removed from the events they are discussing, interviewees are of course susceptible to romanticising the past, or to placing it in a context to fit with their current beliefs. When Thenjiwe Mtintso says the poverty and discrimination she faced gave her 'no choice' as to whether to become a political activist, it doesn't answer the question of why millions of other poor black women did not ascend to the vanguard of the struggle. But the clues it gives us to her political trajectory provide a roadmap to understanding. When viewing her story alongside others, a narrative begins to emerge.

All the Fort Harians I spoke with related how they came to be at Fort Hare. When put together, these individual accounts provide a historical glimpse of the educational opportunities available to black people in South Africa and help elucidate the development of political consciousness among Fort Harians. Finding commonality in seemingly disparate narrators' accounts links together fundamental matters of personal, family and community identity.[42]

Heard in the context of other narratives rather than in isolation, stories are full of resonances.[43] In the case of Fort Hare, piecing together narratives unveils a social history of the university, providing clues as to how it consistently produced political leaders. Through interviews, the political culture of Fort Hare becomes apparent. By looking into individuals' backgrounds and then locating common threads, themes of political development emerge. For example, many students were first sensitised politically by witnessing their parents or other respected elders participate in the Defiance Campaign of

1952. Black teachers at mission high schools who led discussions or provided newspapers influenced others. When examined as a whole, the path of political maturation for Fort Hare students included family influence (with, for many, a large role played by mothers and sisters), mission high school experiences, personal encounters with oppression, the volatile political situation in the country, influential fellow students and staff, and conditions at Fort Hare.

In all, stories were collected from 34 people associated with Fort Hare, beginning with Govan Mbeki, who arrived there in 1933, and ending with people such as Thenjiwe Mtintso and Selby Baqwa, who left Fort Hare in the aftermath of the 1973 tumult. Since my method is oral history, I was forced to start in the 1930s because that was as far back as living Fort Harians' memories reached. However, the 1930s were an appropriate place to start to examine the development of a radical student body at Fort Hare. This decade witnessed the beginnings of an anti-establishment attitude that would develop parallel with the growth of extra-parliamentary politics in the 1940s. Similarly, 1973 is an appropriate time to end this study. Following the 1973 school year, many student leaders abandoned their studies at Fort Hare to work for SASO. The strike that resulted in the expulsion of more than 400 students marked the culmination of more than 13 years of protest that rocked Fort Hare after the 1960 government takeover. As protest spread to the ethnic universities around the country, the importance of Fort Hare in the nation's political landscape began to subside.

I did not limit myself when selecting narrators. Although my initial list of prospective interviewees comprised mostly people who went on to lead politically active lives after Fort Hare – as those were the easiest people to identify – the interviews were eventually conducted with a diverse group of people. While some were political leaders before they arrived at Fort Hare, others became active during their student days. Still others never became overtly active, but developed social and political consciousness by observing and participating in the daily life on campus. When I began, I assumed that I would be interested only in what the political leaders had to say. However, the non-political narrators, many of whom were Indians, taught me a great deal as well. Through a large contingent of Indian ex-students I met in Durban, I learned of Fort Hare's importance in opening them up to a wider, more diverse world.

Many of my findings were serendipitous. Though I carefully constructed a list of people I hoped to interview, most of the time the successful arrangement of an interview depended on who called me back and whose secretary delivered my fax. While Buthelezi, a cabinet minister, answered my fax minutes after he received it, it took me six months to arrange an appointment with Makhenkesi Arnold Stofile (1970–1979), who was premier of the Eastern Cape at the time. Nthato Motlana (1946–1948), an influential ANC Youth Leaguer who was on my original list, did not respond to repeated requests for an interview. Though various administrators in charge of coordinating Nelson Mandela's schedule answered my numerous queries, they never granted me a meeting with the former president.

Luck was on my side when I met with Isaac Mabindisa (1959–1962), who was easy to identify as a narrator, because he was the registrar at Fort Hare in 1998. He suggested I meet with Ambrose Makiwane (1955–1958), the former SRC president, who had not been on my original list. It turned out that Makiwane was a key political figure on campus in the 1950s. Fortune struck again when I visited Durban to meet with Devi Bughwan (1942–1944). When I spoke with Bughwan on the phone, she recommended I speak with Herby Govinden (1947–1949), who in turn suggested I speak with his friend Rama Thumbadoo (1945–1948). When I arrived in Durban, the three had all thought of other people I 'had to interview' while I was there. Govinden arranged an appointment for me with Rev. G.C. Oosthuizen, a white staff member sympathetic to the students' struggles in the 1960s. Their suggestions also led to fruitful meetings with Ratinasabapathy Arumagam Pillay (1950–1954), Loganathan Naidoo (1954–1957), Vadaval Ramsay Govender (1956–1959) and Goolan Suleman Tootla (1959–1962). Tootla, in turn, put me in touch with Marumo Moerane (1959–1961), a friend and patient of his, who studied at Fort Hare in the late 1950s and early 1960s.

Though far from scientific, in the final analysis, I believe my method of selecting narrators was productive. Though I unfortunately did not have the opportunity to meet with any coloured students, I feel that otherwise I interviewed a cross-section of the Fort Hare student population.

To gain a full understanding of the political and social history of Fort Hare, I met with people representing different political tendencies, ethnicities, races and classes. Wycliffe Tsotsi came out of the Unity Movement, while Ambrose Makiwane emerged as an activist in the ANC tradition. Kaiser and George Matanzima supported separate development, while Govan Mbeki, a contemporary of Kaiser's, fought, wrote and philosophised fervently against it. Stofile grew up steeped in the notion of non-racialism, while Selby and Jeff Baqwa (1968–1972) supported SASO, with its black consciousness ideology, from its inception. Thenjiwe Mtintso describes her background as extremely poor, while the Baqwas say they grew up in a middle-class family. I met with Indians and Africans from various ethnic and linguistic groups.

Yet despite the varied origins of my narrators, there are inescapably homogeneous aspects to the group. Having studied at Fort Hare, all the narrators were part of an elite, well-educated sector of society, and all possessed an understanding of politics that rendered them aware of the quasi-political nature of their story-telling. Thus, though socially diverse, the narrators had common experiences and educational backgrounds that must be taken into account when analysing the interviews.

As the history of Fort Hare is so closely connected with that of South Africa, the chapters are organised chronologically. Because of the relationship between Fort Hare and broader South African history this chronological organisation naturally lends itself to a thematic one as well. Chapter 1 shows how campus and national events transformed the consciousness of some of Fort Hare's students from the 1930s, significantly altering the character of the college. Specific attention is paid to the birth of the YL on campus and its role in student politics. Chapter 2 discusses the multi-racial nature of Fort Hare before 1960, preparing for Chapter 3, which focuses on the apartheid government's attempt to crush that incipient rainbow nation and the response from within Fort Hare. Chapter 4 looks at how the government takeover negatively affected both student and academic life at Fort Hare. Chapter 5 shows that the apartheid government takeover of Fort Hare failed to achieve the desired result of quelling student activism. Themes in South African liberation movement history are woven throughout the chapters as they affected life for students at Fort Hare. Some aspects of South African history that are illuminated include missionary education and the birth of an African elite, the explosion of extra-parliamentary politics in the 1940s, the YL, the Defiance Campaign, Bantu Education, university apartheid, and black consciousness. Chapter 6 summarises the role the university played in producing the nation's activists and examines the different political paths that graduates wound up travelling.

Notes

1   Kader Asmal, press statement by the minister of Education, 30 May 2002.
2   University of Fort Hare, available at www.ufh.ac.za.
3   Over the years, Fort Hare has passed through a number of phases, with resultant name changes. Founded in 1916, Fort Hare opened as the South African Native College. In 1951, the institution affiliated with nearby Rhodes University and in 1952 its name changed to the University College of Fort Hare. In 1970, Fort Hare was granted independence and has been known as the University of Fort Hare since that time. (Fort Hare is popularly known as 'The Fort'.)

4　Lovedale, founded by Scottish missionaries in the mid 1800s, was South Africa's best-known African educational institution, comprising a secondary school and teacher training centre.
5　The dates in parentheses refer to the years an individual spent studying at Fort Hare.
6　Students are known as 'Fort Harians', which has long been the title of a student publication.
7　Ivy Matsepe-Casaburri, interview by author, Bloemfontein, 25 February 1999. Except where noted, all quotations from Fort Hare students are taken from interviews I conducted throughout 1998 and 1999.
8　Leslie Blackwell, 'Alice, where art thou?', Cory Library Alexander Kerr Collection, PR4128, 2.
9　Joe Matthews, interview by author, Cape Town, 17 February 1999.
10　Thenjiwe Mtintso, interview by author, Johannesburg, 14 July 1999; see also June Goodwin, *Cry Amandla! South African Women and the Question of Power* (New York: Africana, 1984), 12.
11　Like Mtintso, many interviewees (both male and female) reveal the important roles female relatives played in their politicisation. Though women were admitted to Fort Hare from the start, it was a heavily male institution, with women making up only 8–15 per cent of the student body from 1916–1958. While women were not excluded from politics at Fort Hare – Ivy Matsepe-Casaburri, for example, was elected to the SRC and Manto Tshabalala-Msimang organised for the ANC on campus – men made up the overwhelming majority of students and tended to dominate student politics.
12　Mtintso, interview.
13　*Ibid.*
14　Organisation for the 16 June 1976 protest against the use of Afrikaans as the language of instruction in schools took place at Morris Isaacson High School. The Soweto uprising is often viewed as the event that signalled the end of apartheid.
15　Mtintso, interview.
16　*Ibid.*
17　*Ibid.*
18　*Ibid.*
19　Wycliffe Tsotsi, interview.
20　Terence Beard, 'Background to student activities at the University College of Fort Hare,' in *Student Perspectives on South Africa*, H.W. van der Merwe and D. Walshe (eds) (Cape Town: David Philip, 1972), 158.
21　For a detailed list of notable Fort Hare alumni, see Z. K. Matthews, *Freedom for My People* (Cape Town: David Philip, 1986), 132–136.
22　Beard, 'Background to student activities', 158.
23　Andre Odendaal, *Vukani Bantu! The Beginnings of Black Protest Politics in South Africa to 1912* (Cape Town: David Philip, 1984).
24　*Ibid.*, 8.
25　Peter Walshe, 'The origins of African political consciousness in South Africa', *Journal of Modern African Studies*, 7, 4 (1969), 592.
26　Odendaal, *Vukani Bantu!*, 16.
27　Walshe, 'The origins of African political consciousness', 590.
28　Apollos O. Nwauwa, *Imperialism, Academe and Nationalism* (London: Frank Cass, 1997), 8.

29 Catherine Higgs, *The Ghost of Equality: The Public Lives of D.D.T. Jabuvu of South Africa, 1885–1959* (Athens, Ohio: Ohio University Press, 1997), 17.

30 Steven Gish, *Alfred B. Xuma: African, American, South African* (New York: NYU Press, 2000), 24.

31 Les Switzer, *Power and Resistance in an African Society: The Ciskei Xhosa and the Making of South Africa* (Madison: University of Wisconsin Press, 1993), 33.

32 Switzer, *Power and Resistance*, 179.

33 *Ibid.*

34 Odendaal, *Vukani Bantu!*, 67.

35 Switzer, *Power and Resistance,* 180.

36 Odendaal, *Vukani Bantu!,* 15.

37 SABC, 'Fort Hare at 80', 1996.

38 Selby Baqwa, letter to author, 15 May 1999, in author's possession.

39 Mxenge went on to become an activist and lawyer for the ANC. He was killed in 1981 by a hit squad from the infamous Vlakplaas headquarters of the South African Police Counterinsurgency Unit. Vlakplaas Cmdr Dirk Coetzee recalled the murder in testimony before the Truth and Reconciliation Commission in 1997. 'The decision was made by Brigadier [Jan] van der Hoven from Port Natal Security Police and he told me that ... uh ... he was a thorn in the flesh [of the apartheid government] because he acted as instructing lawyer for all ANC cadres and ... uh ... he stuck by the law. So they couldn't get to him. I never heard of the name before until that day when I was instructed to "make a plan" with Griffiths Mxenge. It means one thing only: Get rid of the guy, kill him. Nothing else, but murder him, kill him'.

40 Allesandro Portelli, 'What makes oral history different', in Robert Perks and Alistair Thomson (eds), *The Oral History Reader* (London: Routledge, 1998), 64.

41 *Ibid.*, 67.

42 Samuel Schraeger, 'What is social in oral history', in Perks and Thompson, *The Oral History Reader,* 288.

43 *Ibid.*, 289.

From Black Englishmen to African Nationalists: Student Politics at Fort Hare to 1955

You sent us the truth, denied us the truth;
You sent us the life, deprived us of life;
You sent us the light, we sit in the dark,
Shivering, benighted in the bright noonday sun
'The Prince of Britain', *a poem by Mqhayi[1]*

When social changes take place, you don't seek the
permission of the founders.[2]
Govan Mbeki

God will look after us

In the winter of 1933, Edward Roux, a member of the Communist Party of South Africa, arrived in Alice on a donkey, with his new wife, Winifred.[3] The two pitched a tent on Sandile's Kop, a hill overlooking the Fort Hare campus, and at a series of outdoor meetings, shared the teachings of communism with students. They discussed organised religion, handing out literature that attacked Christianity. The couple recalled the students relating 'their life in college and how they were disciplined and treated as schoolboys'. In turn, the Rouxs 'told them of the movement and of *Indlela Yenkululeko'* (The Road to Freedom), a recently launched monthly magazine.[4] Wycliffe Tsotsi says that the magazine made the students aware of the extent of political strife in the country and Roux writes that it enjoyed a 'fair circulation' among the students at Fort Hare.[5]

A panoramic view of Fort Hare, undated

While the students listened eagerly to Roux, the authorities felt his teachings ran contrary to those of the college. Alexander Kerr, the school's first principal, was 'squarely against the college becoming a political agency … [He] wanted the Fort Hare authorities to control, channel and domesticate African aspirations.'[6] Tsotsi says: 'The authorities were not interested in us involving ourselves in politics. Any sign of activity by the students which was independent of the authority was crashed down.'[7] Sipo Makalima (1936–1940) describes early Fort Hare as a 'very conservative place', and says that despite what may have been the best of intentions on the part of the missionaries who ran Fort Hare in its early years, it was not an 'open university'. He adds:

> The church people, who were very, very religious, seemed committed
> to black education, black enlightenment, but had very strange attitudes
> towards black advancement. The attitudes to contact with outside
> people, especially black Americans, and especially communists. We
> hardly knew what communism was, but we knew that there were so
> many people who should not be listened to.[8]

Officials barred Roux from campus and forbade students to attend his lectures. Kerr, a little-known headmaster from Scotland, believed religion and education went hand in hand. In the early days at Fort Hare, scripture readings complemented academic lectures. Roux was seen to be rocking the foundation Kerr strove so hard to build. 'The idea was that we shouldn't worry ourselves about the situation there because God is there, God will look after us and change the situation one day,' says Tsotsi. 'We don't have to do anything about it.'[9] When the liberal-Christian basis of the college was thought to be under attack, restrictions replaced open discussion. Roux's visit brought into focus the view of the Fort Hare authorities that it was not the role of a university to critique the political system.

According to Kerr, religion, not politics, was the cornerstone of university life. He was probably the first non-clerical head of an institution for the higher education of Africans, but Kerr saw his role as religious and deeply moral. Trained under a Scottish system that, until 1907, entrusted its education to the church, he was in full agreement with a Christian missionary ethos.[10] 'I saw no sound reason why the Christian tradition and practice should not be fully honoured,' wrote Kerr.[11]

A student studies at the remains of the old Fort Hare, undated

No answers from the missionaries

The birth of student politics at Fort Hare in the 1930s must be viewed within the broader context of the political changes that took place in South Africa during the decade. Colin Bundy writes that the 1930s saw a 'burgeoning sense of African identity, and a new, more forceful assertion of African grievances and demands'. An industrialising economy and an expanding educational system increased the numbers of the black petty bourgeoisie, making it large enough to 'permit awareness of shared identity and interests'.[12] At the same time that their numbers were increasing, educated blacks had to come to terms with an attack on their rights.

Legislative measures of the 1920s and 1930s, particularly those following the rise of the Pact government in 1924, had a crippling effect on black South Africans. The Native (Urban Areas) Act of 1923 codified the pass laws that greatly restricted the freedom of blacks. Labour laws gave preference to white workers, while restricting the rights of their black counterparts. In the depression years from 1929–1933 the number of black workers in manufacturing industries dropped by almost 10 000 while that of whites increased by 3 000.[13] Poll taxes, combined with the attack on and eventual abolition of the already limited Cape franchise through the 1936 Representation of Natives Act proved the notion 'equal rights for all civilised men' to be a farce. With segregation firmly entrenched, this new generation of educated Africans was finding it 'ever harder to follow in their fathers' footsteps'.[14] It became increasingly clear that education alone was not going to bring about equality. 'The terms in which this state was being formed were already ensuring their politico-economic exclusion, and making a mockery of the generalised liberal promises of mission morality.'[15]

A new, more assertive nationalism began to develop in the country. While this fresh outlook took root firmly with the advent of the YL in the 1940s, it had already begun to filter into Fort Hare by the mid 1930s. Speaking at the 1936 graduation ceremony, Edgar Brookes said the legislation had raised two questions for young Africans.[16] 'First, whether a more militant Bantu Nationalism is not called for; and second, whether a reliance on intellectual, moral and spiritual forces is worthwhile, or whether some form of direct action is the only thing which can save the Bantu from servitude.'[17]

An examination of Govan Mbeki's student days shows how the Fort Hare students of the 1930s began to develop along nationalistic and, in some cases, socialistic lines.

◆◆◆◆◆

Govan Mbeki was born on 8 July 1910, the youngest of his father's eight children, spanning two marriages. He began his schooling in 1918 at a Methodist primary school six miles from his home in the Nqamakwe district of the Transkei. Mbeki's father became a staunch Methodist and his mother was the daughter of a Methodist minister. Mbeki himself was strongly influenced by a minister who broke away from the Methodists to form an independent church. 'He used to hold concerts at his church … to raise funds for the ANC … He told us why the ANC came to be and indicated the areas in which the views of the white people differed from the views of the African people,' says Mbeki.[18]

Though the minister stimulated Mbeki's political interest, the greatest early influence on his political life took place at Fort Hare in 1933, where the radical vision of the Rouxs caught his attention. Mbeki, who arrived at Fort Hare in 1931 after four years studying at Healdtown, in nearby Fort Beaufort, recalls their open-air meetings as eye opening:

> We used to go to that tent and Eddie Roux would give us lectures on Marxism, Leninism. He would answer questions about what Hertzog was doing, which the missionaries could not answer. He could show us the way forward, which the missionaries could not do.[19]

Bundy writes that for weeks after Roux's visit, 'excitement gripped some who had heard him. A student from Durban, George Singh, owned a brightly striped blazer, and his friends took it in turn to sport the garment, explaining that "as communists, you see, we must share!"'[20]

Max Yergan, a black American who worked in South Africa from 1922–1936 for the Young Men's Christian Association, also influenced Mbeki. Yergan lived in Alice and worked from the Christian Union Hall on the Fort Hare campus. Though Yergan initially had very little contact with the students at Fort Hare, his interest in them grew after a trip to the Soviet Union. Wycliffe Tsotsi says:

> He did not seem to me to have a real political interest in the students at Fort Hare … But he did talk to me … about the situation in South Africa, especially when he came from … Moscow … He was saying we had to do something more radical … we should strike deep.[21]

Mbeki also noticed the change in Yergan after his Soviet sojourn.[22] He told Colin Bundy that before his trip Yergan was 'very Christian and highly religious', and added, 'when he came back it was not the Yergan we had known'.[23] The new Yergan delivered lectures on communism and fascism to Mbeki's political science class. He also 'fed' the young Mbeki with literature, lending him books such as Lenin's *The State and the Revolution* when the student visited his home.[24]

At the same time, Mbeki and his fellow students were influenced by their surroundings. Mbeki's classmate Wycliffe Tsotsi speaks about the first time he became aware of the tumultuous situation facing blacks in South Africa: 'I remember taking a friend of mine to my home in the Transkei … When we got off the train we had to get transport … My friend and I were made to lie on an open lorry on top of sacks of mealie meal. And the driver was by himself. There was nobody with him in the front seat.'[25] Mbeki recalls the vicious pass laws, which made him aware of the situation in the country:

> When I went out in the evening with a girlfriend, I would be stopped on the streets ... the fact that a policeman, you have to pull something out of your pocket to show a policeman, and he allows you through ... And if there's anything unsatisfactory in those documents you are jailed. Who could not have been aware?[26]

Indeed, as Bundy points out, the students of Mbeki's generation began to construct a 'new identity type'. He quotes Phyllis Ntantala, who remembers Mbeki as part of a circle of 'progressive' and 'politically minded' students at Fort Hare that included A.C. Jordan, Tsotsi, Paul Mosaka and Ernest Mancoba.[27] 'We were the first group of students who ... became nationalistic' says Mbeki. This nationalism began to transform a conservative missionary institution that produced in its first decade and a half, in Mbeki's words, 'Black Englishmen' into one that produced African nationalists. Mbeki says the change could be seen in the students' new vision of their education:

> We were not happy about the fact that when we came there most students had majored in ethics, in English, in logic, things like that. We said it was wrong. Fort Hare was producing Black Englishmen ... They had no contact with the people. They had teas with the students, the missionaries, white missionaries, never mixing with the people ... We said, in the language of the student in those days, 'bugger it', we must not be Black English people. So we changed courses. I majored in political science and psychology ... A move away from the old tradition.[28]

The push to radicalise the Fort Hare curriculum began around 1934. As a constituent college of UNISA, it was possible for students to study the curricula of the broader university, though the authorities did not encourage it. Mbeki and McLeod Mabude became the first two students to major in political science, despite having to study on their own, because there was no qualified staff member to teach the final-year course. According to Mbeki, their interest sparked by Roux and Yergan, students began to abandon courses in English and logic in favour of fields such as history and political science.[29]

Tsotsi led a similar move to diversify the Fort Hare curriculum. Along with classmate Victor Mbobo, he wanted to study history, which was not offered as a subject in 1935. The two approached Kerr and asked to be assigned a lecturer in history. He told them to take psychology. Tsotsi and his friend decided that they were going to do history anyway. They acquired all the necessary reading material, made monthly trips to nearby Rhodes University, and passed the history exam at the end of the year – without the aid of a teacher. Alexander Kerr had warned Tsotsi that his 'blood would be on his own hands', but Tsotsi had the last laugh. After the success of Tsotsi and his classmate, a permanent lecturer in history was added to the Fort Hare staff.[30]

However, the new history department did not help Sipo Makalima in 1940, when he attempted to become the first Fort Hare student to earn an MA in history: 'In my thesis, I brought in new attitudes which were not accepted by the missionary historians. They emphasised that friction between black and white over the frontier was caused by cattle thieving. The Xhosa people were stealing cattle from the whites. And I said the cattle were only an element in the struggle. The main struggle was on land.'[31]

Sipo Makalima

Bundy writes that Mbeki and his contemporaries were 'less patient' than the previous generation of educated Africans, which included Professor D.D.T. Jabavu and Z.R. Mahabane, who served two terms as president-general of the ANC.[32] Visiting Fort Hare in 1937, Ralph Bunche observed that the students resented older Africans who were 'duped' by attempts to divide them from the black masses.[33] Of course, this outlook ignores the complexity of the lives and politics of these older Africans, whose views were often far more deeply rooted in indigenous peasant culture than the students realised. But the events of 1935 and 1936 'whipped up so much feeling' among the students that they would have to be forgiven for thinking their predecessors too timid. With the passage of the Native Representation Act, the enthusiasm over the AAC, and Italy's attack on Ethiopia, Fort Hare students were 'absolutely moved'.[34] Mbeki joined the ANC in 1935 and, though he did not join the CPSA while at Fort Hare, he developed an interest in socialism through Roux and Yergan. In 1936, in part moved by the changing franchise laws, Fort Hare students attended the ANC conference in Bloemfontein.[35] 'Those were serious days,' says Mbeki. 'The students were alive. They were debating these issues [the Hertzog bills] ... We turned around to our missionaries to find an answer ... They were afraid to come out openly against Hertzog. They wouldn't.'[36]

Tsotsi remembers political discussion at Fort Hare over the Hertzog bills prompted him to attend the initial meeting of the AAC, where he became a founding member of the organisation.[37] Professor D.D.T. Jabavu opened his presidential address with an assault on the Italian invasion of Ethiopia, the last independent state belonging to indigenous Africans: 'The brief history of the last eight months has scratched the European veneer and revealed the white savage hidden beneath.'[38] William Nkomo (1935–1937) says that as president of the AAC, Jabavu 'influenced students and some of his thinking naturally was passed on to the students'.[39]

Tsotsi, Makalima, Kaiser Matanzima and William Nkomo recall Mussolini's attack on Ethiopia sparking a great deal of debate among the students. 'We followed that very closely and we began to take an interest not only in the politics of South Africa, but in the politics of the whole African continent,' says Nkomo.[40] Makalima comments: 'There was a great deal of enthusiasm about ... a state in Africa being taken by a state in Europe.'[41] Matanzima states: 'The students were interested. And there was discussion among themselves. The senior students were much involved.'[42] Bundy cites Mbeki's reminiscence of 1936 as 'a year that decided the future course of most of us then at Fort Hare'.[43]

The new political fervour on campus in the mid to late 1930s took many forms. Phyllis Ntantala remembers intense discussions 'during leisure time, or in the reading room and C U [Christian Union], or on the lawn'.[44] Paul Mosaka protested against the employment by Fort Hare of white women as domestic workers when there were so many unemployed Africans in the region. A.C. Jordan wrote a poem in Xhosa, condemning the invasion of

Ethiopia. Successful protests against segregation were organised at the Alice Post Office and at a Lovedale athletics meeting.[45] The 'civilised labour policy', which ensured inflated wages for unskilled white labourers, prompted Fort Hare students to empty tins of jam marked 'Manufactured by white labour' onto the tables and floor in the dining room.[46]

More often than not, the new spirit enveloping the Alice campus could be seen in clashes between the students and the missionary authorities. One of the earliest incidents of student unrest occurred in 1935 when members of Iona House organised a mixed dance, despite the objections of the authorities. 'We wanted to invite the women who were working as domestics in the institution to come in and that infuriated the authorities,' says Tsotsi, an Iona resident. Makalima comments, 'During the proceedings, the authorities ... clashed with the house committee because ... they played the piano and played some drums, and in one of the items, the gentlemen took ladies and had a mixed dance and that was such a big broil.'[47] When the warden tried to stop the party, he clashed with the Iona House Committee. Tsotsi remembers telling the warden to 'go to bed'. He says, 'We were just surrounded by barbed wire rules and regulations. Even our movements. We couldn't go to certain places, we couldn't meet at certain places.'[48]

10. Dining Hall, South African Native College, Fort Hare, Alice, South Africa.

The poor quality of food was a constant source of tension on campus. Here the SRC presides over a meal. Undated

The next decade brought more campus unrest. In 1940, Nelson Mandela got into trouble for flouting college regulations by refusing to sit on the SRC in protest against the poor quality of dining-hall food.[49] The first of countless mass actions embarked upon by Fort Hare students occurred a year later when, in the absence of Kerr, the students demanded the dismissal of the dining-hall boarding master for assaulting a servant in the kitchen. About three-quarters of the students carried out the threat to strike.

In 1942, discontent boiled over in what became known as the Beda Hall Tennis Dispute. Although the reason for the controversy was ostensibly the refusal of the warden of Beda Hall, an Anglican residence, to allow students to play tennis on Sundays, the 1942 disruption was about more than tennis. For the first time, students began overtly to show their contempt for missionary authority. In a statement issued by the committee of Beda Hall, they expressed animosity toward the control of the warden:

> The warden of Beda Hall has refused to understand the students [sic] point of view on any matters affecting the smooth running of the Hostel … This attitude of the warden … culminated in his refusal to allow the Anglican students to play tennis on Sundays … a thing to which the Church of the Province does not object.[50]

The sanctuary at Beda Hall, 1920s. Over the years, students resisted compulsory attendance at religious services.

They also resented the bullying attitude of the principal, who 'insists on treating post-matric and post-grad students as children in a kindergarten school'.[51] Upset over the poor quality of food, interference in holding student meetings, prohibitions on dancing and on visits to the bioscope in Alice, and, yes, playing tennis on Sundays, the students refused to perform their normal hostel duties. After the Beda Hall committee was suspended, 54 students signed a petition in its support. The disagreement culminated in a student boycott of classes from 18 to 20 September.

The authorities viewed the strike very seriously and it dominated discussion in Council and Senate meetings. They

Oliver Tambo and a classmate celebrate rag day, 1941

resolved that it was 'not a question of religious beliefs, but of submission by the students to the authority of the Senate'.[52] Striking students who had also participated in the 1941 strike were suspended for the remainder of the school year. First-year students were suspended until 5 October, and all other students were asked to leave until the commencement of examinations. To be readmitted, students had to pay a one-pound fine each and had to sign a declaration pledging good conduct. In all, 25 students were suspended, including Oliver Tambo, then a post-graduate student.[53]

Z.K. Matthews, one of the few black staff members at the time, recognised that the campus was not isolated from the rest of the country. His insight into the cause of the disturbance augured more unrest. At a Senate meeting to discuss the Beda Hall Tennis Dispute, he pointed out that the situation at the college was 'made difficult because the students regarded any attempt to govern them as a form of oppression. This was probably because the majority of the staff were European.'[54] Though Matthews' warning fell on deaf ears,

Oliver Tambo graduates with a Bachelor
of Science degree, 1941

he had acutely identified the cause of the problem. The students could not help but equate their treatment within the college to that of their people throughout the country. Two sources of activism emerged: one was organised around campus discontent; and the other used campus discontent to express wider political grievances. Bundy writes that the students' politics were shaped 'not only *in* mission schools but also in reaction *against* them'.[55] In the 1930s and 1940s, Jabavu and Matthews were the only black professors at Fort Hare. Both held high national political positions while teaching, but both remained grounded in the Christian liberal philosophy of the university at large. From the 1930s and 1940s, 'the trend was to appoint English-speaking staff with missionary connections or inclinations, and with a strain of paternalism', though exceptions did exist. By 1959, just before the government takeover, 86 per cent of the Senate was white.[56]

Devi Bughwan (1942–1944) states: 'You felt they're treating you as infants, that you haven't sufficiently evolved yet. You're still black. Whether there were shades of blackness and brownness didn't matter. There was a paternal attitude.' In the early 1940s, with the ANC in a sluggish state and extra-parliamentary politics far from the fevered pitch it would reach later in the decade, the students expressed their complaints locally. Campus issues dominated student debate, and grievances were articulated through food strikes, which were annual rites of passage. Bughwan describes how apparently superficial complaints often led to deeper discussion:

They had to get permission to hold a mass meeting. You couldn't hold one to discuss the state of the country. So it would be grumbling about food or the curfew, we shouldn't have to have lights out. That excuse to have a mass meeting. Then one thing would lead to another, that they're treating us like we're black. And it would always lead to a total free-for-all about the state of the country, the oppression, the apartheid. That is how in my recollection the mass meetings became platforms for fiery tirades against the government at the time.[57]

Tsotsi offers a similar view, saying that the students were forced to collaborate among themselves:

> The rules that bound them, they had to obey rules which they thought were not proper in an institution like Fort Hare ... The treatment of the students ... the deficiencies ... were associated with the political situation and it was felt that the authorities were carrying out the government policy against the black man.[58]

Kerr's disciplinarian approach contributed to mounting rebellion over domestic issues among the students. Mandela recalls: 'In those days Fort Hare was little better than a high school ... The principal was a well-informed man, but of course he was white, and he had his own conception of how black students should develop.'[59] Although Kerr seemed to comprehend that the disturbances at Fort Hare and other mission schools had to be viewed in the wider light of opposition to oppression, he was never able to sanction student activism in any form.[60] 'He was not a politician,' says Matthews, who adds that it would not be fair to dub Kerr a conservative. 'He was radical in the sense that he was coming along to prove that blacks were as good as whites in the university.'[61]

Buthelezi recalls Kerr, in later years, walking around campus, referring to Fort Hare as 'my college' and saying, 'Don't do this in my college.'[62] George Matanzima remembers Kerr as

> a very strict man. He sometimes got up in the middle of the night and went around the hostels himself. I remember one day in the night I was studying with the use of a candle. When he saw that his temper came. 'Put it off, put it off, my son. You are going to burn this whole institution.' ... In the morning, he announced it during the prayers. He said, last night, I dreamt Fort Hare was in fire. And when I went to the hostels I saw one student using a small candle and I told him to put it off.[63]

Indeed, Kerr was extremely possessive of Fort Hare, and did not take action perceived to be against his college lightly. It was this heavy-handedness that often led to unrest. Thus, while early protest at Fort Hare can be viewed broadly as a response to the political situation in South Africa, in its initial stages it manifested itself predominantly in domestic confrontations with the missionary authorities of the university.

Just the place for a Youth League

The 1940s brought about a further increase in student militancy. A combination of events radicalised students at Fort Hare, and continued to transform the missionary institution into a political crucible. The revitalisation of the ANC under the direction of Dr A.B. Xuma, coupled with the unsettling events of World War II and the surprising National Party victory in the 1948 elections, all contributed to a heightened sense of awareness at Fort Hare. As politics in South Africa fomented in the 1940s, the student that Fort Hare produced moved further and further away from Mbeki's 'Black Englishman'. The authorities could expel Eddie Roux from the college grounds, but ultimately they were powerless against a growing spirit of nationalism that began to envelop the university in the 1940s as intelligent, educated youngsters came together and increasingly began to relate events outside the campus to their lives within Fort Hare.

The Atlantic Charter of 1941, promulgated by Franklin D. Roosevelt and Winston Churchill, laid the groundwork for a post-fascist, democratic world with political and economic freedom. African political leaders took notice. And during Dr Xuma's presidency, the ANC moved away from its history of deputations and delegations and began to transform itself into a modern political organisation akin to those of the Western world, albeit operating in the exceptional environment of South Africa. Africans' Claims in South Africa was issued in 1943, calling for, among other things, land distribution, trade-union rights and, for the first time, unqualified universal suffrage.[64]

The Second World War accelerated industrialisation and brought more blacks from the rural areas to the cities. Joe Matthews attributes a great deal of the politicisation of students to the events surrounding the war and its aftermath and not to what was happening at Fort Hare itself: 'People took sides, people took up positions, debates occurred.' He describes one such campus deliberation:

> People at first were saying, how can we go to the war when we are not armed, when we haven't got freedom, and so on. And the next thing everybody is saying the attack on the Soviet Union alters the character

of the war and now you must support the war effort. And there were debates going on right there in the university arguing why are you supporting the war now when you were saying you were against it the previous week.[65]

Nelson Mandela writes: 'Each evening, the warden of Wesley House used to review the military situation in Europe, and late at night, we would huddle around an old radio and listen to BBC broadcasts of Winston Churchill's stirring speeches.' He adds that, like his classmates, he was 'an ardent supporter of Great Britain'.[66]

In 1940, the graduation speaker was Prime Minister Jan Smuts. Although the students applauded Smuts's stance on the war, his visit provoked a great deal of discussion on English oppression in South Africa. Matthews recalls another visitor to Fort Hare, a government recruiter, becoming annoyed when he was asked by the students: 'What's the use of us being recruited to the war when it is said that we won't be armed? How will we face Italian and German soldiers without weapons?'[67]

The changes in attitude at this time were not limited to Fort Hare. Similar transformations took place at mission high schools across the country, where students started to express dissatisfaction with a system that was unable to cope with increased demand for education. The schools were too small and poor to cope with growing numbers of urban youth and were in a state of near collapse. Students studied in old, dilapidated facilities, sometimes without electricity and running water. They were fed paltry diets. An uprising at Lovedale in 1946 spilled over into nearby Healdtown. Soon other institutions were in revolt. A combination of a weakening of the missions' infrastructure and the political changes of the time led to a breakdown in the authority of missionaries over their students.[68]

Fort Hare soon moved to the forefront. The seeds of majoritarianism were laid by the Africans' Claims document in 1943, but the transformation of the ANC did not stop there. There were parallel movements within the ANC that would greatly affect both the organisation and the entire South African political scene. The rumblings of change would reach Fort Hare by the end of the decade, profoundly influencing campus life. The YL was established in 1944 in Johannesburg, where white wealth and black poverty were most stark, and where the most skilled, educated, politicised and frustrated portion of the African population lived. The YL saw itself as more radical than its parent organisation. Led by such ex-Fort Harians as Oliver Tambo and Nelson Mandela, its leaders initially considered starting a separate body, but eventually decided to join as a pressure group within the ANC to effect transformation of the organisation. The more militant YL, made up mostly of mission-educated young people who had been politicised during their student days, felt the ANC tended to yield to oppression, and was thus unable to advance the cause of African freedom. Joe Matthews, writing in 1949, summed up the YL philosophy:

> We are not asking for a greater share to be given to the African in the running of the country. We are without apologies going to fight for a S.A. which will be ruled by the majority i.e. by the Africans. We intend to struggle for a return of sovereignty to the rightful owners of the country.

College students, he added, should view themselves 'as part of a nation army preparing themselves for their destiny which is to rule this country and indeed the continent'.[69]

In 1948, the YL began to grow convincingly under the direction of A.P. Mda. Because Fort Hare was home to the leading members of South Africa's black intelligentsia, and because teachers trained at Fort Hare went on to educate people around the country, the university was strategically important for Mda, who grew determined to establish a branch on campus.[70] In the early 1940s, the AAC had received more support on campus, but, with the ascendancy of the National Party, that began to change. The resuscitation of the ANC under Xuma, the unsettling effects of the war, and Malan's victory over Smuts in 1948 had all 'roused the Fort Hare student body to a new pitch of political concern'.[71] The AAC's compliant stance was increasingly looked down upon as a more confrontational position was embraced, especially by the youth.[72]

The change in atmosphere could be seen in *Beware*, a daily commentary on political issues prepared by Robert Sobukwe, Dennis Siwisa (1947–1949) and Pelem Galasi Stamper (1947–1949) that was posted on campus noticeboards. Hand-written, the topic of choice of these daily manifestos was non-collaboration, with fierce attacks on such advisory bodies as the Natives' Representative Council (NRC).[73] Sensing the time was ripe for action, Mda wrote a letter to Godfrey Pitje (1941–1945), a lecturer at Fort Hare, suggesting that the university was 'just the place to start a Youth League. The young people there are the intellectual leaders to be, and a growing consciousness of their role in the national liberation struggle will add a new vigour and force to the struggle for national freedom.' He urged Pitje to 'get together a small nucleus and soak them in our Nationalistic outlook and indicate to them the

Students and staff celebrate the opening of Wesley House

need for youth to train for a greater leadership. This will form the core of the Movement at Fort Hare.'[74]

Following a meeting called by Pitje of about 50 staff and students in August of 1948, the Fort Hare branch was formally founded in November.[75] Prohibited by the college authorities, it was forced to operate off-campus and became known as the Victoria East branch, with meetings in neighbouring villages. Herby Govinden (1947–1949), a student at the time, says: 'There were political problems in the country and we felt we should identify with that. It was the beginnings of students' involvement in politics outside the campus …The student body became more and more active.'[76] Robert Sobukwe, Joe Matthews and P.V. Mbatha were appointed researchers, assigned the task of reading literature on the South African political scene, and reporting back to the group. The YL enlivened the atmosphere on campus. According to Pogrund's account, by the end of 1948, the Victoria East branch was a very 'closely knit group'.[77]

Pitje says Sobukwe began to emerge as its leader. In 1948, he was chosen to speak at the Completer's Social on behalf of continuing students, where he would deliver the first of two impressive speeches. The exact text of the speech is not available, but Siwisa recalls him saying: 'Your starting-point in your struggle for our liberation is non-collaboration, and the boycott of dummy institutions is the first step on the ladder of non-collaboration.' Siwisa calls that speech a 'coming-out party for Sobukwe' as 'an orator of no mean repute'.[78] 'From then onwards he was always called up to make speeches and no meeting – political, cultural, social or even a mass meeting of students – would be regarded as having ended until or unless Robert had spoken.'[79]

From the beginning, the YL had an uneasy relationship with university authorities, who felt education and not politics would bring the African equal rights. The majority of the staff did not understand the intricacies of the political struggle. Joe Matthews, who grew up on the campus before becoming a Fort Hare student, says that it was less a political outlook, attitude or philosophy and more

> just a simple bewilderment at what people were talking about. I mean people were talking about freedom, and freedom in our lifetime, you know, an end to oppression ... And to the average white lecturer or professor ... I don't think they even understood the forces at work ... they thought this was just ... hot air by the students.[80]

The authorities' failure to grasp the desires of the students was particularly evident in 1949, perhaps the most active year for the Victoria East Branch. Walter Sisulu, in his capacity as secretary-general, made frequent visits to Fort Hare to meet with the young members of the YL.[81] A boycott was organised of a segregated showing of *Hamlet* at the bioscope in Alice and a few students who defied the call were attacked on their way back to campus. According to a statement by Principal C.P. Dent, who took over when Kerr retired in 1948, 'stones were thrown at them and one woman student was beaten with a stick, and at least one bed was soaked with water'.[82] Off campus, the Youth Leaguers spearheaded the charge for the Programme of Action, which emphasised extra-parliamentary activity, such as boycotts, strikes, civil disobedience, and non-collaboration. When the programme was up for discussion at the annual Cape provincial conference of the ANC in June 1949, and again at the national conference in Bloemfontein in December, 'it was members of Fort Hare's Youth League who took the lead and together with Mda and the League's Transvaal leaders – Tambo, Sisulu and Mandela – most forcefully pressed for the programme's adoption'.[83] On campus, the students began to involve themselves in more overtly political activity as well. To the food strikes of the early 1940s, a broader, more national platform of protest was added, as student politics at Fort Hare became increasingly militant in line with the thinking of the YL.[84]

Beda Hostel, 1948.

'Inmates' include Alfred Hutchinson (top, fourth from right), who went on to become an ANC leader in the Transvaal and a defendant in the Treason Trial; Godfrey Pitje (3rd row from bottom, 8th from left), who helped start the YL at Fort Hare and went on to become an influential anti-apartheid lawyer; journalist and short story writer Can Themba (three to the right of Pitje); Ntsu Mokhele (seated, first on right), who became prime minister of Lesotho; Joshua Zake (seated, second from right), who became attorney general in Uganda; filmmaker Lionel Ngakane (on ground, third from left); Nthato Motlana (two to the right of Themba), who became Nelson Mandela's doctor and chaired the Committee of Ten in Soweto; and Rama Thumbadoo (on ground, fifth from right).

Banned from campus by the university authorities, the Youth Leaguers found a home in Victoria East and began spreading their gospel around the community. 'We got the nurses at Victoria Hospital involved, politicised them,' says Henry Makgothi (1948–1951).[85] Influenced by the YL, the nurses' strike in 1949 played a large role in the political development of those at Fort Hare. Expelled from their rooms, the nurses spent two weeks sleeping on the hospital lawn, and holding meetings on the banks of the Tyumie River. Fort Hare students brought blankets to the nurses and participated in their meetings. Govinden says: 'We sympathised with our sisters at Victoria Hospital when they had issues. We joined them.'[86] As the strike dragged on, Youth Leaguers such as Sobukwe assumed positions of leadership, with the nurses coming to them for advice and instructions.[87] The strike was finally settled after two months, but its impact on the students stretched far beyond that period. Dent viewed the strike as an example of his students keeping 'trouble alive in a neighbouring establishment', and failed to understand its deeper meaning.[88]

Towards the end of the year many students boycotted a service conducted by the chairman of the Fort Hare Council because he was also chairman of the Lovedale Hospital Board.[89] The nurses' struggle was viewed as victimisation by hospital management. The strike 'hardened attitudes' at Fort Hare towards the authorities, whom the students increasingly began to equate with the oppressors.[90] Rev. E. Lynn Cragg, a long-time warden at Fort Hare, described the evolution of the students' attitudes: 'Anti-white tended to become anti-Church and anti-Christian as Christianity was looked upon as the white man's religion and the church as supporting white domination; opposition to the "white oppressors" and white rule became opposition to all authority.'[91]

To Sobukwe, the strike was more than just a local squabble. It was part of the broader struggle against minority rule. Sobukwe's views on the conflict, which provided him with his first real taste of confrontational politics, were first made public in his memorable speech at the 1949 Completer's Social. Makgothi recounts the evolution of the speech:

> We said, look, this business … of having socials … what was it? Dancing? … we thought we should introduce an element of seriousness here … make people feel that they've got a mission … And we said, look here, the dancing and that kind of jolliness and jollification is going to take a back seat here. We are going to put across the political line and what it really means to complete here politically.[92]

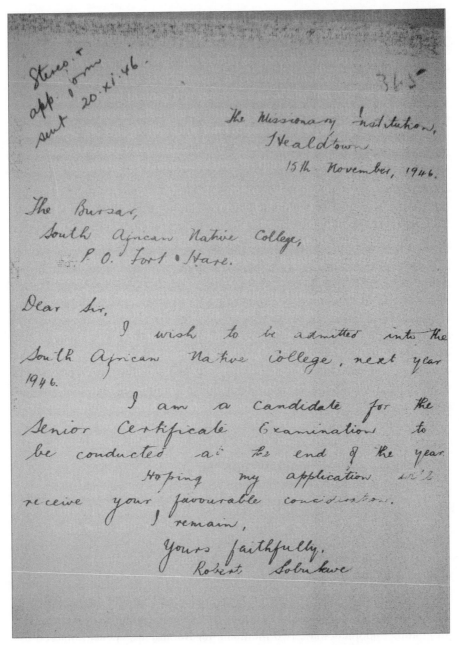

Robert Sobukwe's letter of application to Fort Hare

Students transformed the usually festive end-of-year gala on 21 October 1949 into an exhibition of the political maturation of Sobukwe and the YL. Political speeches replaced music, with Ntsu Mokhehle (1947–1949) and Temba Hleli (1948–1949) joining Sobukwe at the podium. 'It was a hell of a thing,' says Makgothi. 'People came there, "Oh, they're going to have a nice time", and we opened up, and Robbie delivered a most memorable speech.'[93] A complete written record of this speech does exist. Calling the nurses' strike 'part of a broad struggle' and not 'an isolated incident', Sobukwe said it was a struggle 'between Africa and Europe, between a 20th-century desire for self-realisation and a feudal concept of authority'.[94] Mokhehle implored his classmates to avoid complacency, noting that as educated Africans, they were 'like passengers seated most comfortably in some first-class, water-tight cabins of a sinking ship'. He urged them to come out of their 'intellectual luxury cabins'.[95]

For Sobukwe and other Fort Harians, the division between missionary authority and white rule was beginning to blur, and the battle lines were drawn in the fight for the right 'to call our souls our own'. Ignoring the knowledge that his words would irritate university authorities, he strongly criticised the college. He wanted Fort Hare to be to the African 'what Stellenbosch is to the Afrikaner' and bemoaned its failure to become the 'barometer of African thought'. He understood the role Stellenbosch played in the ideological development of apartheid, and envisioned Fort Hare playing just as influential a position in eradicating it. He attacked trusteeship and any form of collaboration with the apartheid regime:

> We want to build a new Africa, and only we can build it …Talks of cooperation are not new to us. Every time our people have shown signs of uniting against oppression, their 'friends' have come along and broken that unity ... I am afraid these gentlemen are dealing with a new generation which cannot be bamboozled.

Exhorting his classmates to 'Remember Africa!' Sobukwe, just two years into his political awakening, gave a speech that Sipo Makalima said 'changed attitudes very much'.[96]

The speech is particularly revealing when examined against the backdrop of the rise of the YL and the ANC's adoption of the Programme of Action. The programme, adopted some two months after Sobukwe's speech, marked the culmination of a growing sense of 'self-determination' among young Africans. Earlier in 1949, Sobukwe and Pitje presented their own programme to the Cape provincial conference in Queenstown, emphasising the boycott of dummy institutions.[97] A Fort Hare YL delegation led by Sobukwe was present at the programme's Bloemfontein adoption, taking particular delight, according to Gerhart, in its emphasis on the method of boycott.[98] Seeds of the later split between the ANC and PAC were laid, as supporters of interracial cooperation and those favouring 'Africa for the Africans' began to take sides.

Anton Lembede and A.P. Mda, 1947

Over the next decade, as the orthodox African nationalists began to separate themselves from the increasingly multi-racial ANC, they often returned to the African nationalism embodied in the Programme of Action, claiming the ANC had to be brought back to the 'unadulterated nationalism' of Anton Lembede[99] and the early YL.[100] As the ANC enunciated a strategy of multi-racial cooperation – forging alliances with coloured, Indian and left-wing white groups that culminated in the 1955 Congress of the People – former Fort Hare Youth Leaguers lined up in both camps: some, like Joe Matthews and Henry Makgothi supported the move towards multi-racialism; while others, like Sobukwe and Frank Mdlalose (1950–1953), remained rooted in the Africanist ideas set forth in the programme and in Sobukwe's graduation speech. The experience of multi-racial cooperation in 1950s' Johannesburg was one factor that caused Fort Harians such as Mandela, Matthews, and Makgothi to moderate their stance against collaboration with non-Africans.

Pogrund explains that the Sobuwke speech is remarkable in that at such an early stage in his development, it 'contains much of what was to be Sobukwe's later political philosophy: the rejection of any trace of white paternalism; the stress on black self-regard … the rejection of colonialism'.[101] Herby Govinden says: 'He was giving some kind of picture of what was going to happen, what he was going to do when he left. So we were not surprised when he formed the PAC because we had insight into his thinking.'[102]

However, not everyone was impressed. The missionary authorities, who 'felt all politics is nonsense and the big thing is to be educated', did not even partially understand the students' transformation.[103] Cragg's recollection of Sobukwe's speech shows how inept the authorities and white staff were in understanding the growing sense of nationalism on campus. He charges Sobukwe with 'attacking both the white staff and white rule in general … The white staff sat silently through it all, but from that time speeches at farewell socials were barred, and many white staff ceased to attend.'[104]

There was little the administration could do to punish Sobukwe and Mokhehle because the two students had already completed their studies. Temba Hleli was not so fortunate. Authorities expelled Hleli, the speaker chosen to represent the continuing students. Dent's response to the evening of speeches is illuminating and provides a framework for understanding the unrest at Fort Hare in the first half of the 1950s. He wrote that the students were trying to turn a liberal institution 'with a purely educational purpose into a recruiting ground for party factions' and that they advocated methods which 'were of the Nazi pattern.'[105] Hleli, according to Dent, was 'responsible for an impertinent and bad mannered speech in which, among other things, he described the Europeans in South Africa "as the scum of Europe, who had come to fill their bellies and their pockets"'.[106] To Dent, the evening's speeches represented

> … a planned attempt to use the opportunity for a propaganda which has no proper place here. To the staff it appeared as a piece of planned impertinence. We had been treated to a show of discourtesy that evening which was a disgrace.[107]

Hleli's sponsor, Dr M. Capcan, wrote back to Dent, complaining that the university gave Hleli a 'raw and unfair deal'. He wrote, 'If a Native College treats the African in the way Fort Hare has treated Hleli, then I am not surprised to find restlessness among the Africans.'[110] Yet Dent never considered listening to the students' political strivings. 'Many young people … imagine that they are free to do and say just what they please,' he wrote. He viewed the students as impetuous and immature, lacking 'restraint and courtesy',[109] a stance that ensured his already poor relationship with them would only worsen.

The politically charged Completer's Social was an attempt to thrust Fort Hare into the national political scene. Recognising what he saw as a deficiency, Sobukwe asked for the college to 'express and lead African thought'.[110] The result was an increasingly strong call on the part of the students, and particularly of the YL, to reject the authority of the college. The missionaries were now more closely associated than ever before with the notion of trusteeship. And although there had been minor grievances against missionary paternalism in earlier years, the new philosophy articulated by Sobukwe indicated a conviction that there was little or no distinction between university and national politics.

◆◆◆◆◆

Henry Makgothi studied at Fort Hare with Sobukwe and was a founding member of the Victoria East Branch of the YL. He was born and raised in Pimville, near Johannesburg, where his father was a schoolteacher and his mother a domestic servant. Education was emphasised in the Makgothi household, and Henry's siblings were all sent to boarding schools after their mother's death when he was five years old. Makgothi stayed with his father in Pimville before the two moved to Orlando. His father was politically active, and Makgothi remembers him going to many meetings. As a child, he was puzzled that his father was constantly on the move. Later he came to realise that it was because of his political activity. 'He knew most of the leaders of the ANC. Sol Plaatje was a personal friend of his and he had a great admiration for him … He was friendly and close to people in the ANC, people like [A.P.] Mda.' Makgothi recalls Mda providing him with some of his first lessons in politics: 'We used to hang around … and he would call us in the street and talk to us about political questions and encourage us to attend political meetings.'[111]

In 1939, his father joined the army and Makgothi went to live with an aunt in Sophiatown. He helped his aunt, who ran a clothes-washing stand, by carrying washing atop his head on his way to school. Although his father had been active politically, Makgothi did not develop a keen interest in politics until high school. He chose to enrol at St Peter's Secondary School in Johannesburg in 1942, where he was a classmate of Joe Matthews. 'When I got to St Peter's, it was a new world to me,' he says.[112]

That choice turned out to be significant for Makgothi, as it thrust him into what Joe Matthews calls the 'political whirlpool' of post-war Johannesburg.[113] At St Peters, Makgothi met Oliver Tambo, who eventually found a job teaching mathematics and science there after being expelled from Fort Hare in 1943: 'He was a man who liked to challenge you to think about things. Bring a problem and talk about a problem to you and get you to think. And then only later on you'd realise, my God, this was related to this, that and the other.' The first impression Tambo made on him was not that of a politician. 'He never came to you and preached and said, look, this is like this. No, no, no. He made you think about things, and that is how I started learning about politics. Not in a direct fashion.'[114]

Makgothi became very close to Tambo, serving as his personal assistant. 'I looked after his room … I was assigned to him … and I really enjoyed that … I'd go to his room, study in his room, and he taught me a lot of things. Not in a direct way, but I just watched him.' As their relationship deepened, Makgothi picked up Tambo's love for music and enthusiasm for politics. At St Peter's, Makgothi also met Joe Matthews, the head of the school's YL branch. Makgothi describes Matthews, the son of ANC leader Z.K. Matthews, as being 'ahead of' the rest of the students in terms of political understanding. As Makgothi grew older and his thinking became more advanced, Tambo began to speak in more overtly political terms. Tambo and Matthews 'would now give us … political education, tell us about the ANC and the whole struggle … interpret our history in the struggle mode'.[115] Influenced by both Matthews and Tambo, Makgothi joined the ANC around 1944, eventually becoming a YL committee member at St Peter's.

By the time Makgothi entered Fort Hare in 1948, he had been formally introduced into ANC politics. However, once at Fort Hare, his political understanding matured: 'Fort Hare, for us, it helped us to find ourselves; to find ourselves in a world in which we could have been swallowed up and ended up being just rubbish.'[116]

In his first year, Makgothi witnessed one of the results of the increasingly politically charged campus atmosphere: 'The first thing that happened at Fort Hare is we opened a branch of the Youth League.' He attributes the development of his political consciousness to being in the right place at the right time. He was again fortunate to come into contact with outstanding political figures. Rubbing shoulders with future Basutoland Congress Party president Ntsu Mokhehle, Sobukwe, future president of Zimbabwe Robert Mugabe (1950–1951), future ANC secretary-general Duma Nokwe (1947–1950), Nthato Motlana (1946–1948), an Africanist who was to become medical doctor to

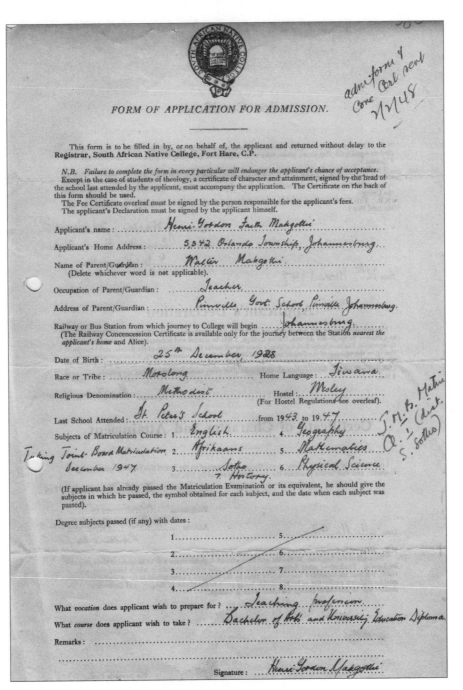

Henry Makgothi's Fort Hare application

FORM OF APPLICATION FOR ADMISSION

Mugabe R.G.

In all future correspondence quote Application No. 230

Failure to complete the form in every particular will endanger the applicant's chance of acceptance.

This form is to be filled in by the applicant and returned without delay to the **Registrar, South African Native College, Fort Hare, C.P.** together with the deposit of £3.

The Certificate of *Character* and *Attainment* must be signed by the head of the school last attended by the applicant in the case of all applicants applying for admission for the first time. Students of Theology should get this Certificate signed by the Church Authority under whose direction they are studying.

The *Fee Certificate* overleaf must be signed by the person responsible for the applicant's fees.

The Declaration must be *Written Out in Full* in the applicant's own handwriting and signed.

Applicant's name: (in BLOCK LETTERS) . ROBERT GABRIEL MUGABE

Important. The names given *Must* be the same as those under which the Applicant registered for the Matriculation or equivalent examination.

Applicant's Home Address: . Kutama, P.O. Makwiro, S.R.

Name of Parent/Guardian: . Peter Matibili
(Delete whichever word is not applicable).

Occupation of Parent/Guardian: . General

Address of Parent/Guardian: . Mutual buildings, P.O. Box 705, Bulawayo

Station from which journey to College will begin . . . Railway Station . KUTAMA (R.R.)

Bus Station (if any) . .

(The Railway Concession Certificate is available only for the journey between the Station *nearest the applicant's home* and Alice which is the station 1 mile from Fort Hare).

Date of Birth: 20th February 1924 . Race or Tribe: . Shona . Home Language: . Shona

Religious Denomination: . R. Catholic . Sex Male . Hostel: . Beda

Last School Attended: . Kutama School . from 19.32 to 19.41

Subjects of Matriculation or equivalent } Course: 1. English A (Nov) 4. Geography (June)
2. Zulu B (Nov) 5. Physiology & Hygiene (June)
Name of Examination . Senior Certificate (JME) 3. History (Nov) 6. Com. Arith (Nov) D. Commerce

Date of Examination: . Nov. 1946 . Candidates Examination No. (if known): . .

(If applicant has already passed the Matriculation Examination or its equivalent, he should give the subjects in which he passed, the symbol obtained for each subject, and the date when each subject was passed).

Degree subjects passed (if any) with dates

1. English I (1947) 5. Philosophy I (1948
2. History I (1947) 6. Education (1948)
3. Shona I (1947) 7. English II (1950)
4. G.I.S Philosophy (1947) 8. History II (1950) 9. Const. Law (1950)

What *vocation* does applicant wish to prepare for? . Teaching

What *course* does applicant wish to take? . Bachelor of Arts

Remarks: . .

DEPOSIT. No application will be considered from new applicants or from students seeking re-admission until the £3 deposit has been paid.
The deposit will be :—

(a) Returned to the applicant if he/she fails to qualify for admission, or notifies the College *before the 10th of February* that he/she is unable to come.

or (b) Credited to the student's account—£2/10/0 as fees and 10/- as library deposit—if the student is accepted and comes to College on time, or, if likely to be late, notifies the College of that fact before the 10th of February, giving the expected date of arrival. The Library deposit of 10/- will be returned at the end of the year to each student who has returned all library books borrowed and has no account outstanding with the Library for books mutilated or kept out over time.

or (c) Forfeited by students who do not comply with the requirements of the College as stated under (a) and (b)

Date . 20th January, 1951 . Signature: . R.G. Mugabe

Certificate of Character and Attainment

Robert Mugabe's Fort Hare application

Mandela and Sobukwe, and Matthews, who moved with Makgothi from St Peter's to Fort Hare, his involvement deepened. He says,

> Look, I went to Fort Hare when I was 18. I left Fort Hare five years later when I was 23 and a lot of my political understanding matured when I was in Fort Hare … I'm telling you we in the Youth League, we said to ourselves, look … we have a role to play out there … We are not just going to disappear in society and we thought that was the weakness of the intellectuals before us, left Fort Hare and just got swallowed up. They didn't seem to make any impact on the lives of people. So we thought we had a mission.[117]

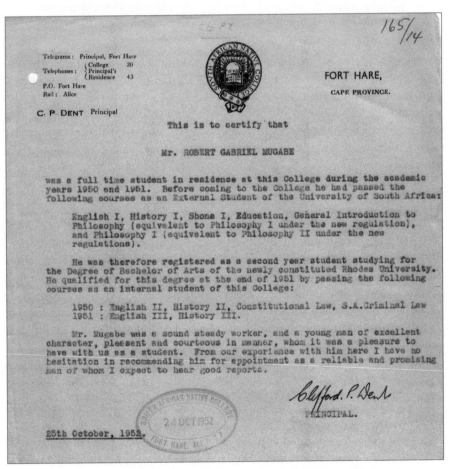

Clifford Dent offers a testimonial on behalf of Robert Mugabe

Start jiving on your books

The revitalisation of the ANC under Xuma, coupled with the war and the National Party victory of 1948, impacted the development of student political activism at Fort Hare. However, one of the more intangible influences on student activism was that of Z.K. Matthews. Though Professor Jabavu was president of the AAC until his retirement from Fort Hare in 1944, Matthews had a far greater impact on students' political development. In Matthews' autobiography, editor Monica Wilson writes:

> Few people realise what an influence he was to generations of students at Fort Hare. This naturally applied more specifically to those who actually attended lectures given by him, but many to whom he did not formally lecture admired him and came under his influence.[118]

Born in Barkley East in 1900, Matthews went to Lovedale before enrolling in a matriculation class at Fort Hare in 1918. He finished his BA degree at Fort Hare, becoming the school's first graduate on 3 May 1924. After a stint as headmaster at Adams College in Natal, Matthews travelled to the United States, where he received an MA under C.T. Loram at Yale University. He then moved on to the London School of Economics, where he studied under Bronislaw Malinowski.[119] Matthews returned to Fort Hare, accepting a lectureship in native law and social anthropology in 1936. In 1944, following Jabavu's retirement, Matthews was promoted to professor and made head of the African Studies Department.

Although Tim White calls Z.K. Matthews an educational 'elitist' and more of a liberal than a nationalist, he acknowledges that many students became active through contact with him. He writes: 'Students were drawn to hear the man who was able to dissect the many social problems they faced. Many learned the art of politics from Matthews.'[120] Often, it would be in the form of argument or debate. Through this discussion, the students developed a reverence for their teacher. Joe Matthews says:

> Students would argue with him. And he wouldn't say, 'Look here, I'm the professor. I'm not prepared to discuss politics with you chaps; you must study your subjects.' He would hone the arguments and exchange heated arguments with students and that is why a lot of them when they left the university would say that he was the man who inspired them. Because of what he was and what he was prepared to discuss, both in class and outside it.[121]

Pitje, who was a critic of Z.K. Matthews later in the 1940s, spoke of the professor's influence during the 1942 Beda Hall student strike: 'I remember several science students discussing his influence … Z.K. offered to speak to the students, but they turned down the suggestion on the grounds that once he had spoken, the strike would collapse.'[122] A fearful respect developed for Matthews. Although the militant Youth Leaguers thought Z.K.'s views were accommodationist, they were in awe of his ability to win any debate by calmly dissecting and analysing the political situation in the country or on the campus. Makgothi talks of Matthews' prowess:

Professor Z.K. Matthews

> So the professor … he was a brilliant man, absolutely brilliant. We would go at him … take up certain positions on certain issues and we'd go and clear it up with him and he'll say, sit down here and let's talk about this thing. And then when you leave, you feel, no man, you've been cheated somehow.[123]

Intent on showing off their militancy, the students provoked a conflict with their professor and mentor. Matthews, an extremely serious man, was staunchly independent-minded and this led the more militant students to label him a conservative. He would not allow the YL to dictate his thoughts and actions, and was therefore regarded with suspicion at times. However, Matthews was not interested in a popularity contest and would never give up his independence for political gain. Isaac Mabindisa (1959–1962) says,

> Some of the students thought Z.K. Matthews was a very conservative man because students wanted adventure, that you could always challenge the government and it was going to fall tomorrow … I remember when Mandela was first sentenced to a prison term. We were standing outside the dining hall … and there was an announcement on the notice board that he had been sentenced to, I think, three years' imprisonment. We thought, oh well, when he comes out, by the time he comes out, we'll

> be free. I think people like Matthews knew that this was going to be a
> very long struggle and therefore he didn't encourage these adventures,
> and some students didn't like him because of that.[124]

White points out that the clash between Matthews and the YL was inevitable.
He writes: 'Matthews' influence at Fort Hare was seen as being too strong
and his political stance was too moderate for the likes of Mda.'[125] Matthews
was reared with a liberal Cape worldview, marked by a belief in assimilation
and the notion that there was 'room for all races in Africa'. His worldview,
according to Williams, had much in common with whites on the Fort Hare
staff who believed in the Cape liberal tradition.[126] Calling Matthews 'most
disgusting', and his views close to those of 'the European liberal', a 'positive
danger to African freedom', Mda, along with Pitje, generated anti-Matthews
sentiment among the YL members.[127]

The rift between Matthews and the Youth Leaguers eventually grew so wide
that the professor and Pitje were not on speaking terms. A vote of no confidence
in Matthews as the president of the Cape Congress was even passed. Makgothi
explained:

> At one stage, when I was secretary of the Youth League, we got a bit
> annoyed. There was a conference of the ANC coming and we thought
> we'll have it out, we'll say some nasty things about the professor, that
> he's not supporting us. I think we sent Sobukwe as our representative
> to the conference to go and state our case, the difficulties we had in
> organising at Fort Hare despite the fact that the Professor was there.[128]

Buthelezi was another of the Youth Leaguers that came under Matthews'
influence. He recalls that some of the YL members questioned the fact that
Matthews had participated in the NRC. He remembers the students inviting
Matthews to a meeting to respond to demands that he should resign his
position in the ANC because the NRC was a government structure. Buthelezi
says, 'I remember actually with amusement that some of us who knew how
competent Professor Matthews was were not overly keen that he should be
invited because we thought he would just scuttle us. Because he was very,
very able.'[129]

YL pressure did not disturb Matthews, and he never gave in. Makgothi
comments: 'The professor, that didn't ruffle him. He took it in his stride. He
was a very level-headed person.'[130] Buthelezi recalls Matthews calmly getting
the best of the students. When Ntsu Mokhehle asked the professor if he

believed in democracy, Matthews replied, 'Yes, Mr Mokhehle, I do believe in democracy, although I sometimes have no confidence in the *demos*, that is, the people. It's not so much the hands that you count when it comes to voting that matters, Mr. Mokhehle, but the heads behind them.' Buthelezi adds, 'Now, for some of us at that age, it was just the sort of thing that we were afraid of when the suggestion was made that Professor Matthews should be invited.'[131]

Z.K. Matthews was uninterested in responding to the superficialities of political rhetoric and intrigue, and his prime concern was always the education of the African at Fort Hare. White writes, 'Matthews would never have been able to sacrifice his independence for support based on restrictive conditions.'[132] Joe Matthews says that his father never gave in to pressure:

> Are you going to give in, just give into everything that people say, because you want to be a hero and militant? Or are you going to tell them, sorry, this is my policy and I don't agree with that? And that's what Z.K. did, always. He didn't shrink from saying, no, I don't agree with that. And people would say, well, he's a reluctant revolutionary. And I would say, no, it's just his viewpoint.[133]

In spite of the apparent differences in philosophy, Matthews's influence on the political scene at Fort Hare was unquestionable. His courses naturally attracted students interested in public affairs, and classroom discussion ranged from current legislation to witchcraft and sorcery.[134] Students often made their way to the Matthews's home in Alice for hours of discussion. Frieda Matthews feels that the depiction of the 'angry young men' of the YL pitted against the older leaders of the ANC is not entirely accurate. In her memoir, she wrote of this 'misconception': 'I was often present when members of the Youth League of the ANC held discussions with older leaders in our home in Alice. These were frank and open on both sides, each treating the other with respect and admiration for their points of view.'[135] Although the relationship between Matthews and the Youth Leaguers might appear ambiguous when viewed from the outside, discussion with his students yields an image of a more positive relationship. A picture of a stern, dedicated teacher emerges from their recollections and the contact, although occasionally confrontational, contained an underlying respect.

Makgothi says that although, at the time, they thought Matthews was conservative, students could still sit down and talk with the professor: 'He made you feel. He made you think.'[136] It may have been Matthews' firm belief in the importance of study that caused the students to doubt his political militancy. Frieda Matthews writes:

> Time and again young students would visit us to discuss with their teacher and leader the part they wished to play in our political predicament, and after listening attentively and respectfully to their proposals, my husband would quietly reply, 'The best you can do at this stage for the liberation of our people is to study and study hard and pass. We want qualified men who have learnt to think things out so as not to be pushed blindly into situations which will do no good at all and which may retard our progress.'[137]

On close examination, the differences between Matthews and the Youth Leaguers are less stark. Gerhart writes: 'The underlying conception of political change still revolved around ideas of reforming, rather than totally scrapping, South Africa's system for the distribution of power.'[138] The Youth Leaguers advocated new tactics of mass action and non-collaboration, but ambiguous

Z.K. Matthews receives his honorary degree, 1961

goals of 'national freedom', political independence', and 'self-determination' were never clearly defined.[139] Makgothi says, 'We were interested in action, you know, action, 1949, we had a Programme of Action, which we wanted to see implemented. It meant certain things to us. It meant we must be militant.'[140] Gerhart writes that this militant rhetoric gave the impression that the perception of the struggle was changing more than it was in reality.[141]

Indeed, although the foundation of the new spirit of nationalism was undoubtedly racial exclusiveness, the 1948 'Basic Policy' of the national YL outlined a distinction between two streams of African nationalism that were developing. 'Garvey's slogan of "Africa for the Africans" and its implications that whites must be driven into the sea was disavowed as "extreme and ultra revolutionary"'. Instead, the YL opted for a more 'moderate' stream of nationalism, declaring, 'We of the Youth League take account of the concrete racial situation in South Africa, and realise that the different racial groups have come to stay.' Thus, while expecting 'national freedom', 'political independence', and 'self-determination', the Youth Leaguers accepted whites would participate in any future democracy.[142]

Although he loved to debate politics with his students, Z.K. Matthews was first and foremost a university staff member. As such, he took any disrespect for college authority seriously. He was extremely careful to separate his political affiliation with the ANC from his role as Fort Hare professor. Frieda Matthews writes:

Z.K. Matthews and Dr Alexander Kerr after receiving honorary degrees, 1961

Xhosa poet K.H. Billie sang the praises of Matthews and the graduates, 1961

Z.K. Matthews with his daughters after receiving his honorary degree in 1961

It did not matter how unhappy my husband was about a Senate decision
… I have never known my husband to give students, our sons included,
his own stand against a move in Senate, and thus he missed what might
be called popular approval from the students as a result.[143]

Repeatedly, Matthews would chastise the students for not concentrating on
their studies. Buthelezi recalls one such time fondly:

The Professor wasn't very happy when we were at rag and we dressed
ourselves in all sort of things and we'd jive and so on. I remember one
day I saw him sitting there in his black tie and so on, he was shaking his
head … And then on Monday morning, I think we had a Roman Dutch
Law class, his class, and he asked us some questions about the lessons
we had done the previous week. And we were all very blank. And I
remember him saying that, 'sirs', you know he was saying sirs, he was
poking fun at us, calling us sirs. 'Sirs, stop all these nonsensical things
you do about the place. Start jiving on your books.'[144]

◆◆◆◆◆

Though Matthews clearly influenced a wide spectrum of students at Fort Hare,
he had a particularly profound effect on his son Joe. 'I can't say I got my
political consciousness from Fort Hare,' says Joe Matthews, who adds, 'I got
it from my parents, obviously.'[145] In response to a question about the influence
Tambo had on him while studying at St Peter's, Matthews says, 'When you
are the son of Z.K., you won't be influenced by anyone. You don't need any
other influences.' Born in Durban on 17 June 1929, the eldest son of Z.K.
and Frieda, Matthews describes his family as 'very political'. He completed
his primary education at Lovedale, before moving on to St Peter's, where he
joined the YL. 'We had our own library, which was full of political material
and books.' Matthews remembers consistently learning from his father:

There was a lot of argument and discussion, every day. You had
discussions and sometimes they would be quite profound. I remember
discussing with him the whole issue of civilisations … that had
gone virtually without a trace. The question was, what is it that each
civilisation did which was a change that led to disaster … Now you
don't often [see] a father and son discuss the merits or otherwise of
change and the roles of civilisations, but with him, you could do it …
He would even point out books that you could read.[146]

Thus, when Matthews arrived at St Peter's, other students felt that politically speaking he was ahead of them. He became the chairman of the YL branch at St Peter's and earned a reputation as a die-hard. Matthews entered Fort Hare in 1947 and became the secretary of the YL when it was founded in 1948. 'By the time we got to the college, we had ideas,' he told Gerhart. 'We were members of the movement; we had been in that movement for some time, and we knew all the ins and out of the ANC.'[147]

Matthews was part of the militant YL group that fought for the Programme of Action and condemned collaboration with non-Africans and communists. In 1951, he was still arguing against multi-racial cooperation when Mandela tore into what he called Matthews' 'emotional, nationalist attitudes'.[148] In time, Matthews' stance towards whites and liberals softened, a combination of the erosion of youthful exuberance and experiences in 1950s' Johannesburg.

> You meet white people who say they entirely support you … and you feel, well I don't think there can be such whites, but anyway, here they are. And then you see them being arrested, you see things happening to them, you see them banned … There are all sorts of factors operating … the immediate needs of the struggle … contact with people … You start to learn more; you start to build up; you start to understand a bit more.[149]

Buthelezi and the Dettol

By 1950, the Victoria East Branch had made its mark. It was influential in pushing for the adoption of the Programme of Action, had helped lead the nurses in their strike at Victoria Hospital, and was the context for the political maturation of Robert Sobukwe in his Completer's Social speech. David Burchell writes: 'By the 1950s, the impetus underlying most of the troubles on campus could be traced to a strong black nationalism.'[150] In May 1950, the entire SRC resigned, charging Principal Dent with abrogating the constitution of the SRC for refusing to grant permission for a mass meeting of students to discuss the decision of a relay race judge.[151] However, by 1950 it was the YL, and not the SRC, that controlled the campus, and the resignation of the SRC members had little effect on political activism at Fort Hare. On 9 September 1950, the Youth Leaguers continued their move towards overtly political action when they decided to boycott the visit to the campus of the governor-general, G. Brand van Zyl. Frieda Matthews wrote:

The Senate met and made feverish arrangements for this august occasion. Tea at such and such a place, lunch in the neighbouring town (for Whites only) and a meeting with the students from three to four that afternoon. The students, without the knowledge of the staff met to discuss this: How can we welcome the head of State of which we are not citizens?[152]

Upset over the showing of a segregated film at Beacon Bioscope in Alice, the student meeting Frieda referred to was actually called to discuss boycotting the cinema.[153] R.A. Pillay (1950–1953) says:

> [Dewey] brought a picture called 'Unfaithful' ... And when we went to go ... he said, no, we can't come in there. This picture's banned for the non-whites. So we got really angry. We came back to the university and had a big meeting there outside the dining hall and said, look this chappy is insulting us. He depends on our custom, now he embarrasses us by bringing pictures like this ... So we'll boycott this Dewey fellow; we won't go to the films anymore.[154]

It was at this meeting outside the dining hall, just two days before the governor-general's arrival, that the idea came up of staying away from his visit to campus. Pillay continues: 'One up-start called Dennis Merckel ('50) ... jumped up there and said, Let's boycott the governor-general. ... He's a symbol of our oppression in this country. Now why must we go there and listen to him. So that's all he had to say and it was decided we're boycotting this fellow.'[155] Calling the governor-general an 'embodiment of British imperialism', the Youth Leaguers led the move against attending the meeting he was to address.[156] In the principal's report on the incident, Dent wrote: 'This was not a case of a few students deciding to absent themselves from an official function; it was an organised boycott, and was therefore a serious matter.' The effort was indeed organised. When Saturday afternoon came, more than two thirds of the student body stayed away from the mandatory meeting. Dent continued: 'By 3 p.m. it was apparent that a large proportion of the students were boycotting the meeting.'[157]

Dent had made attendance at the assembly compulsory and the students' open defiance was taken seriously. In the Matthews home, Joe and his cousin Peter felt the wrath of Z.K. The professor had been away during the governor-general's visit and was shocked to learn that his son and nephew did not participate in the festivities. Frieda Matthews wrote:

He asked, well, how did the governor-general's reception go off? Silence. After what seemed like an eternity, but must have been only a second or so, Joe said, 'We did not go.' 'You did not what?' 'We did not go because the students decided to boycott the meeting and, after all, we are right, this man stands for all that we are fighting against.'[158]

Joe says: 'My father was very, very angry. You see, he was now in a difficulty. The authorities had to take action against the students and both my cousin and I had been in the boycott.'[159] Buthelezi recalls that the boys were 'not even allowed to sleep at home that night'.[160]

Outside the Matthews home, Senate meetings were called and long discussions were held on how to deal with mass disobedience. The Senate affirmed its right to require students to attend functions arranged by the college, and absence from the assembly was considered an act of insubordination. Students were forced to sign a declaration acknowledging their disobedience and pledging to honour all college rules.[161] Only the clemency of the governor-general prevented the Senate from taking strong action against the students. Communicating with Dent, Van Zyl made it known that he would rather have the incident swept under the carpet.[162] Yet the governor-general's goodwill did not close the incident. As was becoming customary at Fort Hare, those who chose not to participate in the boycott paid for their cooperation with the authorities at the hand of campus vigilantes. Dent wrote:

> Some students assume the right to enforce the boycott by secret persecution called 'lynching' of students who do not obey the instructions of the 'caucus'. This lynching has in the past taken various forms: attack in the dark, or soaking a students' bed with water.[163]

Following a lengthy but unscientific investigation, the authorities implicated Buthelezi in the wetting of W.M. Chirwa's bed and expelled him from Fort Hare shortly before he was due to graduate.[164] The evidence against Buthelezi, from a student deposition, was as follows:

> Muhoya (1945–1950) washed in a bucket of water, in which he had put some Dettol, in the bathroom. F. Simon (1950–1953) and Buthelezi were washing there at the same time. When Muhoya had finished washing, Buthelezi asked if he might have the bucket of water, and took it away, leaving the other two men still in the bathroom. When Muhoya went from the bathroom to his room, he found Chirwa's bed soaked with water. Leaving to go to breakfast, he met Chirwa in the courtyard of the Hostel and told him about it. At breakfast, Muhoya noticed that

> Buthelezi also was late in finishing his meal. Soon after … both Chirwa
> and Muhoya claim that they could smell Dettol in the water on Chirwa's
> bed and Mrs Rodgers confirms this.[165]

On these grounds, Buthelezi was expelled, along with two other students,
including Rosette Ndziba (1948 –1950), setting off a string of events that
would involve some of the nation's future well-known political figures.

Because Buthelezi was the successor to a chief, his expulsion had implications
outside Fort Hare. Letters from people such as the secretary for Native Affairs
arrived at Fort Hare, inquiring about the incident. A telegram asking Dent to
reconsider arrived from Councillor A.W.G. Champion, saying that Buthelezi
may have 'been influenced badly'.[166] Buthelezi himself appealed to Dent
on 27 September 1950 to allow him to write his exams outside Fort Hare.
However, he refused to admit his guilt in the incident and it was only after
his uncle, Cyprian Buthelezi, another uncle, Pixley Seme, and Senator Edgar
Brookes interceded on his behalf that Dent agreed to allow Buthelezi to write
his exams in Durban.

Once granted permission to take his exams, Buthelezi finally came clean, but
he refused to apologise. In a lengthy letter written to Principal Dent, Buthelezi
outlined the circumstances that led to the 'lynching' of Chirwa. Buthelezi
describes how Chirwa advocated the boycott of the governor-general's
meeting, pretended to stay away from the meeting, and then 'turned right
around and went to the CU Hall to give the official welcome to the governor-
general against which he had advised quite a number of students.'[167] Buthelezi
continues:

> There is nothing to be ashamed of in it as far as I am concerned. I felt
> and still feel that Mr. W.M. Chirwa's behaviour was very cowardly and
> mean in the extreme … I was not a member of any 'pressure group'
> … The only case I know is that of Chirwa and the reasons are those I
> have stated above, i.e. his cowardly and mean behaviour … I am not
> apologising for this.[168]

◆◆◆◆◆

Although Buthelezi says he learned politics at his 'mother's knee', his real
political education occurred at Fort Hare under the watchful eye of Z.K.
Matthews. Born on 27 August 1928 in Mahlabathini, Zululand, his mother
was the granddaughter of King Cetshwayo and daughter of King Dinizulu.

His father was the grandson of Chief Mnyamana Buthelezi, prime minister to King Cetshwayo. Buthelezi grew up in a traditional household, spending his early years as a herd-boy. As a child, his mother regaled him with tales of Zulu rebellion, particularly of the Bambatha Rebellion of 1906.[169] He remembers in his early childhood the Zulu regent, Prince Mshiyeni, calling a big political convention that was attended by Chief Albert Luthuli. Dr J.L. Dube frequented the regent's quarters, along with Edgar Brookes, with whom Buthelezi came into contact at Adams College.[170]

Buthelezi attended Impumalanga Primary School from 1934 to 1943 before enrolling at Adams College in Amanzimtoti in 1944. His formal political education began at Adams, where Brookes was the principal. Brookes was, at the same time, a senator in Cape Town representing the Africans of Natal. Qualified Africans at that time elected several whites to represent them in parliament. At Adams, Brookes had an influence on Buthelezi's political development, along with many graduates of Fort Hare who had joined the academic staff.[171]

After he matriculated from Adams, some members of the Buthelezi family opposed the continuation of Buthelezi's education. Led by Chief Maliyamakhanda, the regent of the family and Buthelezi's uncle, the call was made to discontinue Buthelezi's schooling. Temkin suggests this was because Maliyamakhanda saw a relationship between Buthelezi's education and his interest in politics. Once, Buthelezi had been seen in the company of radical journalist Jordan Ngubane. Family members even branded Buthelezi a communist and follower of M.B. Yengwa, a leading member of the YL.[172]

Maliyamakhanda felt Buthelezi had to steer clear of politics in order to prepare to serve his people later in life, and thus refused to pay for his nephew's further education. However, Buthelezi's mother stepped in. Believing the tribe required learned leaders, and fulfilling her dead husband's wish to educate their son, she supported Buthelezi as he entered Fort Hare in 1948.[173] Buthelezi's classmates at Fort Hare included Joe Matthews, Ntsu Mokhehle, Robert Sobukwe, Robert Mugabe, Duma Nokwe and Henry Makgothi. Among his first-year roommates in an Iona rondavel were Njoroge Mungai, a future Kenyan foreign minister and Orton Chirwa (1948–1950), a future minister of justice in Malawi, who was kidnapped and imprisoned by the Hastings Banda regime. Perhaps most importantly, Matthews taught one of Buthelezi's major subjects, Bantu administration, and two of his minor subjects, Roman Dutch Law and criminal law. 'I regarded him not only as my teacher, but really as one of my mentors,' says Buthelezi.[174]

At Fort Hare in the early and active days of the YL, Buthelezi could not help but become politically involved. He explains the decision to join as 'a natural step' in that his uncle was Dr Pixley Seme, the founder of the ANC, and he grew up in that tradition.[175] In 1949 Buthelezi's roommate was Temba Hleli and Buthelezi led the protest against his friend's expulsion after the Completer's Social speech. And although Hleli was never reinstated, the incident gave Buthelezi a chance to test his leadership skills for the first time.[176] R.A. Pillay recalls Buthelezi being constantly engaged in discussion with Joe Matthews and Abdool Karrim Essack ('50), an Indian student:

> These three fellows always used to be locked in political discussions. They'd walk from Beda Hall and go right up to the dining hall, which was some half a kilometre away. These chaps would be talking from this end to that end, and they'd stop 20 times in between. They had missed their lunch. But they were still carrying on. And what they'd be arguing about at the time was, Gatsha and Joe were talking about passive resistance as being the key political solution to the country. And there was this Indian, on the other hand, this fellow Essack, who was saying, you fellows are talking nonsense … This was quite a funny thing to see. An Indian on one side saying, no passive resistance and the ANC boys on the other side saying, they should go for passive resistance.[177]

Revolting against liberals

Despite Buthelezi's expulsion, the YL continued to enliven the atmosphere at Fort Hare in the early 1950s. National politics dominated the students' agenda in 1952, an especially busy year. It was not unheard of for a visiting preacher whose sermon did not meet with the students' approval to 'later find that their tyres have been deflated under cover of darkness'.[178] When the Report of the Eiselen Commission on Bantu Education was published, the students totally rejected it. And when Dent gave a speech to the Transkeian Bunga (General Council) in King William's Town, expressing his approval of some parts of it and urging 'reasonableness' in the African fight for equality, the students abandoned lectures and staged a sit-down protest in front of Stewart Hall.[179] At an assembly shortly after the speech, when Dent called for silence, someone shouted: 'Oh, shut up!' According to Selby Ngcobo, the affair damaged Dent's stature and 'moral authority' irreparably.[180]

The principal took another hit when, in response to a government warning, he urged Z.K. Matthews not to speak before the Political Committee of the United Nations. In an interview with the *Daily Dispatch,* Dent said: 'As a member of the College, which is subsidised by the Government, Professor

Matthews is not free to speak, and I would think the Government would take a serious view if he did speak.'[181] Matthews, who was on leave in New York at the time as a visiting professor at Union Theological Seminary, did not take to Dent's attempt to control his decision, which he deemed intimidation. In the end, Matthews was never invited to speak before the UN, but he did circulate among delegates an ANC memorandum opposing apartheid.[182] White notes that there was a 'certain amount of tension' between Dent and Matthews after the incident that never fully subsided.[183]

The matter did not end there. When Matthews returned to Fort Hare in 1953, he found the Department of Education, Arts and Sciences had again approached the Fort Hare Governing Council, requesting action against him for certain speeches he had made in the United States. Dent persuaded Matthews to issue a statement, in which he wrote:

> ... as a South African national and leader of African thought, I have never hesitated to express my disagreement with schemes or policies which I believed to be detrimental to the development of harmonious relations between different sections of the population, but I submit that I have always done so with due regard to the views of those who are of a different persuasion.

He recalled an incident when, after a speech, three American women complained that he was not radical enough: 'I had not, as they had hoped, espoused the policy of "Africa for the Africans", but had spoken about "Africa for the Africans too", which was not in keeping with their view on the subject.' Dent sent the statement to the department and nothing further was heard about Matthews' 'alleged activities' in America.[184]

Yet despite a growing disenchantment with Dent's parochialism and the missionary atmosphere on campus, Fort Harian discontent with the National Union of South African Students (NUSAS) dominated discussion. The growing disillusionment with NUSAS indicated a continuing movement towards the ideas of black nationalism and anti-trusteeship Sobukwe had first articulated three years earlier. As government apartheid legislation grew more stringent, NUSAS became less and less of an option for Fort Hare students. Frank Mdlalose comments:

> We got into the groove of saying the liberals, like the missionaries, are people that cannot be trusted because they will talk fine and smoothly to us but they won't act properly. So let's have a clear-cut difference

between us and them. Cut them off completely. NUSAS is one of them. Cut them off from our action.[185]

NUSAS, founded in 1924, initially served as a forum for association between white students at Afrikaans and English-language universities. Over the years, as progressive English-speaking whites pushed for the admittance of Fort Hare to NUSAS, the Afrikaner students withdrew from the association. NUSAS leaders maintained a tenuous relationship with the Afrikaans universities until 1948, when the National Party victory quelled any lingering hope at uniting English and Afrikaner students. From that point, the debate in NUSAS shifted to whether the organisation should involve itself in the issues of national politics or confine its agenda to student matters.[186] In the early 1950s the students at Fort Hare felt NUSAS leaned too far to the former focus, sparking a lively series of events on campus.

In June 1952, NUSAS president Patricia Arnett came to Fort Hare with a small delegation to convince the students not to pull out of NUSAS. She met with SRC members. According to Mdlalose, Arnett had no chance of convincing them. 'I was on the SRC,' he says. 'We were all against it and said, "Forget about it, we are pulling out."' Mdlalose recalls it as a time that 'we were revolting against liberals'.[187] The students believed that the stance assumed by NUSAS did not fit in with the African nationalism they felt was required to gain political equality. NUSAS' refusal to enter the realm of politics was unacceptable to the students, who felt the organisation's failure to adopt a stance of 'political and social equality for all men in South Africa' left them no choice but to secede.[188]

At national level, similar discussions about multi-racial cooperation were taking place. The disintegration of the SACP after the passage of the Suppression of Communism Act of 1950 led many African communists to make the ANC their political home. When, on May Day 1950, the ANC worked with Indians, coloureds, and communists to organise a national strike, many Youth Leaguers and African nationalists felt attention was being diverted from their Programme of Action. Mandela, Tambo and Sisulu all objected to ANC participation, but 'the extent of the popular response' and the government's increasing hostility, combined with their own experiences of close cooperation with radicals of different races, prompted a 'shifting toward acceptance of a multi-racial front and cooperation with the left'.[189] This multi-racial cooperation grew over the 1950s, upsetting some Africans who felt a more exclusive African nationalism was needed, and resulting in the Africanist split from the ANC and subsequent 1959 formation of the PAC.

Meanwhile, after being rebuffed by the SRC, Arnett wanted to talk to the students. Mdlalose explained what happened next: 'We didn't want Patricia Arnett to bamboozle the students, to fall for her and NUSAS. So we had to organise.' Mdlalose and others devised a scheme whereby it would be impossible for Arnett to sway the student meeting in her favour. He described how they strategically positioned detractors of NUSAS in the crowd:

> We put Galera in the gallery – he was a powerful man – to argue against NUSAS. We put so and so there; we put so and so there. But our most powerful man, a gallery man only. When Chirwa [SRC president W. Chirwa] asked for speakers, everyone raised their hands. I was up there with Chirwa [calling on people to speak]. That's the hand I see. That's the hand. Then at that time, all the time I'm working up to it, Galera is getting restless, stomping the ground. So I say, let's have someone from the gallery. It was in the CU Hall. Then Galera came up and blasted the whole issue of NUSAS. And I could see the fingers of Patricia Arnett trembling.[190]

Having gained the upper hand, Mdlalose relates how he orchestrated the defeat of NUSAS:

> At that stage, everyone wanted me to talk. So I said, Mr Chairman, I want to make an appeal to you. We've heard a powerful argument against NUSAS, but you know we are democratic. We must hear the opposite view … Those that are for NUSAS put up your hands. Then of course few are brave enough to put up their hands after Galera's powerful argument. And I know who is a great debater. I wasn't going to point at the great debater. I point at the weakest man among the lot. He came up and couldn't express himself, until it ultimately became clear that we wouldn't lose. [191]

It is likely that the rejection of NUSAS would have taken place without Mdlalose's plot as 'it had become apparent that the commitment of the national organisation [NUSAS] to building a new dispensation was rather half-hearted'.[192] When on her visit to campus Arnett reiterated that her organisation, since its foundation, had pursued an avowedly non-political role and that politics did not fall into its activities, it was clear the rift between NUSAS and Fort Hare students was wide. There was also some sensitivity on the part of Fort Harians to alleged racial slights, especially at conferences, and further dismay when, in 1950, NUSAS pulled out of the International Union of Students because it claimed the organisation had become communistic.[193] After the chicanery of Mdlalose and his compatriots, a vote was taken, and withdrawal from NUSAS was approved by a count of 147 to 67. The statement presented to the Fort Hare administration read,

> That in view of the fact that the policy and activities of NUSAS fail to satisfy the non-Europeans on the whole, and as this body has openly and unequivocally refused to recognise even the principle of political equality and, seeing that it is of no positive benefit to us we resolve that Fort Hare students as a Body secede from it.[194]

According to Mdlalose, the administration did not take kindly to the students' secession from NUSAS. Dent identified himself with the liberals and took the students' revolt personally. The students' rejection of both the liberals and missionaries hurt Dent, and he could never quite come to terms with their disapproval.[195]

We are going to defy

The growth of anti-NUSAS sentiment at Fort Hare coincided with the onset of the nationwide Defiance Campaign.[196] And, as had become customary, Fort Harians were in the middle of the action. With Z.K. Matthews in the United States, Dr James Njongwe took over as acting president of the ANC in the Cape, and interacted frequently with the Fort Hare students. He sent A.P. Mda, Walter Sisulu, Oliver Tambo and Moses Kotane to educate the students and prepare them for the Defiance Campaign. Mdlalose comments:

> These are the people we interacted with in 1952, before the Defiance Campaign. And they put us into the mould of it. Njongwe, particularly as the president in the Cape, interacted with us a great deal. We were learning freedom songs in Ntselemanzi ... ANC Youth League was alive in Ntselemanzi. We talked to people in the surrounding areas, Upper Qamasha, Lower Qamasha, Fort Beaufort ... We got so involved that we did not even go to classes.[197]

It is safe to say that if Matthews had not left for the United States, such academic delinquency would not have been tolerated. However, Njongwe did not intend students to miss classes and he eventually put his foot down. As the Defiance Campaign took off, the Fort Hare group pressed to be involved. The SRC passed a resolution commending the Defiance Campaign, saying that the students 'take pride in its heroes'.[198] However, the students were not content to remain on the sidelines. Discussions in 'bush meetings' high above campus under the cypress tree on Sandile's Kop, where years earlier Eddie Roux had conducted lectures on communism, centred on how the students could participate. Mdlalose states:

> We wrote to Njongwe saying, now, we are going to defy. I don't know how to transmit to you, we were all so powerfully strong, wanting to go to jail. Virtually 90 per cent of the students at Fort Hare were behind us. Ready to go to jail. Njongwe sent a telegram back, saying you have done very well so far. Your work over the eastern province is well known. Now the next duty you have is to go to the classroom and pass. I had to read that notice before the students. It was a most painful thing on our part … We were told not to defy. We couldn't go against the leader. We were crying, but we were to obey.[199]

Although the students themselves did not defy, they organised the protest in and around Alice. Karis and Carter note that the students were 'active as organisers in the towns and villages of a wide area during the night and at weekends' and that some 70 per cent of those arrested in the early period of the campaign came from the small cities and towns of the Eastern Cape.[200] The students arranged for people to ignore curfew laws and to sit on benches reserved for whites in the train station. In a letter to a friend, Williams underscored the fervour with which the students organised.

> The headquarters of the movement seems to be centred somewhere in this area. Joseph Matthews and Co. are always on the move here, talking in groups to others, mainly students. The students are flooding the area with the necessary amount of unrest. One sees, on a Sunday afternoon, huge groups of students returning to the hostels from the veld, excited and glowing.[201]

In August, the day after a particularly large group of volunteers had been arrested in Alice, Fort Hare students marched into town and rallied in front of the courthouse in support of the detainees. Mdlalose says: 'We'd organise the whole of Fort Hare to come and sing around the courthouse to disrupt things.' The peaceful protest of the students soon turned violent as police were called in. Mdlalose adds:

> They brought police from King William's Town, from Fort Beaufort, from all over, a big group. We, as the students, we just sang. Then

we got the baton charge. That's when I saw the ferocity of the police hitting us. We ran. I could never forget that the policeman who was the strongest in attacking us had a label, had a number, E331. I'm talking of 1952 and I want to tell you that I can never forget that number to my grave. Today I still see it clearly, E331. Hitting us, jumping over us. You fall down, he stands over you; you run away, he pushes you.[202]

The police baton charge marked the last Defiance Campaign activity for the Fort Hare students, who by the end of the 1952 were wearing ANC colours on their sleeves.[203] After the incident in Alice, they took up legal action against the police. Many of the students had seen E331. However, their case was futile from the start. Mdlalose explains: 'When they brought over the people to identify who had done this, that, and the other and we saw the man with E331, pushing his chest out to show that he was E331. Of course we all booed that, that's not E331. The real man was not there.'[204]

♦♦♦♦♦

After the Defiance Campaign, Victoria East Youth Leaguers elected Mdlalose as their president, a remarkable achievement for a student who had become interested in politics only two years earlier. Mdlalose was born on 29 November 1931 in Nqutu, a rural area. He was the last of five children, all boys. His father owned a small business and his mother was a teacher. 'My father was very poor until he began a small business of his own,' says Mdlalose. He attended a local primary school in Nqutu up to Standard 4 before moving on to the Polela Institution, a 'semi-high school.' Mdlalose did his Standards 5 and 6 at Polela, in what he describes as two rather uneventful years. The only disturbance was a strike of students in 1944, protesting against the expulsion of some black teachers. The instructors had assaulted white students who insulted them. This incident provided Mdlalose with one of his first glimpses of what he calls the 'racial clash' in the country.[205]

Mdlalose left Polela to do Standard 7 at St Francis College, Mariannhill, where he studied until he matriculated in 1949. Mariannhill was a Roman Catholic school and Mdlalose was taught by Roman Catholic sisters and some black teachers. It was a conservative school where 'there were no politics', according to Mdlalose. 'It was uneventful in terms of clashes between the races, but it was very good in terms of English, maths, botany.' In 1950, Mdlalose entered Fort Hare, uninitiated politically. 'When I got in there, I'd heard nothing about politics,' he says.[206]

However, the YL was at the height of its powers, and Mdlalose's interest would soon be awakened. His older brother Edward was also at Fort Hare and was a member of the YL. 'But he thought I was too young to join politics. He wasn't interested in telling me much about that,' says Mdlalose. It was Buthelezi, doing his third and final year, who got the younger Mdlalose brother involved. Mdlalose comments:

> I met him on a Saturday and he told me there was a meeting of the Youth League over at Ntselemanzi. 'Have I heard about that?' 'No, I haven't heard about that.' 'Didn't your brother tell you?' 'No. Come, let's go.' So I went to Ntselemanzi. To my surprise, my brother was one of the speakers at Ntselemanzi. And so I got interested in this Youth League and I became a member.[207]

Disregarding his brother's thoughts on his level of maturity, Mdlalose became increasingly involved in YL activity. He was struck by the controversial nature of politics when the governor-general's visit was boycotted: 'The whole college became alive with events like that. It was black/white clashes at the social and political level in the country with resultant activity at the college.' As a younger member of the YL, the group's more senior radicals educated Mdlalose. 'We got into … groups, or cells.' 'We had groups that were given lectures on politics. Fifty, fifty-one, there was a lot of that.' Joe Matthews was a powerful influence on Mdlalose:

> He was informed. He read African newspapers. He told us about Dr Kwame Nkrumah. We did this in small groups because the Youth League was banned at Fort Hare. Our bible was *Time Longer than Rope* by Edward Roux. Then of course we also studied the *Communist Manifesto* and the introduction by Harold Laski.[208]

'You must have heard about this,' Mdlalose says, readying to relate one of his favourite stories. 'I did not touch her,' he says. He proceeds to recount the tale of Frieda Matthews' graduation from Fort Hare in 1951, an event that influenced his political development a great deal. Mdlalose tells of one of the incidents that made him aware of the extent and absurdity of racial strife in South Africa:

> Dr A.J. van Ryan who was chancellor to Fort Hare had capped Mrs Frieda Matthews … And then the parliament and the NP were taunting him, saying, we saw you in the pictures with Mrs Matthews. And he said, 'But I didn't touch her.' Now that was put in

the newspapers, the *Daily Dispatch* ... And then it touched me that here is the wife of Professor Matthews, whom we respect so much, the vice-principal of Fort Hare, she is the librarian. And she's doing private studies and being capped. This one said, I did not touch her. That infuriated us.[209]

Buthelezi recalls the incident as well, saying, 'We have never forgotten that, that he was boasting that he didn't touch her, as if she was a leper.'[210]

Mdlalose was of course influenced by the events of 1952 at Fort Hare. He was an active participant in organising the Defiance Campaign, even receiving a beating from the police. He also led the movement for secession from NUSAS. Mdlalose's incipient African nationalism is already evident in this reaction to NUSAS. Despite reading Edward Roux and the *Communist Manifesto* at Fort Hare, Mdlalose says that his

> political thinking at the time was completely against communism ... When I read about communism, it was hard to understand it. The more I understood it and the more I read about what was happening in Russia, the more I disliked communism ... I found myself going more and more towards Africanism.

In 1955, while in medical school, Mdlalose spoke out against the Freedom Charter, which he felt was evidence of 'the communist element, which we had seen creeping into the ANC, gaining the upper hand'.[211] When the PAC was formed, Mdlalose was invited to join, but he decided to remain with the ANC to reform it from within. The political nationalist in him, first visible in the 1952 battle opposing NUSAS, would remain a strong element of Mdlalose's political ideology throughout his career.

After the Defiance Campaign, the government launched a systematic effort to halt the ANC's most experienced leaders through banning and prosecution. The nationwide crackdown on opposition groups made 1953 a difficult year at Fort Hare for Mdlalose and the Youth Leaguers. At the end of July 1952 Nelson Mandela was arrested and charged with violation of the Suppression of Communism Act, which had been passed in 1950. Along with 20 others, including Walter Sisulu, Mandela stood trial in Johannesburg in September. On 2 December, all 21 were found guilty of 'statutory communism' and sentenced to nine months' imprisonment. The sentence was suspended for two years, but the government onslaught continued. Fifty-two leaders around the country were served with six-month bans from attending any meetings or gatherings.[212]

The government response to the Defiance Campaign, which included the new Public Safety and Criminal Law Amendment Acts, undoubtedly affected life at Fort Hare. Capitalising on white fears sparked by the campaign, the National Party won an enlarged majority in the 1953 general election. Government banning orders now restricted many of the YL leaders that had frequented campus earlier in the decade. Leaders such as Nelson Mandela and Walter Sisulu were prohibited from attending public gatherings and had restrictions placed on their movement.

As chairman of the YL, Mdlalose and fellow Youth Leaguer Z.B. Molete (1951–1953) wanted to continue teaching YL principles in the cell system, as Joe Matthews had done a few years earlier. Yet post-Defiance Campaign South Africa provided new obstacles to organisation. In addition to new nationwide government oppression, 'spies were put into Fort Hare as students, but they were not students. We could see there was a man of 30 who was supposed to be studying,' says Mdlalose.[213] Logan Naidoo says: 'There were informers funded by the government and planted there to feed back information. So there was a climate of suspicion. You couldn't talk as we did, even with your friends because anyone could be a spy.'[214] Activism at Fort Hare was dealt a serious blow by the infiltration. Mdlalose says: 'Fifty-three was a difficult year and ANC work went down throughout the country because of the infiltration of the government.'[215]

Behave, read the Bible, and go to sleep

With extra-parliamentary activity hampered nationwide by the government crackdown, the next two years witnessed a decrease in national political activity at Fort Hare and a return to the earlier, more domestic targets of protest, which nonetheless cloaked deeper grievances: missionary authority, food and stringent rules and regulations. The activism of the first few years of the decade was replaced by suspicion, 'suspicion of the college authorities, suspicion of (not all) Europeans, suspicion of one another'.[216] Cragg notes that the 'growth of apartheid and African passive resistance movements of the 1950s ... intensified political feeling and one never knew what small incident might spark off trouble'.[217] The tenure of Principal Dent, which began in 1948 when Alexander Kerr retired, and had been somewhat overshadowed by militant YL activity, now became the pith of student attention.

Burchell writes that authoritarianism and repression increased at Fort Hare under Dent, who had spent his entire professional career at the university, beginning in 1922, when he came to teach physics and chemistry. Calling Dent's attitudes on political and campus issues 'dictatorial', Burchell charges that he alienated both staff and students.[218] Logan Naidoo, a student from 1954 to 1957, says that Dent was 'a missionary who felt everybody must behave, read the Bible at night and go to sleep'. His lasting image of Dent was of the principal prowling the streets for students breaking the college curfew. Naidoo tells how Dent, whose first initials were C.P., earned the nickname 'College Private Detective' among the students:

> The Tyumie River was virtually the boundary as far as Dent was concerned. If you got into Alice and were there after eight o'clock you were out of bounds. So he would stand on the bridge with a big trench coat and find out who came and who didn't. And if he got you, you were in for a lathering the next day. But he never got us. We would run and he couldn't run.[219]

Others, including Frank Mdlalose, preferred to call him 'College Public Disgrace'. Buthelezi says Dent was 'authoritarian by nature', and Mdlalose describes Dent's reign as a bumbling one where the professor 'lost his fibre, lost his respect … He made impromptu criticisms, wrong decisions and then Professor Matthews had to come and protect him, smooth things over.'[220]

Although Cragg describes Dent as 'conscientious and hard-working', the principal was never able to gain the complete trust and esteem of the students.[221] Kerr's disciplinary legacy seeped into Dent's management of the college and resulted in a growing tension between principal and students over domestic issues. Cragg notes that college and hostel rules often caused clashes, with the students ultimately ignoring regulations on hours of study, out of bounds and lights out.[222] Compulsory daily morning services, a mandatory Sunday service and Wednesday night sermons annoyed the students. A declaration by the SRC shows that the object of the students' ire was less the religion than the compulsion, as many of them came from at least somewhat religious families. As the SRC resolution put it: 'Roll-signing in morning assembly is childish and responsibility for daily attendance should be left up to the student.'[223] The principal and wardens often went around the hostels during the Sunday service to look for absentees. Yet many students devised clever ways to avoid the proceedings without being caught, and agitation against this service caused the authorities to make it optional after 1952.

In the first half of 1955, trouble began when a film entitled *Africa Untamed* was scheduled to screen in the CU Hall. Students felt the film would 'ridicule the personality of the Black Man of Africa; that it would be an insult to the university and students and the whole of Africa' and organised a boycott.[224] When an estimated 120 students showed up for the film, someone threw a large stone through a window, injuring a student and damaging the projector.[225] Extensive discussions on student discipline ensued in Senate as the staff attempted to put a lid on the 'simmering Fort Hare kettle'.[226]

Meanwhile, discontent spread to Iona Hostel and Wesley House, which the students had taken to calling 'Wesley High School'.[227] At a mass meeting, members of Iona drew up a resolution expressing their 'grave dissatisfaction with their warden'. They declared 'a permanent struggle against [the warden's] despotism' and demanded, 'THE IMMEDIATE RESIGNATION OF THE WARDEN OF THIS HOSTEL'.[228] Notices appeared on campus bulletin boards attacking the warden, James Rodgers, and other staff members. At the same time, the authorities issued new rules governing the visits by male students to the women's hostel, Elukhanyisweni. Logan Naidoo says: 'The high school attitude really became bad when they closed the women's hostel.'[229] When the students asked Dent to convene a mass meeting to discuss the new rules, he refused. Subsequent mass meetings, unauthorised by the authorities, were held on Sandile's Kop, including one organised by SRC president Sikota Wina the night before the graduation. The SRC decided to resign and the students resolved to boycott hostel prayers, meals, inter-institution sports and graduation, to crowd the women's hostel with visitors and to mix men and women in seating at morning assemblies.

Elukhanyisweni, the women's hostel

The boycott of graduation brought matters to a head late in April 1955. The students felt they were provoked into this action by Dent. Although the impetus for the boycott was the implementation of the new visiting hours, Andrew Masondo (1955–1957, 1959), who arrived at Fort Hare three months before the strike, explains that the issue was much larger:

> When we went on strike, many people, I think some of our parents thought, what were we doing? Why do we want to sleep in *mzana*?[230] But you see there was a principle that was involved. And the principle was that the Senate had taken that decision to prohibit people going to *mzana* without consultation with the SRC.[231]

Naidoo agrees that the factors underlying the strike were never acknowledged by the authorities. 'The real motive was suppression that was applied to us,' he says.[232] On the eve of the graduation, Wina convened another meeting in which he called the SRC a 'toothless bulldog', a phrase that was remembered years later by both Masondo and V.R. Govender.[233]

Fort Hare officials reacted strongly and swiftly to the students' boycott. Dent was offended by their action, panicked, and began to lose control of the college. The Senate viewed the boycott as the culmination of a 'long process of defiance' and felt that strong action had to be taken.[234] Senate meetings were held, Dr Thomas Alty, the vice-chancellor of Rhodes University, was consulted, and the Council executive met. It was decided to close the college temporarily and send all students home. Preparations were made in secrecy for the closure and the railway agreed to provide a special train to take students home. At a college assembly on the Wednesday morning after the graduation boycott, Dent directed the students to campus bulletin boards where they were to receive instructions. Afraid of their reaction to the closure, he let notices posted on these boards do the talking. Most students were to leave on a train at noon.[235] The police were called in to see that the proceedings went smoothly. Naidoo recalls: 'Police surrounded Fort Hare and we were marched out of there. The first time we saw police armoured vehicles was when they entered Fort Hare. Guys with guns came in. They accompanied the train right up to Durban.'[236]

As with Sobukwe's speech at the 1949 Completer's Social, the college authorities, particularly Dent, failed to comprehend the complexity of the events of 1955. Terence Beard notes the 'inability of most staff to comprehend the very meaning of the political struggle', with only two members of the Senate voting against the proposal.[237] Externally, the college concentrated on the alleged existence of a secret ring of students whose orders were followed by classmates, often through fear of physical violence and other forms of intimidation, at the expense of the constituted authorities.[238] As Dent put it in a memorandum:

> There has developed unmistakable evidence of the existence within the student body of a secret authority, sometimes referred to as the caucus, whose instructions are obeyed by the students ... The result has been that, under the influence of the caucus, the students have resorted to irregular methods, such as boycotts, threats and even violence.[239]

The alleged presence of a caucus, or secret group, took on a life of its own. Many staff members suspected this mysterious group of being pro-communist, and former principal Alexander Kerr even referred to the group as a 'junta'.[240] If there was a caucus, the students didn't know about it. In the press, they expressed bewilderment about such as organisation.[241] Writing 45 years later, Williams, one of the staff members who bought into the paranoia of the time, noted that, 'Dent, the Senate (including myself), and the Governing Council, succumbed to a collective neurosis which permeated the campus periodically in times of high tension.'[242]

Senate meetings continued in the wake of the closure of the college. Officials drafted letters to parents, telling them why their children had been sent home. As a precondition for re-admission, all students had to say whether they had attended the graduation ceremony, and make available whatever information they had about the ringleaders of the boycott movement. When the college reopened at the end of June, 14 students – allegedly the force behind the protest – were refused readmission. Five of the 14 appeared before the disciplinary committee and were readmitted on varying terms.[243] A commission was established, consisting of Dr J.P. Duminy (principal of Pretoria Technical College), Dr Edgar Brookes and Professor M.C. Botha (former director of education in the Cape) to look into the disturbance and recommend the changes necessary to prevent the repetition of such an occurrence.

The Duminy Commission, as it was called, met with the students, wardens and the principal, and inspected hostels over a two-week period. Yet in making its final report, the commission, like most of the college staff, failed to grasp the forces behind the student grievances. The main thrust of the report was that Fort Hare should work to temper its 'missionary high school' atmosphere and strive to become a university comparable with Rhodes. The commission believed that all new hostels should be under college, and not church control, and that attendance at religious functions should be optional.[244]

Yet instead of trying to understand the students' political strivings, the commission dismissed their action as testimony to 'the exaggerated sense of self-importance of the students'. At no time were the students portrayed as adults capable of making their own judgments. Duminy and his colleagues gave no credence to their political concerns, condemning the students for 'feeling that the College must be looked on as being in the vanguard of the political and racial struggle'. The commission recommended that 'those who claim freedom of speech should ... learn not to obtrude political and racial speeches into any and every kind of discussion'.[245]

While calling for a loosening of missionary control, the commission made the same mistake as the missionaries in failing to recognise the capabilities and initiative of black students. At its worst, student activism was not taken seriously, and was viewed by the authorities as the machinations and mischief of a select few comprising the 'caucus'. Beard suggests that this seemingly paternalistic attitude resulted at least partially from an inability to understand the meaning of the political struggle.[246] Calling on the YL and the Society of Young Africans (SOYA) to temper their activity, the commission noted, 'One could not ask the organisations not to stand for their principles, but they could be asked to direct their members at Fort Hare not to confuse the political struggle outside the college with resistance to discipline and authority inside it.'[247] Yet the students were not confused, according to Masondo, who says, 'It was clear that it was political. The university attacked the SRC. They were not prepared to recognise the SRC as an important aspect of the college.'[248] Reflecting on the events of the 1950s in his memoir, Cragg acknowledges the root of the disturbances:

> Underlying all, and the cause of most of our troubles, was the strong
> African nationalism and opposition to apartheid and white domination.
> This had been present before 1948 but was intensified by the victory of
> the Nationalist Party.[249]

The students equated their disenfranchisement within the college to that of their people outside campus. The consistent failure of the authorities to note the relationship between national and student politics served as a springboard for student activism and, more than any student 'caucus', caused activism to simmer on campus. In an interview with Williams, D.G.S. Mtimkulu summed up the situation best when he said the closure of the college could have been prevented if the administration had understood it was faced with a political situation rather than what they regarded as a 'schoolboy uprising'.[250]

◆◆◆◆◆

Andrew Masondo was one of the many who were misunderstood by the authorities. A new student at the time of the strike, he was not a ringleader. However, examination of his background shows just how far off the university was in thinking that the students were blindly following a 'caucus'. Masondo was born on 27 October 1936 in Sophiatown. His father was a barber and his mother worked for various doctors as a receptionist. Masondo began his education at the Albert Street Methodist School, where he did kindergarten up to sub-B. In 1946, he left for the St Agnes School, a Swedish mission boarding school, where he completed Standard 6 in 1949. Like Thenjiwe Mtintso, Masondo had a female political mentor. His father, Eloise, was 'strictly apolitical', leaving his lessons to his mother, Elsie. He says that she was 'an admirer of Communists' and 'a very fanatical member of the ANC'. It was during vacations from St Agnes that his lessons began:

> She taught me politics when I was about 13 years. She made me read papers. Every time when I was away she would stack the papers of the Communist Party of South Africa and when I come back I would read those things. Whatever material was to do with liberation, she tried to get me to read. She bought me books, political books ... She was a very inspiring person.[251]

On the advice of Father Trevor Huddleston, who was friendly with the Masondo family, Masondo entered St Peter's School in Rosettenville in 1950.[252] His appetite whetted by the books his mother gave him, Masondo delved further into politics when he entered St Peter's and came into regular contact with Father Huddleston, the school's superintendent.

In 1953, the Bantu Education Act was passed, and Masondo witnessed the response from the leaders of St Peter's. 'It was a missionary [school]. And the Anglican Church was proud of its institutions and particularly proud of St Peter's. So when Bantu Education took over schools, they could not accept that ... So that started to give you some political background.'[253]

At St Peter's, Masondo excelled in history, although he did not enjoy it. 'I thought the history we were taught was biased. You know I couldn't understand how people who came here and didn't have cattle suddenly talked about other people stealing their cattle.' Masondo also began to sharpen his leadership skills, leading revolts against the school's prefect system and poor food quality and earning himself the label of malcontent. Although there were no formal political organisations at the school, Masondo first came into contact with the YL at St Peter's when Joe Molefe, a former student, returned to mobilise the students. He brought them to hear Youth Leaguers talk. Masondo recalls listening to Alfred Hutchinson recount tales of his travels in Czechoslovakia.

> And then he described socialism for me, for us … the way it works, why it is, what is the aim, what it is doing. And I must say, I was attracted, very much attracted. Because I couldn't understand the vast differences between the impossibly rich and the diabolically poor. And I thought the system he described was a good one.

Complementing the lectures were his mother's books: 'I think when I was about 15, I read the biography of Stalin. And I kept reading.'[254]

Masondo steeped his mind in Marxist literature before he arrived at Fort Hare. His mother was a friend of Mark Shope, who was the general secretary of the South African Congress of Trade Unions and a member of the Communist Party. Shope supplemented the readings provided by Elsie, inviting Masondo to his house for discussions on trade unionism.[255] Thus, when Masondo arrived at Fort Hare, he was politically aware. And although he did not mature into a real position of leadership until he became a lecturer at Fort Hare in 1960, he understood the forces at play in the 1955 boycott.

The Duminy Commission Report marked the end of the line for Dent. Although the official reason given for his resignation was the 'unsatisfactory state of his health', it was clear that Dent had worn out his welcome.[256] He finally realised and accepted that he had no support among the students. When he took charge of Fort Hare at the end of 1948, he was publicly told, 'This is no sinecure to which you have been called, but one of the heaviest tasks in the Union.' Indeed, Dent's term turned out to be turbulent. His tenure coincided with the increasing racial tension in South Africa and the subsequent transformation of Fort Hare into a 'storm centre' of activism. The growing conflict 'greatly affected the life of Fort Hare' and Dent was never able to operate in this atmosphere.[257]

In addition to the resignation of Dent in the wake of the report, James Rogers, the Iona warden, and Mollie Smith, the warden at Elukhanyisweni left Fort Hare. Yet these were the only major changes that came about. There was much discussion of the report at Fort Hare, but few of the recommendations were adopted because Fort Hare suddenly had new problems, more severe than a student boycott of graduation, about which to worry. Shortly after the students absented themselves from the 29 April ceremony, the government made an even louder political statement. It was announced that the minister of Education, Arts and Science had appointed an Inter-Departmental Commission on the Financial Implications of the Provision of Separate University Facilities for non-Europeans. The proclamation in the press made it clear that the government was intent on introducing apartheid into universities.[258]

Dent's departure marked the end of an era at Fort Hare. The mission atmosphere that dominated the college from its inception was somewhat tempered when Z.K. Matthews became acting principal. Although religious services were still a part of college life, compulsory attendance was not. 'The question was whether the staff and students could get the College back on track during 1956,' wrote Matthews.[259] At least temporarily, the answer was 'yes', as Z.K. was able to create a calm atmosphere on campus. He addressed a meeting of students in 1956, acknowledging that Fort Hare was going through a difficult time, but reminding them of the dignity and resilience of black people in South Africa.[260] According to Monica Wilson, 'minutes of the SRC reflect a striking difference in tone between meetings with the acting principal during 1956 and earlier meetings with the principal'.[261]

So, with Matthews in charge, there was the possibility of a new beginning of sorts. Under the 1951 Rhodes University (Private) Act, Fort Hare had been affiliated with Rhodes, with the eventual goal of assuming the independent status recommended in the 1947 Government University Report. The Universities Act No 61 of 1955, which provided for the inclusion of Fort Hare among the universities of the country, made it eligible for full government funding. An initial enrolment of 16 students in 1916 had swelled to 368 by 1956.[262] However, Matthews was not the principal of Fort Hare under ordinary circumstances. Thrust into the difficult position of trying to repair relations between the students and the authorities, he took the helm when the prospect of government interference began increasingly to colour the daily experience at Fort Hare for staff and students.

Yet Matthews did not forecast doom. He pointed out to the students that when Hertzog came to power in 1924, everyone was sure it was the end of the African race. Then came the 1936 Land Acts and the crisis over Bantu Education in the early 1950s. He assured them, 'we are still living in spite [of] all these happenings. Ours is to go on with our work, discharging the duties in front of us.'[263] But in addition to the prospective implementation of university apartheid, Matthews had to deal with his arrest on charges of treason in December of 1956. Improvements to the physical plant and educational life of Fort Hare were put on hold as the university's perilous position took centre stage.

Notes

1   Mqhayi (trans. Robert Kavanaugh), 'The Prince of Britain' (1925), in *The Making of a Servant and Other Poems*, 14–16, quoted in A. Sampson, *Mandela* (New York: Knopf, 1999), 23.
2   Govan Mbeki, interview.
3   President Thabo Mbeki posthumously awarded Roux (1903–1966), botanist, activist, author and teacher, with the Order of Ikhamanga in Silver on 21 September 2007. The citation read: 'For excellent contribution to the struggle for a non-racial, non-sexist, just and democratic South Africa under trying apartheid conditions.' Generations of Fort Harians remembered Roux for his groundbreaking account of black protest movements, *Time Longer Than Rope*, a book he started writing just two years after his visit to Sandile's Kop.
4   Colin Bundy, 'Schooled for life' (Cape Town: University of Cape Town [UCT] Africa Seminar, 1994), 18. In his groundbreaking book on black protest movements, Roux writes that the students also served up an alternative theory for the Xhosa cattle killing that focused on a European conspiracy to assuage a labour shortage in the developing colony. Edward Roux, *Time Longer than Rope: The Black Man's Struggle for Freedom in South Africa* (Madison: University of Wisconsin Press, 1948), 40.
5   Tsotsi, interview; Roux, *Time Longer than Rope*, 276.
6   D. Burchell, 'Alexander Kerr', *Acta Academica*, 23, 2 (1991), 20.
7   Tsotsi, interview.
8   Sipo Makalima, interview.
9   Tsotsi, interview.
10   Burchell, 'Alexander Kerr', 2.
11   Alexander Kerr, *Fort Hare 1915–1948: Evolution of an African College* (New York: Humanities, 1968), 41.
12   Bundy, 'Schooled for life', 21.
13   Govan Mbeki, *The Struggle for Liberation in South Africa* (Cape Town: David Philip, 1992), 34.
14   Helen Bradford, *A Taste of Freedom: The ICU in Rural South Africa, 1924–1930* (New Haven: Yale University Press, 1987), 64–65, quoted in Bundy, 'Schooled for life', 21.
15   Jean and John Comaroff, *Of Revelation and Revolution: Christianity, Colonialism, and Consciousness in South Africa*, volume 1(Chicago: University of Chicago Press, 1991), 230.
16   Brooks was principal of Adams College in Natal and, beginning in 1937, a Senator from the Liberal Party in Parliament.
17   Kerr, *Fort Hare 1915–1948,*196.
18   Mbeki, interview.
19   *Ibid*. Hertzog founded the National Party and was the mastermind of the 1936 acts that rendered the African vote in the Cape useless and further entrenched white control of South Africa's land.

20   Bundy, 'Schooled for life',19.

21   Tsotsi, interview.

22   Mbeki, interview.

23   Bundy, 'Schooled for life', 19.

24   David H. Anthony, 'Max Yergan in South Africa: From evangelical pan-Africanist to revolutionary socialist', *African Studies Review*, 34, 2 (September 1991), 43. In 1948, disillusioned by the onset of the Cold War, Yergan abandoned leftist activism in favour of ultra-conservatism. For more information on Yergan, see Anthony's article.

25   Tsotsi, interview.

26   Mbeki, interview.

27   Bundy, 'Schooled for life', 23.

28   Mbeki, interview.

29   *Ibid.*; see also Bundy, 'Schooled for life', 18.

30   Tsotsi, interview.

31   Makalima, interview.

32   Bundy, 'Schooled for life', 23.

33   Robert Edgar (ed.), *An African-American in South Africa: The Travel Notes of Ralph J. Bunche* (Athens: Ohio University Press, 1992), 134–136.

34   Bundy, 'Schooled for life', 23.

35   William Nkomo, interview by Thomas Karis, April 1964, Pretoria.

36   Mbeki, interview.

37   Tsotsi, interview.

38   D.D.T. Jabavu, 'Presidential Address', in Thomas Karis and Gwendolyn Carter (eds), *From Protest to Challenge, A Documentary History of African Politics in South Africa*, volume 2, *Hope and Challenge 1935–1952*, 48.

39   Nkomo, interview by Karis.

40   *Ibid.*

41   Makalima, interview.

42   Kaiser Matanzima, interview.

43   Bundy, 'Schooled for life', 22.

44   *Ibid.*, 23.

45   *Ibid.*

46   Mbeki, *The Struggle for Liberation in South Africa*, 33.

47   Makalima, interview.

48   Tsotsi, interview.

49   Though Mandela attributes his 'expulsion' from Fort Hare to the aftermath of this student protest, the details surrounding his exit are cloudy. In a letter responding to Alexander Kerr's inquiry about a newspaper article that mentions Mandela's expulsion, W.W. Shilling, who was on the staff at Fort Hare in the 1940s, wrote: 'To the best of my knowledge Mandela was not suspended from Fort Hare' (Shilling to Kerr, 11 September 1962, Cory Library, PR 4095). See also Nelson Mandela, *Long Walk to Freedom* (Boston: Little Brown & Co., 1994).

50   'Statement by Beda Hall Committee', undated, Fort Hare Papers.

51   Burchell, 'Alexander Kerr', 15.

52   Senate Minutes, 17 September 1942, Fort Hare Papers.

53   Senate Minutes, 10 November 1942, Fort Hare Papers. According to the minutes, the Senate later recommended that Tambo be invited back. In her biography of Tambo, Luli Callinicos writes that Tambo had trouble finding work because of his expulsion. In a

letter to the author, she writes: 'OR talked about the opportunity to return in his taped memoirs, but he felt that on principle, as leader of his SRC, that he could not renege on his stand by apologising. He did, though, make it clear that other students should not jeopardise their future by emulating him. He already had his degree and was doing a post-graduate teacher's diploma. Nevertheless, although he played down his own situation, it significantly affected the size of his monthly pay cheque until he was able complete his diploma through UNISA. This is a typical illustration of Tambo's rather refined moral standards and also his conscientious concept of the responsibilities of a leader.' For more on Tambo, see Luli Callinicos, *Oliver Tambo: Beyond the Engeni Mountains* (Cape Town: David Philip, 2004).

54 Senate Minutes, 9 March 1942, Fort Hare Papers.

55 Bundy, 'Schooled for life', 22, Bundy's emphasis.

56 Donovan Williams, *A History of the University College of Fort Hare, South Africa, the 1950s: The Waiting Years* (Lewiston, New York: Edward Mellen, 2001), 77. For biographical information on Fort Hare staff, see chapter 2.

57 Devi Bughwan, interview.

58 Tsotsi, interview.

59 Nelson Mandela, interview by Mary Beale, Johannesburg, 15 January 1999, quoted in M. Beale, 'Apartheid and university education' (MA thesis, University of the Witwatersrand, 1996), 56.

60 Burchell, 'Alexander Kerr', 19.

61 Matthews, interview.

62 Buthelezi, interview.

63 George Matanzima, interview.

64 Africans' Claims in South Africa was adopted by the ANC in Bloemfontein on 16 Dec. 1943 in response to the Atlantic Charter, which set forth a new world order emerging out of the Second World War. The document, sometimes referred to as 'The Atlantic Charter from the Africans' Point of View', insisted that any new order must be based on justice and self-determination for all people. The document outlined a Bill of Rights that called for political, social and economic rights for Africans.

65 Matthews, interview.

66 Mandela, *Long Walk to Freedom*, 42.

67 Matthews, interview.

68 Jonathan Hyslop, *The Classroom Struggle: Policy and Resistance in South Africa, 1940–1990* (Pietermaritzburg: University of Natal Press, 1999), 14.

69 Joe Matthews, 'The significance of the African nationalist programme,' *Inkundla ya Bantu*, 5 November 1949, quoted in G. Gerhart, *Black Power in South Africa* (Berkeley: University of California Press, 1978), 69.

70 Gerhart, *Black Power in South Africa,* 127.

71 *Ibid.,* 128.

72 T.R.H. White, 'Z.K. Matthews and the formation of the ANC Youth League', *Kleio*, XXVII (1995), 129.

73 B. Pogrund, *How Can Man Die Better* (Johannesburg: Jonathan Ball, 1990), 28.

74 Karis and Carter, volume 2*, Hope and Challenge, 1935–1952*, 319–322.

75 Williams offers a slightly different version of events, based on an interview with P.N. Tshaka, an Honours student at Fort Hare in 1948. Williams writes that Tshaka helped to establish a YL branch in Victoria East, with an offshoot at Fort Hare, with the help of students at Fort Hare and 'a few people from surrounding villages'. See Williams, *A History,* 35.

76   Herby Govinden, interview by author, Durban, 17 April 1999.

77   Pogrund, *How Can Man Die Better,* 29.

78   *Ibid.* A written record does exist of the second speech – Sobukwe's memorable oration given at the Completer's Social a year later. Details of this speech follow.

79   Pogrund, *How Can Man Die Better,* 32.

80   Matthews, interview.

81   Buthelezi, interview.

82   C.P. Dent, statement by principal, volume 2, SRC, Fort Hare Papers.

83   Gerhart, *Black Power in South Africa,* 128.

84   White, 'Z.K. Matthews', 124.

85   Henry Makgothi, interview.

86   Govinden, interview.

87   Pogrund, *How Can a Man Die Better*, 33.

88   Dent to Dr M. Capcan, 19 January 1950, Temba Hleli student file, Fort Hare Papers.

89   SRC documents, volume 1, Fort Hare Papers.

90   White, 'Z.K. Matthews', 131.

91   E. Lynn Cragg, 'Fort Hare and other memories', unpublished manuscript in Rhodes University Cory Library Collection, 34.

92   Makgothi, interview.

93   *Ibid.*

94   Robert Sobukwe, 'Address on behalf of the graduating class at Fort Hare College, delivered at the 'Completer's Social', 21 October 1949, in Karis and Carter, volume 2, *Hope and Challenge, 1935–1952,* 331.

95   Ntsu Mokhehle, 'A sinking ship', *The Commentator*, Lesotho, July 1968, 15, cited in Gerhart, *Black Power in South Africa,* 110–111.

96   Sobukwe, 'Address on behalf of graduating class', 332; Makalima, interview.

97   Karis and Carter, volume 2, *Hope and Challenge, 1935–1952*, 337.

98   Gerhart, *Black Power in South Africa,* 186.

99   Lembede was one of the founders of the YL. He died in 1947 at the age of 33, but his Africanist ideas lived on and formed the basis of the Africanist bloc that split from the ANC to form the PAC.

100 Gerhart, *Black Power in South Africa,* 179.

101 Pogrund, *How Can a Man Die Better*, 39.

102 Govinden, interview. Sobukwe founded the PAC in 1959, but was imprisoned in 1960 for three years. On serving his sentence, he was detained for six more years on Robben Island, after which he was released and banned to his home of Kimberley, where despite facing severe restrictions, he opened a law practice.

103 Matthews, interview.

104 Cragg, 'Fort Hare', 37.

105 C.P. Dent, letter to Dr M. Capcan, 23 January 1950, Temba Hleli student file, Fort Hare Papers.

106 C.P Dent, letter to Dr M. Capcan, 19 January 1950, Temba Hleli student file, Fort Hare Papers.

107 C.P. Dent, letter to Dr M. Capcan and B.C. Hleli, 13 January 1950, Temba Hleli student file, Fort Hare Papers.

108 Dr M. Capcan, letter to C.P. Dent, 26 February 1950, Temba Hleli student file, Fort Hare Papers.

109 C.P. Dent, letter to Dr M. Capcan, 23 January 1950, Temba Hleli student file, Fort Hare Papers.
110 Sobukwe, 'Address on behalf of graduating class', 332.
111 Makgothi, interview.
112 *Ibid.*
113 Gerhart, *Black Power in South Africa,* 189.
114 Makgothi, interview.
115 *Ibid.*
116 *Ibid.*
117 *Ibid.*
118 Z.K. Matthews, *Freedom for My People* (Cape Town: David Philip, 1986), 116.
119 Matthews's studies at Yale led him to adopt the 'culture-contact' approach popular among anthropologists at the time. He continued to hope for a constructive synthesis of African and Western cultures, and the influences of Loram, Malinowski and others continued to exercise restraint on his political decisions.
120 White, 'Z.K. Matthews', 128.
121 Matthews, interview.
122 Matthews, *Freedom for my People,* 116.
123 Makgothi, interview.
124 Isaac Mabindisa, interview.
125 White, 'Z.K. Matthews', 130.
126 Williams, *A History,* 40.
127 White, 'Z.K. Matthews', 134.
128 Makgothi, interview.
129 Buthelezi, interview.
130 Makgothi, interview.
131 Buthelezi, interview.
132 White, 'Z.K. Matthews', 142.
133 Matthews, interview.
134 Matthews, *Freedom for my People,* 117.
135 Frieda Matthews, *Remembrances* (Cape Town: Mayibuye, 1995), 32.
136 Makgothi, interview.
137 Matthews, *Remembrances,* 37.
138 Gerhart, *Black Power in South Africa,* 68.
139 *Ibid.,* 83.
140 Makgothi, interview.
141 Gerhart, *Black Power in South Africa,* 93.
142 Karis and Carter, volume 2, *Hope and Challenge, 1935–1952,* 106–107 and 329.
143 Matthews, *Remembrances,* 38.
144 Buthelezi, interview.
145 Matthews, interview.
146 *Ibid.*
147 Gerhart, *Black Power in South Africa,* 189.
148 Sampson, *Mandela,* 65.
149 Gerhart, *Black Power in South Africa,* 115.
150 D.E. Burchell, 'The emergence and growth of student militancy', *Journal of the University of Durban-Westville,* 3 (1986), 154.
151 Minutes of Senate Meeting, 14 June 1950, Fort Hare Papers.

152 Matthews, *Remembrances,* 38.
153 Beacon Bioscope was located in Alice and run by a Mr Dewey. Fort Hare students and staff frequented the bioscope, as it was one of the few sources of entertainment in Alice. From time to time, segregated films were shown, and over the years the bioscope was a consistent target of student protest.
154 R.A. Pillay, interview by author, Durban, 29 April 1999.
155 *Ibid.*
156 Buthelezi, letter to C.P. Dent, 18 October 1950, Buthelezi File, Fort Hare Papers.
157 Dent report, volume 2, SRC, Fort Hare Papers.
158 Matthews, *Remembrances,* 38.
159 Matthews, interview.
160 Buthelezi, interview.
161 Minutes of Senate Meetings, 11 and 12 September 1950, Fort Hare Papers.
162 Minutes of Senate Meeting, 13 September 1950, Fort Hare Papers.
163 Dent, letter to native commissioner, 18 October 1950. Fort Hare Papers.
164 W.M. Chirwa later became a representative in the Legislative Assembly of Rhodesia and Nyasaland.
165 Student deposition, volume 1, SRC, Fort Hare Papers.
166 W. Champion, telegram to Dent, November 1950, Buthelezi File, Fort Hare Papers.
167 Buthelezi, letter to Dent, 18 October 1950.
168 *Ibid.*
169 Buthelezi, interview.
170 Ben Temkin, *Gatsha Buthelezi* (Cape Town: Purnell, 1976), 31.
171 Buthelezi, interview.
172 Temkin, *Gatsha Buthelezi,* 31.
173 *Ibid.*, 30.
174 Buthelezi, interview.
175 *Ibid.*
176 Temkin, *Gatsha Buthelezi,* 36.
177 Pillay, interview.
178 Beale, 'Apartheid and university education', 57.
179 Cragg, 'Fort Hare', 37. Williams cites a letter from Selby Ngcobo, head of the Economics Department, writing that Dent said 'Africans were not fit to go to Parliament and there is not a single African who is competent enough to run Fort Hare': Williams, *A History,* 151.
180 S. Ngcobo to Z.K. Matthews, 21 October 1952, cited in Williams, *A History,* 153.
181 *Daily Dispatch*, 1 November 1952, 7, cited in Williams, *A History*, 157.
182 Matthews, *Freedom for my People,* 163.
183 T.R.H. White, 'Student Disturbances at Fort Hare in 1955', *Kleio,* XXIX (1997), 116.
184 Matthews, *Freedom for my People,* 165–166.
185 Frank Mdlalose, interview by author, Johannesburg, 25 May 1999.
186 Thomas Karis and Gail Gerhart, From *Protest to Challenge*, volume 5, *Nadir and Resurgence, 1964–1979* (Bloomington: University of Indiana Press, 1997), 66.
187 *Ibid.*
188 SRC minutes, p. 200, 25 July 1951, cited in Williams, *A History*, 116.
189 Karis and Carter, volume 2, *Hope and Challenge, 1935–1952,* 404.
190 Mdlalose, interview by author.
191 *Ibid.*

192 Burchell, 'The emergence and growth of student militancy', 157.
193 *Ibid.*
194 Mass Meeting Resolution, 31 May 1952, volume 2, SRC, Fort Hare Papers.
195 Mdlalose, interview.
196 The Defiance Campaign was a civil disobedience campaign, waged by the ANC and the South African Indian Congress, beginning in June 1952, that sought to bring about changes in government policy on pass laws, Bantu Authorities, group areas, separate representation of voters, and the suppression of communism. For a few months, the protesters disobeyed regulations such as curfew and pass laws, inviting arrest. They were moderately successful in clogging prisons and courts and wreaking havoc in the administration of the apartheid regime. The government responded by introducing the Public Safety and Criminal Law Amendment Acts, putting an end to the protest. By the time the campaign petered out in November, 8 326 people had been arrested. The main achievement of the Defiance Campaign was to swell the ranks of the ANC to 100 000 people.
197 Mdlalose, interview.
198 SRC resolution, 17 August 1952, volume 2, SRC, Fort Hare Papers.
199 Mdlalose, interview.
200 Interview with Tennyson X. Makiwane, cited in Karis and Carter, volume 2, *Hope and Challenge, 1935–1952*, 420.
201 Williams, *A History,* 60.
202 Mdlalose, interview.
203 Williams, *A History,* 61.
204 Mdlalose, interview.
205 *Ibid.*
206 *Ibid.*
207 *Ibid.*
208 *Ibid.*
209 *Ibid.*
210 Buthelezi, interview.
211 Mdlalose, interview.
212 Mandela, *Long Walk to Freedom*, 125.
213 Mdlalose, interview.
214 Logan Naidoo, interview.
215 Mdlalose, interview.
216 Beale, 'Apartheid and university education', 58.
217 Cragg, 'Fort Hare', 34.
218 Burchell, 'The pursuit of relevance', *CON-TEXT,* 1 (1988), 62.
219 Naidoo, interview.
220 Buthelezi, interview; Mdlalose, interview.
221 Cragg, 'Fort Hare', 33.
222 *Ibid.*, 35.
223 Volume 2, SRC, 31 May 1952, Fort Hare Papers.
224 Interview with anonymous student, cited in Williams, *A History,* 173.
225 Williams, *A History,* 174.
226 *Ibid.,* 177.
227 Cragg, 'Fort Hare', 35.
228 Volume 2, SRC, May1952, Fort Hare Papers.
229 Naidoo, interview.

230 Women's residences at Fort Hare are popularly called *mzana*.

231 Andrew Masondo, interview by author, Pretoria, 25 May 1999.

232 Naidoo, interview.

233 V.R. Govender, interview; Masondo, interview.

234 Cragg, 'Fort Hare', 39.

235 *Ibid.*, 40.

236 Naidoo, interview.

237 Beard, 'Background to student activities', 165.

238 'Closed down: Police force stands by', *Natal Daily News*, 5 May 1955.

239 Minutes, Executive Committee of Council, 3 May 1955, Fort Hare Papers.

240 Williams, *A History,* 245.

241 See clipping collection in Howard Pim library.

242 Williams, *A History,* 245. In an interview with Williams, former student A.W.Z. Kuswayo surmised it was all one big linguistic mistake. He said that the students planned their annual graduation braai at Wesley House, complete with the roasting of three sheep. Word circulated that a 'carcass' would be braaied and this was caught by Dent, who thought there was a 'caucus'.

243 Report of Governing Council, 31 December 1955, Fort Hare Papers.

244 Cragg, 'Fort Hare', 41.

245 Report of Fort Hare Commission, 1955, Fort Hare Papers.

246 Beard, 'Background to student activities', 165.

247 The Duminy Report, cited in Beard, 'Background to student activities', 166.

248 Masondo, interview.

249 Cragg, 'Fort Hare', 34.

250 Williams, *A History,* 279.

251 Masondo, interview.

252 Huddleston, who died in 1998, was a Johannesburg-based Anglican priest who wrote of the forced removal of people from Sophiatown in *Naught for Your Comfort* (1956). He was eventually banned from South Africa and moved to London, where he served as president of the British Anti-Apartheid Movement.

253 Masondo, interview.

254 *Ibid.*

255 *Ibid.*

256 Report of the Governing Council, 31 December 1955, Fort Hare Papers.

257 Minutes, Governing Council, 30 August 1955, Fort Hare Papers.

258 'New move for student apartheid', *Cape Times*, 7 November 1955.

259 Matthews, *Freedom for my People*, 190.

260 Williams, *A History,* 290.

261 Matthews, *Freedom for my People,* 191.

262 Student statistics, 1956, Fort Hare Papers.

263 SRC minutes, 10 August 1956, cited in Williams, *A History,* 290.

_2_

A 'Diversity': Multi-Racial Life and 'Possibility' at Fort Hare before 1960

Fort Hare has striven to show during the last forty years that it is possible for people of different racial backgrounds, different cultural backgrounds, different political affiliations, and different faiths, to live together in amity ... I think due credit will [one day] be given to Fort Hare for having pioneered the way and been among those who have shown that it is actually possible for this thing to happen.
Z.K. Matthews[1]

A colourless lot

At a debate in the House of Assembly on the bill that would transfer control of Fort Hare to the government, a minister said one of the real reasons officials wanted to assume control of the university was the danger it posed to the policy of apartheid. Saying that it was essential to put 'a stop to the continued existence of Fort Hare in its present form', Minister G.P. van den Berg called the college 'a colourless lot of people, a university without a character of its own'.[2] In reality, it was not the absence of character, but the presence of a colourful cross-section of the multi-racial South African population that angered the government. For Fort Hare showed that the races of South Africa could live, work and play together. To Isaac Mabindisa, a student at Fort Hare in the late 1950s, the college's multi-racial nature was its biggest asset:

> Fort Hare was a place where young people ... Indians, Africans, coloureds, could meet on an equal footing and form friendships and belong to the same organisations, play together. And of course this was anathema to a government that believed in racial segregation and ethnic segregation.[3]

At the last official college function before the takeover by the government in 1960, Gertrude Darroll, an English lecturer, said that Fort Hare was not a university, but a 'diversity'.[4] Terence Beard calls pre-1960 Fort Hare a 'microcosm of a non-racial society in the heart of apartheid South Africa'.[5] With the National Party elected to power on its apartheid platform, to have a place where Indians, coloureds, and blacks mixed freely and happily powerfully showed, as Ivy Matsepe-Casaburri suggests, 'what was possible'.[6] Yet this possibility was precisely what the Nationalists wanted to break down. In 1955, word reached Fort Hare that the government intended to assume control of African university education. The announcement of a government commission to look into the feasibility of separate university facilities for non-Europeans hit Fort Hare hard and signalled the beginning of the end of its multi-racial days.

Yet up until the takeover, diversity within a larger unity was the cornerstone of an extremely vibrant student life. The official policy of the council was that there should be no racial or ethnic discrimination on campus. Beard writes that the 'university community comprised to a significant degree a racially integrated society within, and largely protected from, the white, racially dominated society which surrounded it'.[7] Indeed, while it lasted, multi-racial Fort Hare was a place that, to a certain extent, defied apartheid.[8]

The melting pot

Fort Hare's original constitution indicated that the university was founded to provide for the education of Africans, but coloureds and Indians contributed greatly to campus life before 1960. By 1955 Indian and coloured students numbered 80, accounting for 22 per cent of the student population at Fort Hare.[9] Fort Hare was the first tertiary institution in South Africa to open its doors to Indians and coloureds when residences at the universities of Cape Town, Natal and the Witwatersrand (Wits), for example, were reserved for whites.[10]

Correspondence between A.D. Lazarus and Alexander Kerr in 1925 indicates that although Indians were a vital part of campus life, the authorities were sensitive to the desire of the founders to maintain the African nature of the college. There was also a scarcity of housing at Fort Hare. Because the churches provided the accommodation and were invested primarily in educating blacks, a limit to the Indian and coloured population was deemed necessary. However, while recognising Fort Hare's commitment to African education, Kerr did not want students of other backgrounds to be left out. In a letter to Kerr, George Singh (1930–1933), an Indian, spoke of a 'spirit of fraternisation' at Fort Hare 'which should continue to exist among the non-European groups in South Africa'. Singh continued, 'Even if Indians and coloureds have to live in tents … the spirit of fraternisation should not be brought to an end.'[11] In response, Kerr wrote, 'The presence of different groups in the college has made for interest and widening of outlook, and we should be the last to exclude any person except on the absolute grounds of want of accommodation.'[12]

In 1940, the Senate recommended to Council that 'in admitting students preference shall be given to qualified Bantu applicants and that the proportion of other races admitted shall not exceed 25 per cent of the total'. It was further recommended that at least 15 per cent and a minimum of 12 per cent should be reserved for Indian and coloured students.[13] In 1946, Rama Thumbadoo, an Indian, was denied admission because the cap on Indian students had already been reached. His application was rejected and stamped, 'stereotyped refusal'. Thumbadoo gained admission the following year.[14] And despite the limits on Indian and coloured enrolment, the multi-racial atmosphere at Fort Hare flourished.

Maurice Peters was the first Indian student at Fort Hare and, by 1918, Indians and coloureds made up 18 per cent of the student body.[15] Occasionally, a sprinkling of white students, mostly the children of Fort Hare or Lovedale staff members, filtered in. Fort Hare played a particularly powerful role in opening Indians up to a wider world. Unlike many of the black students who had studied at mission boarding schools before proceeding to Fort Hare, for many of the Indians, Fort Hare marked the first time they had left home. The road to Fort Hare was determined by necessity and not choice. There was very little opportunity for Indians to pursue science or medicine elsewhere in South Africa. The medical school in Durban did not open until 1952 and prior to that, students interested in science had to go to expensive Wits or Cape Town, where they were not allowed to reside on campus. Devi Bughwan says that the university residences at these schools were reserved for whites: '[Indians] were only allowed to attend the lectures and do the work and back they went to their own homes.'[16]

In a letter to Kerr, the high commissioner for India wrote of 'a number of instances of Indian students experiencing difficulty in securing entry into the law and medical faculties of South African universities'.[17] Bughwan attributes the increasing attraction of teaching to Indians to the difficulties, both financial and logistical, they faced on the path towards medicine. Others who did not want to give up the dream of a medical career went to Fort Hare to complete their first-year science course, studying 'in one of the few places where you could go and be a student in the full sense of the word,' Bughwan said.[18]

Rama Thumbadoo's initial application to Fort Hare was rejected because the quota for Indian students had already been reached

Fort Hare students came from across southern and eastern Africa. Here, Charles Njonjo, who would become Kenya's attorney general, plays chess with Loga 'Doc' Pillay, September 1945.

In addition to providing access to science classes, Fort Hare offered Indians an affordable education. The Natal Provincial Education Department gave bursaries to Indians to encourage them to go to Fort Hare and return to Natal as science teachers. The Indian schools were short of science teachers and the few people who came out of Fort Hare with BSc degrees found employment easily. Though some Indians at Fort Hare came from the Cape and paid their own way, most originated in Natal, as the scholarship from the Education Department financed their schooling. Eventually about 90 per cent of the science teachers in Natal were trained at Fort Hare.[19]

♦♦♦♦♦

R.A. Pillay was one of the Indian students who followed that route to Fort Hare and beyond. One of eight children, Pillay's father was a mine labourer in Natal and he describes his background as 'very poor'. On matriculating, Pillay had aspirations of becoming a doctor. 'I always wanted to do medicine,' he says, 'but if you had to do medicine it was either Wits or Cape Town … it was too expensive for a fellow of my background.' With no other choice, Pillay decided to postpone his medical dreams temporarily and pursue teaching with the hope of saving up enough money to study medicine at a later time. He received a bursary of about 50 pounds a year from the Natal Education Department and entered Fort Hare in 1950 to study for a BSc degree. Pillay says that the funds from the Education Department were enough to cover tuition, accommodation and laundry. 'You needed a little just for pocket money,' he says. Pillay looked at studying at Fort Hare as 'a stepping stone … I'll take that at least and then I will have a chance to get a degree and then probably teach for a while and save money and be able to do medicine afterwards.'[20]

Though Pillay initially viewed his journey to Fort Hare as a temporary diversion on the road towards medical school, his years in Alice did more than prepare him for a career in medicine. Fort Hare gave him a strong science background and Pillay eventually succeeded in becoming a doctor. But he learned more than just chemistry and physics at the university. Like many of his Indian colleagues, the college provided Pillay with his first opportunity to interact with Africans on an equal footing.

> When you came to Fort Hare, for us, for the first time, you were exposed … to African students. Now for us, the type of exposure we had in Durban, an African was a chap who was doing gardening or that kind of menial job. You never even saw any African who was educated, a degree or anything of that sort. So it was quite a revelation the first time we went to Fort Hare.

Although, generally speaking, Indians did not become as politically active as the African students, they did become politically conscious. 'You started thinking politically too … I don't know, they were doing a bad job, if they wanted to keep politics down, herding all the fellows together there.' Pillay describes study and discussion groups awakening his political consciousness. 'We were just green fellows at the time, still very young with politics [on arrival at Fort Hare].'[21]

♦♦♦♦♦

Like Pillay, Goolam Suleman Tootla came into contact with black students for the first time at Fort Hare. 'I was put into a dormitory with 14 students: 13 black students and I was the only Indian. It came as a cultural shock to me,' says Tootla. Nowhere else in South Africa were youngsters being thrust into such 'uncomfortable' positions. 'For the first six months I wanted to go back home,' says Tootla. However, the initial uneasiness provided a tremendous learning experience.

The environment, not having been exposed to the kind of interaction with other groups ... You had a perception about you being the only people around ... Blacks were basically to us ... there to serve your needs, to work for you and so forth. The perception that the white government had created, that they're hewers of wood and carriers of water.[22]

The son of a labourer turned small businessman, Tootla grew up in The Bluff, a conservative, white area in Durban. He first became aware of the racial situation in South Africa at the age of 11 when he was called a 'coolie' and thrown out of a moving bus. 'But the issue of living together in an environment that we had never experienced, I don't think anybody experienced that before getting to Fort Hare.' Tootla credits Fort Hare with breaking down the mental barriers that apartheid had thrust in his face.

For me to get into a room with 13 blacks and they're chatting away and I say what the hell is going on here, I need to sleep. Then six months later I'm chatting away with them past midnight. It's a question of coming to understand people's cultural beliefs.

After a difficult first few months, Tootla's comfort level at Fort Hare increased as his perceptions of the other students, now based on experience and not government dictate, changed:

What Fort Hare did to me in my life was create something in terms of human relationships. I don't think anybody could ever, ever have done that to any one single individual in terms of learning to respect, looking at different lifestyles, knowing the difficulties of students from different backgrounds. It was a tremendous kind of educational process.[23]

Tootla, like Pillay, put his medical ambitions on hold to attend Fort Hare. Unable to secure a place at Natal University to do medicine, he enrolled at Fort Hare to study for the BSc degree. After completing, he went to study dentistry at Wits, an experience he describes as 'the most traumatic' of his life. 'I was the first black student to be admitted to the dental faculty,' he says. 'That was a nightmare.' Contrary to the inclusive atmosphere at Fort Hare, Tootla was forced to reside off campus at Wits. His attitude 'completely redeveloped' from his experience at Fort Hare, Tootla was stunned to be thrust into a 'lily-white' atmosphere.[24]

Devi Bughwan's Fort Hare experience mirrored that of Tootla and Pillay. Bughwan started school at the age of five, doing her primary education at a church mission school in Durban. She did Standards 5 and 6 in one year, before moving on to Dartnell Crescent, which was the girls' high school in Durban. Bughwan entered Fort Hare in 1942 at the age of 15, much younger than the other students, after what she describes as a 'sheltered' childhood. Owing to her age, she was afforded special treatment upon arrival at the college:

> Mrs Kerr [the principal's wife] realised there was a child of 15 at this college. Because of that, my roommate and I got an invitation to come over and have supper with them [the Kerrs]. We were honoured, went along and had this special meal. He [Principal Kerr] asked me a thousand questions about where I came from, my community in Durban and so on.

She says, 'It was the first time I'd ever been away from home or thrown together with people from different cultures.' Like many of the Indians who studied at Fort Hare, life at the college helped to break down stereotypes that had been ingrained in them by their families and the government:

> It did, as sheltered Indian students … a world of good to have this exposure. One tended to be very insular. There was very little mixing in your day-to-day life in your homes. And I think a lot of Indian students went back to their homes and educated their families. They educated their families in what it means to be in a country like South Africa. Because we tended to think the world began and ended with ourselves. That was the policy of the government, to keep us apart. But a lot of Indians didn't even need encouraging in that respect. Prejudices are inbred in all societies. And so often we're accused of having come from a very caste conscious society. It's true. I think Fort Hare was a salutary experience for … me.[25]

The atmosphere at Fort Hare stimulated Bughwan. 'We didn't go there as Indian students just to study. We did have a very good university life,' she says. 'It was such a dynamic place to be. People got together simply to talk, to exchange notes, to read together, to be together.' Bughwan became politically aware for the first time at Fort Hare as she came into contact with new people and concepts:

> There were many political meetings. I recall the meetings at which people like Oliver Tambo, I mean Oliver Tambo was sitting there as a grown man as president of the SRC when I was a 15-year-old. I do

remember him and what dynamism he had even then. He was there in my first year … I can still recall him at the main table, president of the SRC. They held meetings ranging from complaining about the dreadful food to much more weighty matters. You learned an awful lot. And you realised that we'd been sheltered and unaware. I think we became politicised at Fort Hare.[26]

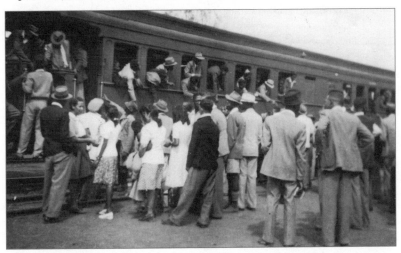

The Alice railway station, 09:00 a.m., 16 November 1945

Fort Hare did not open the eyes only of Indian students. For many Africans, arrival at Fort Hare meant coming into contact with other cultures for the first time. Multi-racial Fort Hare expanded the horizons of all involved. Matsepe-Casaburri says,

> I remember people exchanging stories about some people who had never seen Indians and then having to experience Indians. It's quite a cultural shock. How do they eat? What do they do? The myths that you have to then get over. And Fort Hare was able to do that.[27]

The diversity of Fort Hare worked to break down ethnic barriers within the African community. Z.K. Matthews wrote,

> The supposed stupidity of the Zulu, the so-called stinginess of the Sotho, the alleged treachery of the Fingo, the Xhosa distaste for modesty in matters of dress – all these fallacious theories are being exploded by the rising generation in their common life at a place like Fort Hare where tribal affiliation of a student is of no account whatever.[28]

With a government intent on separating the population, Fort Hare was consolidating it. Matsepe-Casaburri says,

> And you didn't hear about fights between Indians and coloureds and Africans. It wasn't there. And for me it was a good thing that, as a person who eventually ended up studying sociology, to say that these things are possible if the atmosphere is created for people to live.[29]

◆◆◆◆◆

'What Fort Hare did,' says V.R. Govender (1956–1958),

> It did not only give young ladies and men an education of a first class nature. It transformed our thinking as well, not [all] into people who rebelled against the entire country, although some did become leaders of the rebellion, but the vast majority rebelled against the way people were treated … Many of us who came out of Fort Hare tried to change people's thinking.

Govender was born in a small country town in Natal called Mooi River and grew up on his father's dairy farm. Because there was no Indian school in Mooi River, he did his primary education at a Zulu school, where he developed an affinity for the Zulu language. Although he describes his father as conservative, Govender says his upbringing on the farm and in the Zulu school, where he interacted daily with blacks, prepared him for arrival at Fort Hare. '[Growing up] I lived among black people … I used to sleep with the herd boys,' says Govender, who integrated himself into the life of the college shortly after he arrived on campus. 'I think I'm correct in saying that I was the first Indian second-year student to be selected for the SRC,' he adds.

Though his home environment was less sheltered than Bughwan's, Govender did not become interested in politics until he got to Fort Hare and joined the SRC. 'I went into Fort Hare not knowing the ABCs of politics,' he said. 'But in my dorm there were people who spoke of the Unity Movement. They took me to secret meetings.' Govender was recruited into the youth wing of the Unity Movement by friends in his dormitory who invited him to speak at a meeting on the banks of the Tyumie River. Although he eventually joined SOYA, the then head of the YL at Fort Hare, Ambrose Makiwane, also influenced Govender.[30]

To live here is to be free

While Govender fondly recalls his political involvement at Fort Hare, he is most enthusiastic when talking about the vibrant student life there. Mary Dick, a staff member at Fort Hare in the 1930s, writes of Indian students 'mixing well with the African students and having proved themselves an asset both in academic work and sporting activities, as well as having the more general cultural influence'.[31] Burchell quotes Rev C.F. Andrews of India, who after visiting Fort Hare, wrote, 'There is an absolute liberation from all sense of the inhumanity of racial prejudice. Here at last there is perfect equality reigning throughout. To live here is to be free.'[32] Logan Naidoo at one point lived with three Zambians, an Indian and a Xhosa and says,

> We never saw race. My pals were the guys I stayed with in the same room, or were in the same course with me, or sat at the same table in the dining room. It didn't matter what ethnic or race group they came from … We were all in the melting pot, one nation in the true sense of the word.[33]

The mixing of the races could be seen on the cricket team, where Rama Thumbadoo, an Indian, played with Dennis Brutus, a coloured student. Thumbadoo says the members of the 'completely integrated team' got along very well. 'The soccer team had two Indian players, three coloured students and the rest blacks,' he says, and the rugby squad was integrated as well.[34]

Beda Hall cricket team, including Rama Thumbadoo (top, centre) and future poet Dennis Brutus (on ground, first from left) before a match against Wesley Hostel, 1947

Beda Hall cricket team, 1957

Beda Hall football team, 1948

On reflection, four or more decades removed from their college experience, many Fort Harians realise that multi-racial Fort Hare was indeed special. The experiment that defied apartheid was successful daily. However, in talking with the students, it was the more normal, everyday aspects of college life that stood out at the time. The college gave its students the chance to live and act freely, just like their white counterparts at Wits, UCT and Rhodes. Because the African students were, in general, more politically active than the other students, it is the student life that most Indian students recall fondly. Even though there were constant grievances with missionary authority, life at Fort Hare was a complete one. Compulsory daily assemblies, including a special Sunday college service, while irritating, did not stop the students from enjoying themselves. Some students even took advantage of the assemblies to raid the lockers of other students.[35]

V.R. Govender describes with glee the treatment given to first-year students, dubbed 'freshers' by their older colleagues: 'Initiation was great. Making fellows sweep the floor with their toothbrush.'[36] Ismail Dada (1959–1961) was on the receiving end:

> All of us were initiated. If I describe it to you, we were stripped naked and we had to take out our toothbrushes, I was staying in a rondavel, and they made me sweep the entire rondavel with my toothbrush. And then we were taken to hall and all freshers were standing on tables and they polished us with shoe polish. They took us to the river. Always a senior student claimed a fresher and made him do his chores.[37]

Rama Thumbadoo relates how, in his time, the senior students would borrow a scale from the college nurse, have the warden impersonate a doctor, line up the freshers, and give them makeshift physical exams. The older students would get great pleasure out of watching the newcomers squirm when told they were afflicted with various maladies.[38]

Despite rules governing male and female contact, intermingling of the sexes was common.[39] Thelma Appavoo (1943–1945) says: 'We used to have at the women's hostel a social. You invited your men friends down. But other than that, men were not allowed in the women's hostel. And neither were the women allowed in the men's hostel.' The students managed to get around the regulations. 'There was a term they used to use if a chap walked you from the dining room to the hostel. They'd float you down,' says Appavoo. For those male students who couldn't find girlfriends among the small number of female students at the college, the nurses, dubbed 'blue bottles', of nearby Lovedale

Hospital, which earned the nickname 'City Lights', provided a welcome respite. Appavoo says: 'The boys, of course, they, boys are boys. They knew how to duck and dive. And there are stepping stones that cross the river on the road where Davidson Stadium is. And the chaps used to go across those stones on their dates to the City Lights.'[40]

Dating was common on campus and original customs developed. Appavoo says: 'If someone dated you and took you to the cinema, when you got home to go down for supper, they'd give you a geranium and ask you in the presence of everyone to take that geranium and take it to your date.'[41] V.R. Govender says nobody wanted to end up as fodder for the campus notice boards. 'Early in the morning when you go for breakfast … you see a big chart, "V.R. Govender was hoofed". It means kicked, not successful the night before.'[42]

Govender says: 'When you've gone to a place like Fort Hare, the entire experience becomes a part of you.' Though they attended college under far from normal circumstances, the college stories Fort Hare students tell could be those of any college student in any country. Govender recalls: 'At Beda, you had to hand in your laundry and write your name. But sometimes the ink didn't work well and you lost your clothing. So once a month, all laundry was auctioned and one time I had to buy back my own underpants.' Campus dances, held in the dining hall, were favourite events. 'We couldn't dance, most of us,' says Govender. 'We used to only go in for the fast numbers where nobody could see you making a mistake.'[43] Matsepe-Casaburri remembers rag days, when the students created a 'court of injustice', and took great joy in dishing out penalties to those who were charged with offences.[44]

Food played a big part in the socialisation and interaction of the students. Nelson Mandela wrote, 'The students unanimously felt that the diet at Fort Hare was unsatisfactory.'[45] Logan Naidoo says that food was 'a major problem', especially for Indians who didn't eat beef. Students spanning decades relate their daily diet in gruesome detail. For Naidoo: 'Breakfast was porridge. Lunch alternating every other day, one day was beans, boiled; one day was a chunk of beef in stew. Supper was a bit of beef soup, jam, bread, about six slices, and a cup of milk.'[46] R.A. Pillay jokes,

> I always thought I could never get the recipe of the soup they had, some gelatinous, gooey stuff with no taste at all … Hindus didn't eat beef … but fellows who used to eat their beef couldn't eat the one that was prepared there … One year they decided to fortify the mealie meal porridge and they put this oil in the damn thing. I couldn't even eat that. The only thing that kept us going there, I think, was milk.[47]

Ismail Dada says,

> Going to the dining hall, the smell used to make me feel nauseous. When it came to supper, you are really hungry. Four slices of stale brown bread. We used to have fresh bread in the morning. I don't know where the stale bread came from. A mug or a cup of neither water, nor milk, in between, not hot, not cold, no sugar. And they gave a glob of something they called jam and we called something else. That was our supper for three years.[48]

For V.R. Govender, the food memories entailed porridge that was stored unhygienically: 'Believe me, without a word of exaggeration, we always just pushed the worms aside and carried on with the porridge.' Govender also remembers meat that 'couldn't be cut with a knife'. Over the years, the culinary offerings in the dining hall sparked a great deal of protest by the students. Govender remembers these revolts, saying: 'We took pots and pans, boom, boom, boom, and that's how songs came about.' He jokes that Mr McGillivray, the dining room chef, should 'be given a knighthood', as the poor food he prepared brought out 'the latent potentialities of the future leaders of South Africa'.[49]

Though former students recall the Fort Hare food with humour, it was often a serious matter during their student days. Strikes frequently erupted over its poor quality. The action that resulted in Nelson Mandela's exit from the university began with student complaints about food. Wycliffe Tsotsi says that the students often felt that they were given poor quality food because they were black.[50] Jonathan Hyslop writes that the issue of food in mission schools often emerged 'as one which embodied the unjust relations, the authority, power and politics of a racist society: a universal focus of consistent discontent which could unite students motivated by disparate grievances'. Food often served as a metaphor for issues of power and authority in the mission schools. He notes that although the students had legitimate complaints owing to inadequate food, the inferior diets 'became a symbol of, and a matter of protest against, the social domination they experienced in their daily lives'.[51]

At Fort Hare in Logan Naidoo's days, the students went on a hunger strike and Z.K. Matthews' wife, Frieda, was forced to take up utensils in the kitchen in an effort to improve the food. Naidoo says,

> Every day when it came eating time, we came to the CU Hall and had a meeting there. No food to eat. The third day they said, well, we've improved things tremendously in the dining hall, so they're bringing the food to sample. So they brought six or eight plates of boiled cabbage.

As it came there, we couldn't see much of the difference. But the guys when they saw the food and they smelled the food, they saw all of the improvement. They had to eat. [52]

To supplement the paltry Fort Hare diet, Indian students who missed the curries of their home kitchens formed small groups called 'syndicates'. Wednesday and Saturday afternoons were holidays and the students took advantage of the free-time to cook. 'This thing was determined by whether you received money by post,' says Rama Thumbadoo. 'If you didn't, you couldn't participate.'[53] With cooking known by the slang term 'functioning', the syndicates provided many of the African students with their first tastes of curry. 'We invited the other students to join us,' says Herby Govinden. 'I had a very good friend from Uganda who joined us because he couldn't take it either.'[54] R.A. Pillay says, 'Some of them hadn't touched the things before … In fact, if you ask Frank Mdlalose, he'll say, hey, he misses that curry.'[55] For Matsepe-Casaburri, who belonged to a syndicate at Eluk, Fort Hare food never became a problem: 'I had a lot of Indian friends, so I shared whatever food they ate,' she says.[56] Thus, the deficiency in the dining hall was transformed into a cross-cultural learning experience.[57]

The Fort Hare student community developed into an extremely close group. 'You knew nearly everyone there, including the female students,' says Pillay.[58] Part of the togetherness of the student body was because of the college's size, but it could also be attributed to the physical location and the residential nature of the school. Logan Naidoo says, 'All you had was Fort Hare … So the lifestyle was very insular. The outside influences were limited.'[59] Forced to turn inward, the students, as Govender suggests, developed their own customs and even their own language. Men chasing women were after 'jaguars'; Beda students with time to waste would 'lavy', or hang out; and the awful food in the dining hall was dubbed 'magile', after the man who cooked it, Mr McGillivray. Residents of Iona were called Porcupines; students in Beda were Philistines; and Wesley dwellers were nicknamed Barbarians.[60] Pillay says, 'There was nothing else to do except find all the fun with yourselves …You didn't have a town to run away to. So everybody was involved … ballroom championships … science societies … sporting life.'[61] Isaac Mabindisa says, 'There was a vibrant social life at Fort Hare. Love of ballroom dancing by some people. We were a small community, in many ways close knit.'[62]

Fee: One Pound (£1).
File No. 20468 (A)
Sum deposited
Bedrag gedeponeer waived
(£ _____ : _____)
by/deur

Koste: Een Pond (£1).
Lêer No.
Pounds.
pond. № 94090
Rev. Receipt no.
L 50118 dd. 31/7/59

(The deposit hereon will be refunded on production of this Permit when the holder leaves the Province upon satisfactory evidence that the conditions and requirements imposed hereunder have been fulfilled.)

(Die deposito sal by vertoning van hierdie permit terugbetaal word wanneer die houer die Provinsie verlaat en nadat bevredigende bewys gelewer is dat die voorwaardes en vereistes hieronder gestel, nagekom is.)

Subject to the conditions and requirements stated hereunder the holder

Behoudens die voorwaardes en vereistes hieronder gestel word die houer

HERBY SILVESTER GOVINDEN
van
DURBAN

is permitted to enter the Province of— toegelaat om die Provinsie—
CAPE OF GOOD HOPE
at te
CAPE TOWN
for the purpose of— binne te gaan met die doel om—
LECTURER AT UNIVERSITY OF FORT HARE

Authority of Certificate No. Magtiging van Sertifikaat No.
Date of issue Datum waarop uitgereik.
Place of issue Plek waar uitgereik.

Immigration Officer./Immigrasiebeampte. (CAPE PROVINCE)

This permit is issued subject to the following conditions and requirements and to the provisions of the Immigrants' Regulation Act, No. 22 of 1913, and the Regulations thereunder.

Hierdie permit word uitgereik behoudens onderstaande voorwaardes en vereistes en die bepalings van die Wet tot Regeling van Immigratie, No. 22 van 1913, en die Regulasies daarkragtens uitgevaardig:—

1. The holder of this permit registers his address as:— 1. Die houer van hierdie permit registreer sy adres as volg:
(a) Postal address C/O UNIVERSITY FORT HARE Posadres.
P.O. FORT HARE
(b) Residential address CAPE PROVINCE (b) Woonadres.

2. The holder of this permit ... JANUARY ... of op ... Die houer van hierdie permit ...
before 28TH FEBRUARY ... verlaat sonder koste vir die Regering.
without expense to the Government.
3. The holder of this permit shall report to the— 3. Die houer van hierdie permit moet hom by die—
PRINCIPAL IMMIGRATION OFFICER
at te
CAPE TOWN
at intervals of— by gereelde tussenpose van—
AS REQUIRED
and shall keep that officer duly advised of his whereabouts.

aanmeld en moet daardie amptenaar behoorlik op die hoogte hou van waar hy hom bevind.

4. The holder of this permit shall give at least twenty-four hours notice (excluding Sundays and Public Holidays) of intended departure.
5. The holder of this permit shall secure proper endorsement on the reverse hereof of any extension of the period of availability of this permit from a duly authorised Immigration Officer.
6. This permit will be held to be invalidated, and the deposit thereon shall be forfeited to the Government, if the permit-holder or the depositor named herein or other person concerned is shown to the Immigration Officer to have made a false declaration or false representations in applying for, or securing, this permit.

4. Die houer van hierdie permit moet minstens vier-en-twintig uur (Sondae en openbare vakansiedae uitgesluit) vooraf kennis gee van sy voorgenome vertrek.
5. Die houer van hierdie permit moet verseker dat alle verlengings van die geldigheidstermyn van hierdie permit behoorlik op die keersy hiervan aangeteken word deur 'n immigrasiebeampte wat daartoe gemagtig is.
6. Hierdie permit sal as ongeldig beskou en die deposito aan die Regering verbeur word as daar aan die immigrasiebeampte bewys word dat die permithouer of die deponeerder wat hierin genoem word of 'n ander betrokkene 'n vals verklaring gedoen of vals vertoë gerig het toe daar om hierdie permit aansoek gedoen is of toe dit verkry is.

I/We, HERBY SILVESTER GOVINDEN Ek/Ons,
and en

agree to the above conditions, and clearly understand that any breach of such will involve the forfeiture of the deposit lodged hereunder and will render the holder liable to be further dealt with according to law.
It is further specially agreed that the deposit lodged as security for this permit shall be regarded as continued and extended by any extension of the permit made, or authorized to be made, by an Immigration Officer.

stem in met bostaande voorwaardes en begryp ten volle dat 'n verbreking daarvan sal meebring dat die deposito hiervolgens gestort, verbeur word en dat daar verder volgens wet met die houer gehandel kan word.
Voorts word daar spesiaal ooreengekom dat die termyn van die deposito wat as sekerheid vir hierdie permit gestort word, beskou moet word as voortgesit en verleng deur enige verlenging van die permit deur of gesag van 'n immigrasiebeampte.

Holder's signature Govinden Handtekening van houer.
Place Alice Plek.
Witness Getuie.
Depositor's signature Handtekening van deponeerder.
Date 25-8-59. Datum.

The conditions of this permit interpreted by me to the persons concerned in—

Die voorwaardes van hierdie permit is deur my vertolk vir die persone betrokke in—

Herby Govinden and his Indian colleagues had to apply for a permit to travel from Durban to Fort Hare

Students from various eras describe the academic life before 1960 as more than adequate. Mdlalose says 'the quality of the education was high, very high', singling out Professor James Davidson in physics and Professor A.S. Galloway in chemistry.[63] Joe Matthews recalls that Professor A.J.D. Meiring of the Zoology Department, who was 'a National Party man', produced top students such as Ntsu Mokhele. 'They were taught by a rabid Nationalist and they won the gold medals as the best students in the country.'[64]

The missionary influence was mitigated a bit with the onset of Fort Hare graduates returning to teach. By the 1950s, there were four black heads of department, all of whom had graduated from Fort Hare and were ANC members, including Sibusiso Nyembezi (Bantu languages), who encouraged a strong sense of cultural awareness among blacks through his promotion of the Zulu language. Selby Ngcobo, another Fort Hare graduate, obtained an MA at Yale University and a PhD in economics from London University, and returned to Fort Hare as head of the Economics Department in 1951.

Extra-curricular politics

The environment that spawned a vibrant student life gave birth to a lot of the student politics. 'As something that was part of the social engineering of the time, to have all these black students there created the atmosphere,' says Ivy Matsepe-Casaburri. She attributes the growth of student politics at Fort Hare to the circumstances under which the students – all members of oppressed racial groups in South Africa – lived: 'You lived in a close community, in a small town. It was a university town. Activities of the town had all to do with Fort Hare … So Fort Hare simply gave an opportunity which other universities were not able to do.'[65] With little on the outside to entertain them, the students were forced to turn inwards, resulting in what Beard calls 'a highly integrated society with its own *mores*, its own mutually recognised identity, and a cherished *esprit de corps*'.[66]

Though students were well rounded and busied themselves with a variety of endeavours, Herby Govinden says that politics was the main extra-curricular activity on campus. Many of the students belonged to African youth organisations, with the majority of the students joining the YL, SOYA or, when it was founded in 1959, the PAC. 'I never fell in love with any women,' says Govan Mbeki of his student days. 'I didn't have the time. I was all up to here in politics.'[67] Cragg notes that politics could be dragged into everything, even 'a mathematical lecture'.[68] And Beard writes, 'Politics was the main topic of conversation at Fort Hare, even when it was only peripherally relevant, and sometimes when it was not relevant at all.'[69]

Describing their student days, Fort Harians say that the peaceful, non-racial campus erupted when it came to politics. The only squabbles within the student body were because of the friendly, but fiery nature of politics. 'You never heard of a racial incident,' says Thumbadoo, while Matsepe-Casaburri adds that politics at Fort Hare existed 'across racial barriers'.[70] Ambrose Makiwane says that although some coloured students joined the Teachers' League of South Africa (TLSA), the students' politics did not create racial divisions. 'There was no coloured organisation,' he says. 'They belonged to the ANC. The Indians belonged to the ANC, some to the Unity Movement. We interacted very cordially.'[71]

From around the time Eddie Roux first arrived on campus, discussion and debates permeated daily life. In Tsotsi's days in the mid 1930s, the forum for discussion was the Historical Association, which he founded. In 1935, the AAC[72] was formed, and though Professor Jabavu himself did not engage in political discussion with the students, the founding of the organisation was a cause of much discussion.[73] Devi Bughwan remembers trips to Rhodes University as a member of the college's debating team.[74] Yet argumentative discussion wasn't always through formal, inter-institutional debates. The Christian Union Hall was often the site of meetings that generated impromptu discussion. 'The CU was part of the daily life of the university,' says Mabindisa. 'That's where people cut their teeth in debates … Some of them were howlers. They liked heckling … We used to enjoy ourselves.'[75]

Many students took advantage of Z.K. Matthews's hospitality, spending hours engaged in debate at his home in Alice. Matthews' lectures sparked political discussion in the classroom as well. Most black staff were ANC members (including Matthews, Nyembezi, S.B. Ngcobo and Joseph Mokoena), while some supported the NEUM (A.M. Pahle, Sam M. Guma and Cecil S. Ntloko). And, as with Z.K. Matthews, discussion was not limited to the classroom. Both Mokoena and Phahle held 'small meetings at their houses … to politicise the students'.[76] And discussion in Ntloko's native administration course 'morphed' into 'free-wheeling debates – often heated arguments – at his house at night, sometimes until 3 a.m.'. Sobukwe credits Ntloko with 'having done more than any other person to open his mind to the society around him'.[77]

The hostels were also a favourite place to debate, with small groups of ANC, SOYA and African People's Democratic Union of South Africa (APDUSA) members meeting in dorm rooms.[78] Naidoo and Govender were first drawn into politics at Fort Hare through discussions within their hostels. Pillay recalls study groups meeting frequently, 'making you aware of what was going on'.[79] Rama Thumbadoo (1946–1949) says hostel meetings often transmuted

Students honed their political skills in debates at the Christian Union Hall

into political debates and that students soaked up news from outside campus from the East London *Daily Dispatch* and a radio in the CU Hall.[80] Students frequented open-air gatherings known as 'bush meetings'. Matsepe-Casaburri says that Fort Hare was 'a hive of political activity and debate' that 'catapulted one to take one's social experiences and begin to look at them in a slightly different context … not only asking questions, but seeking answers'.[81]

Non-collaboration, highlighted by Robert Sobukwe in his 1949 speech, dominated discussion at Fort Hare in the late 1940s. Frieda Matthews recalled the passion of campus debate saying,

> There can be no doubt that political consciousness grew among most students during their period of study … There was hot debate on how far and in what way government institutions should be boycotted and in what way members of the ANC should co-operate with those of other racial groups.[82]

At times, the ire of the students fell on her husband, Professor Z.K. Matthews, who participated in the NRC that the militant students despised so much. These discussions mirrored those taking place in the ANC.

The 1950s brought new topics that charged the intellectual atmosphere on campus. The issue of withdrawal from NUSAS was paramount in 1952.

However, throughout the decade, the most heated debates were between the YL and SOYA, the latter group an outgrowth of the NEUM. Over the years, both organisations were popular among the students. The YL was founded in 1948 and gained the upper hand, but SOYA – which had opposed the Defiance Campaign – made inroads in the period following the campaign when the ANC was hampered by bannings and infiltration. In the later 1950s, the YL reasserted itself under the strong leadership of Makiwane, who led the resistance to university apartheid. 'When I arrived ... the Youth League ... was rather weak,' says Makiwane. 'It seemed to me when I got there that it was dominated more or less by the Unity Movement.'[83]

Senate estimates from 1953 place the number of students in one group or the other at nearly 75 per cent.[84] By the time Makiwane arrived and the fight against university apartheid came to the forefront, most students belonged to the YL. From 1957 to 1959, an estimated 10 per cent of students were SOYA members, most coming from rural areas of the Transkei that supported the AAC and, later, the Unity Movement.[85] Youth Leaguers tended to hail from the country's urban centres and favoured action above the theoretical politics of SOYA.

Yet, no matter which group had majority support at a particular time, the interaction between SOYA and the YL dominated campus debate, particularly in the 1950s. Matsepe-Casaburri says that both SOYA and the YL 'articulated themselves very, very well'.[86] Makiwane says, 'When we had the meetings, we were quite strong against the Unity Movement and they were also of course most vociferous.' The friendly but intense rivalry generated debate that politicised many students. 'We organised students, new students, into the Youth League,' says Makiwane. 'I suppose the Unity Movement was doing likewise.'[87] Even the non-leadership was forced to choose sides. 'It was ANC and the Unity Movement,' says Govender, who 'fell into the Unity Movement because of a few friends in my dorm', although most students from Natal joined the YL.[88]

The fiery rivalry is remembered fondly among students of the 1950s. Makiwane says the YL eventually got the best of SOYA:

> We finally crashed it. ... We rendered it helpless. ... But there was no animosity. We were just political opponents. We were friends. You'd find that even a man from the Unity Movement, we were calling each other names and so on and still living there at the hostels.[89]

The Unity Movement members were particularly susceptible to name-calling. Mabindisa, a Youth Leaguer, says: 'We used to call people who belonged to SOYA "beans" because you know, the acronym referred to it.' SOYA members responded by dubbing the Youth Leaguers 'Stalinists'. Always prepared to fire back, the Youth Leaguers would seek to have the last word, calling the Unity Movement members 'Trotskyites'.[90]

The SOYA and ANC groupings held their own meetings, getting together only to discuss issues that affected the college as a whole. Frank Mdlalose describes how, as a leader of the YL, he kept abreast of SOYA's discussions:

> I felt I must know what all the other political organisations are thinking and I must be informed. So I planted a new student in SOYA. I planted him there. The Unity Movement, they used to meet behind Beda Hall in the bush. I had to send somebody to give me information and he had to behave like he didn't know me. He had to report to me ... as a spy ... on Sunday nights, room number 75, Ferguson Davie ... an eye in the other movement ... Not for the sake of killing or assaulting, but just for the sake of being part of the thought process.[91]

Mabindisa recalls the debate on campus about the 1959 potato boycott as delineating the difference between the YL philosophy of action and SOYA's emphasis on theory. He describes the divergent philosophies of the two movements in his account of the events, saying, 'There were these potato farmers in the Transvaal who actually were getting labourers from the prisons ... This was a form of slave labour ... Some of the people who were working there were killed in the farms.' The ANC called a boycott of potatoes to protest against the unfair labour practices of the farmers; some 2 000 people burned potatoes at an ANC meeting in Sophiatown in June 1959. The Youth Leaguers supported the call by their parent organisation. 'The ANC Youth Leaguers felt that we shouldn't eat potatoes,' says Mabindisa. 'We used to take potatoes and throw them out.' SOYA did not approve of the Youth Leaguers' methods. Mabindisa says,

> The people who belonged to the Unity Movement, the beans, thought that we were childish. They were waiting for the peasants to start their revolt and we were doing all these silly things. ... They were always harping on the fact that you have to prepare peasants for a revolution and it's only the peasants who can lead this revolution.[92]

Beard notes that SOYA members 'tended to be theoreticians rather than activists, and their approach to "theory" more often than not was of a scholastic kind, involving the debating of the logomachies of political doctrine'.[93] Another staff member, D.G.S. Mtimkulu, told Williams SOYA generally preferred boycotts to direct action, despite its members' unwillingness to participate in the potato action: 'SOYA was aware of the might of the South African government. They feared all possible physical confrontations. The ANC, on the other hand, encouraged protests and all forms of confrontation with the government.'[94]

◆◆◆◆◆

Discussion permeated the university and, like many students, Matsepe-Casaburri was propelled into politics by the debates between the ANC and the Unity Movement at Fort Hare. Born in Kroonstad on 18 September 1937, the daughter of teachers, she was aware of the racial hostilities in South Africa from an early age. Though her parents were not members of any political organisations and they did not encourage their daughter's involvement in politics, the environment in which she grew up awakened Matsepe-Casaburri's social consciousness. Some memories from her childhood are revealing. 'I remember as a young girl, old [Z.R.] Mahabane, who was once the ANC president, used to be a minister in Kroonstad and active in his politics there.' She recalls her sensibilities being roused by the vicious pass laws:

> My own principal was marched off by police for having not carried his pass on him. And this was a respectable citizen, the most educated person in the community. And that made a real mark on many children, that something is wrong with a system that would denigrate someone who has such a high standing in the community.

Many of the forced removals of the 1950s touched Matsepe-Casaburri. Twice, her family was driven out of their home by the government. The second forced removal occurred immediately before she left for Fort Hare. Thus, when she arrived in Alice, she was well aware of the racial strife in the country, though she had not yet become politically active.[95]

She was unprepared for the level of activity that would greet her, however. Her earliest Fort Hare memory is of participating in the fresher versus freshette debate. She remembers the subject of the debate being William Shakespeare. 'I'm glad there were no tapes at the time,' she says. 'But that was one of my first learning experiences.' Her arrival, in 1959, coincided with a peak of activity surrounding the implementation of university apartheid. Though mostly an observer, she picked up a great deal:

> It's only then that I got to really understand what the Unity Movement was all about. I just used to hear about it and really not understand. That's when one began to pick up the differences between the different strands of politics ... And there was quite a great deal of passion about it.[96]

Eventually, she did become involved in campus politics. In her second year, she was the only woman elected to the SRC. The questioning, intellectual atmosphere awed Matsepe-Casaburri.

> Billy Modise and Ambrose Makiwane were people who could debate politically in a manner that you had never really heard people engage in debates ... Fort Hare was the first place where one was thrown into the real world of adult people that seemed to be so knowledgeable and so educated about certain kinds of things.

Though Matsepe-Casaburri did not become active in the ANC until she graduated and went into exile, she describes her Fort Hare days as politically formative:

> As one's experience began to shape, you made your connections with the roots that had been formed at Fort Hare. Then once you got into those politics, your commitment was not ambivalent at all. The groundwork had been done for you ... You came to a position where you now said I may have come here later, but I have come with convictions that clearly say, backwards I cannot go.[97]

However, with the impending government takeover, student life at Fort Hare was soon to take a huge step back. G.S. Tootla and Marumo Moerane (1959–1961) were at Fort Hare during the takeover and stayed on to witness the after-effects. 'The whole basic structure of Fort Hare was destroyed,' says Tootla. 'Everything was breaking up. This was the beginning of the destruction of Fort Hare, what it believed in.'[98] Marumo Moerane says that after the takeover, 'there was hardly any student life', and Sipo Makalima, a long-time observer of Fort Hare says: 'It went down in spirit, down in everything. It was terrible.'[99] This was a far cry from the Fort Hare that Ivy Matsepe-Casaburri loved so much:

> You had a core of a cross-section of the population ... And you all had to live together, eat together, dance together, play together ... And what I have dreaded most about the loss of Fort Hare was that microcosm of South Africa that was not allowed to bloom and be able to reproduce itself.

Matsepe-Casaburri knew only the multi-racial Fort Hare.

> Years later some people had even forgotten how integrated a community Fort Hare was. I found students not knowing this. 'By the way, you mean to tell me you lived as Indians, coloureds and everybody?' Because in their experience, it was a Xhosa university. And that for me was just absolutely shocking, that that can be the memory of any Fort Harian of Fort Hare.[100]

The Student Christian Association, 1959, including Isaac Mabindisa (top, third from left); Ivy Matsepe-Casaburri (middle, third from left); Gertrude Darroll (in hat); and Manto Tshabalala (later Tshababala-Msimang), who would become minister of Health in the ANC government after 1999.

Students participate in rag festivities, 1959

Yet with the takeover, this was the reality. Fort Hare was to become an institution exclusively for Xhosas, stripping it of its multi-racial character and wiping from existence the shining example of what was possible.

Notes

1   Matthews, *Freedom for my People*, 197.
2   Fort Hare Senate, 'Memorandum on University Apartheid', Fort Hare Papers.
3   Mabindisa, interview.
4   Herby Govinden, 'Tribute to Fort Hare at 80', in author's possession.
5   Beard, 'Background to student activities', 157.
6   Matsepe-Casaburri, interview.
7   Beard, 'Background to student activities', 157.
8   At this time, blacks were still being admitted (albeit in very small numbers) to the 'open' universities – Wits, Natal and UCT – but they were not permitted to live in residences with white students and partake fully in student life.
9   'Student statistics', 1955. Fort Hare Papers.
10   'Fort Hare decisive role', *The Leader,* 25 October 1991.
11   George Singh, letter to Alexander Kerr, 11 June 1945, George Singh student file, Fort Hare Papers.
12   Alexander Kerr, letter to George Singh, 18 June1945, George Singh student file, Fort Hare Papers.
13   Senate Minutes, 1928–1945, 15 March 1940, Fort Hare Papers.

14 Rama Thumbadoo, student file, Fort Hare Papers.

15 'Student Statistics', 1918, Fort Hare Papers.

16 Bughwan, interview.

17 High Commissioner of India, letter to Alexander Kerr, 10 March 1944, The high commissioner for India 1942–1954 file, Fort Hare Papers.

18 Bughwan, interview.

19 Pillay, interview.

20 *Ibid.*

21 *Ibid.*

22 G.S. Tootla, interview.

23 *Ibid.*

24 *Ibid.*

25 Bughwan, interview.

26 *Ibid.*

27 Matsepe-Casaburri, interview.

28 Matthews, *Freedom for my People*, 126.

29 Matsepe-Casaburri, interview.

30 V.R. Govender, interview.

31 Mary Dick, 'The higher education of a minority group as exemplified by the group at the South African Native College, Fort Hare' (BEd thesis, UCT, 1934), cited in Burchell, 'The pursuit of relevance', 56.

32 C.F. Andrews, 'Fort Hare and the future', *Indian Opinion,* 1 April 1927, cited in Burchell, 'The pursuit of relevance', 54.

33 Naidoo, interview.

34 Thumbadoo, interview.

35 Pillay, interview.

36 Govender, interview.

37 Ismail Dada, interview.

38 Naidoo, interview.

39 Rules for pregnancy were particularly strict. In 1948, Dennis Siwisa was expelled after he impregnated a fellow student (Dennis Siwisa, student file, Fort Hare Papers). By contrast, at the ANC's Solomon Mahlangu Freedom College in Tanzania, if a young woman became pregnant, she was moved to a centre for pregnant girls. The young man was dropped as a student and had to go to work to help support her.

40 Thelma Appavoo, interview, East London, 1999.

41 Appavoo, interview.

42 Govender, interview.

43 *Ibid.*

44 Matsepe-Casaburri, interview.

45 Mandela, *Long Walk to Freedom*, 44.

46 Naidoo, interview.

47 Pillay, interview.

48 Dada, interview.

49 Govender, interview.

50 Tsotsi, interview.

51 Hyslop, *The Classroom Struggle*, 16.

52 Naidoo, interview.

53 Thumbadoo, interview.

54 Govinden, interview.
55 Pillay, interview.
56 Matsepe-Casaburri, interview.
57 Not everyone loved the syndicates. In an informal conversation with the author in New York City in December 2004, Gail Gerhart vividly recalled an interview she conducted with Z.B. Molete, a Fort Hare student in the early 1950s who later became a member of the PAC Executive Committee. Gerhart remembers Molete saying: 'You'd come back from the dining hall and the hostel would be stinking of curry.' Gerhart says the conversation 'stuck in my mind', and wonders whether race relations at the time were really as rosy as the students, years later, were to portray them. Molete's comment to Gerhart could indicate that the growing Africanist movement in the country had started to filter into Fort Hare.
58 Pillay, interview.
59 Naidoo, interview.
60 Govender, interview.
61 Pillay, interview.
62 Mabindisa, interview. Govan Mbeki enjoyed ballroom dancing while at Fort Hare. 'I used to be very fond of dancing. I used to go to Ntselemanzi and I would dance there,' he says. He also talks of how he passed the time on Robben Island practising his steps. Mbeki, interview.
63 Mdlalose, interview.
64 Matthews, interview.
65 Matsepe-Casaburri, interview.
66 Beard, 'Background to student activities', 159.
67 Mbeki, interview.
68 Cragg, 'Fort Hare', 34
69 Beard, 'Background to student activities', 162.
70 Thumbadoo, interview ; Matsepe-Casaburri, interview.
71 Ambrose Makiwane, interview.
72 Under the chairmanship of D.D.T Jabavu, a professor of Bantu languages at Fort Hare, the AAC (All African Convention) was formed at a meeting in Bloemfontein in mid December 1935. It functioned as an umbrella political movement to fight against the passage of legislation abolishing the limited African Cape franchise. When the legislation was passed in 1936, the AAC remained in existence, receiving particularly strong support in the Transkei, but it died out with the ANC's resurgence in the 1940s.
73 Tsotsi, interview.
74 Bughwan, interview. Though Fort Hare and Rhodes did not formalise their institutional ties until 1951, there was prior contact between the two institutions on cultural and social levels from the 1930s. Separated by about 100 kilometres, Bughwan remembers a 'dusty, bumpy drive. They had a driver take us to Rhodes. The roads weren't like they are today.'
75 Mabindisa, interview.
76 Williams, *A History,* 69.
77 Pogrund, *How Can Man Die Better,* 20.
78 Naidoo, interview.
79 Pillay, interview.
80 Rama Thumbadoo, interview.
81 Matsepe-Casaburri, interview.
82 Matthews, *Remembrances,* 126.

83 Makiwane, interview.
84 Karis and Carter, volume 2, *Hope and Challenge, 1935–1952,* 435.
85 Williams, *A History of the University College of Fort Hare,* 31.
86 Matsepe-Casaburri, interview.
87 Makiwane, interview.
88 Govender, interview.
89 Makiwane, interview.
90 Mabindisa, interview.
91 Mdlalose, interview.
92 Mabindisa, interview.
93 Beard, 'Background to student activities', 168.
94 Williams, interview with D.G.S. Mtimkulu, cited in Williams, *A History*, 31.
95 Matsepe-Casaburri, interview.
96 *Ibid.*
97 *Ibid.*
98 Tootla, interview.
99 Marumo Moerane, interview; Makalima, interview.
100 Matsepe-Casaburri, interview.

3

The Road to Takeover

There are worse things that can happen to a person than
the loss of his 'bread'. One's soul is much more important.
Z.K. Matthews[1]

Winds of change

In the *Brown vs. the Board of Education* decision in 1954, the United States Supreme Court ruled that distinctions based on race or colour violated the equal protection clause of the 14th Amendment to the United States Constitution. The decision provided the legal framework for the United States civil rights movement of the 1960s. That same year, the fall of Dien Bien Phu brought an end to French Indochina, and signalled the beginning of the end of French and British colonial empires. Around the developing world, the defeat of a colonial power by a small Asian nation augured the collapse of colonialism and was a source of great pride.

Increasingly, what racists in South Africa saw as the natural order was becoming out of step with the rest of Africa and the world. In October 1958, the United States government shifted its policy of abstaining from resolutions critical of apartheid, voting for a mild declaration expressing 'regret and concern' over South Africa's racial policy. Shortly afterwards, the All-African People's Conference in Accra, Ghana, pushed Africans in South Africa – particularly those who were Africanists – to identify more closely with movements for independence elsewhere on the continent.[2]

'Self-government has become the cry of the peoples throughout the length and breadth of the continent,' noted the ANC report in December 1959. 'That cry can no longer be resisted by the imperialists who are making a last desperate bid to withhold the legitimate rights of the African people.'[3] Nigeria,

124

Cameroon and Congo were among those colonies on the cusp of independence, sparking a renewed sense of hopefulness that South Africa would overcome white domination. Africanists in South Africa pointed to the growing spirit of independence to claim their movement was in concert with the rest of the continent.

In Britain, Prime Minister Harold Macmillan took note of the burgeoning nationalist movements and, on a trip to Cape Town, declared before the South African parliament that 'winds of change' were blowing throughout the African continent.[4] Yet while Britain and France were acknowledging that their colonies would have to be granted majority rule, and the civil rights movement was taking hold in the United States, the Nationalists in South Africa dug in and increasingly turned to the manipulation of ethnicity to entrench their power.

In 1959, eleven years after coming to power, the National Party secured the passage of the Promotion of Bantu Self-Government Act, which recognised eight distinct homelands on ethnic grounds, and provided the machinery for these areas to be led to self-government. That same year, the government brought university education into line with its ethnically defined goals. Speaking in June 1959, Minister of Bantu Education W.A. Maree said that the provision of separate universities had 'a very close connection with all the other legislation of this government which deals with the development of the Bantu as separate national groups'.[5] With the passage in parliament of the Extension of University Education Act and the Fort Hare Transfer Act, university apartheid became an integral component of a government strategy to defuse political opposition through the Bantustan policy.

The ironically named Extension of University Education Act called for the 'establishment, management and control of university colleges for non-white persons; for the admission of students to and their instruction at university colleges; and for the limitation of the admission of non-white students to certain university institutions'.[6] Under the new law, the so-called open universities (namely Wits, UCT, Rhodes and Natal) were reserved for whites only. While the correspondence institution, UNISA and the medical school of the University of Natal remained open to blacks, four new university colleges were established and designated for distinct population groups as defined by the apartheid government. The University College of Zululand at Ngoye was for Zulu and Swazi students; the University College of the North (called Turfloop, after the settlement where it was situated) for North Sotho and Tswana students; the University College of Durban-Westville for Indian students; and the University College of the Western Cape for coloured students. Under the Fort Hare Transfer Act, the government seized Fort Hare, and the registration of non-Xhosa students (with a few exceptions) was no longer permitted.

The smouldering and undesirable

In her study of the development of university apartheid, Beale writes that the National Party came to power in 1948 without a blueprint for university education. Before 1955, little thought was given within the NP to how university policy would be incorporated into apartheid planning. She notes that racial discrimination was the only concept agreed upon throughout the party, writing that it 'was the common starting point for members of the NP'.[7] The only conclusion reached by the government before 1955 was that white students should study in institutions separate from blacks.

> In the early 1950s the direction taken by the new apartheid government was a source of controversy within the NP. At every level, including the cabinet, the NP combined a range of people and interests, who worked together because they shared a general commitment to Afrikaner nationalism and to the vaguely defined idea of apartheid.[8]

Ideas about the shape and scope of university apartheid were in flux until the NAD and the Suid-Afrikaanse Buro vir Rasse-Aangeleenthede/South African Bureau for Racial Affairs (SABRA) took control of policy in 1955. Previously, university education had fallen under the jurisdiction of the Department of Education, Arts and Science. Spurred on by African political opposition exhibited in actions such as the Defiance Campaign and the Congress of the People and shifts in power within the NP, senior members of the Native Affairs Department (NAD) increasingly took charge of university policy, shaping it into the form it took in 1959.

As the NAD and SABRA wrested control from the Department of Education, the government's university education policy became more clearly defined. Political concerns were now paramount and educational policy for the new institutions was left unresolved:

> Since ethnic self-segregation at university level had helped to foster a separate Afrikaner identity, educational planners in the National Party expected that tribally-based universities would provide similar psychological underpinnings for the future 'independent' African homelands. Segregation of Indians and Coloureds would minimise tendencies for the subject races to identify with one another ...[9]

With the passage of the two acts, politics and university education were brought together, since the primary function of the university colleges was to contribute to the success of the government's Bantustan policy.

The groundwork for university apartheid was laid in 1949 when the government appointed the Eiselen Commission to study African education. The commission recommended 'resorting to radical measures' for the 'effective reform of the Bantu school system'. Some four years later, the Bantu Education Act was passed, removing control of African education from the churches and provincial authorities, and placing it under a separate government department. The act ceded control of most mission schools, including nearby Lovedale,[10] to the government and resulted in a startling disparity between money spent on educating African children and that spent on whites.

Fort Hare students rejected the Eiselen Commission report in part because they saw it as a precursor to the 'heavy hand of Government descending on university education, with control of Fort Hare as a prime target'. The longstanding fears were made more immediate late in 1952 when Prime Minister Dr D.F. Malan addressed a graduation ceremony at the University of Stellenbosch, shaking a 'warning finger at those universities which admit non-European students'. An editorial in the *Daily Dispatch* made it clear the government was intent on conforming higher education policy to the 'Procrustean bed of party ideologies'.[11]

The road to the passage of the two acts had begun in 1953, when Minister of Education, Arts and Science J.H. Viljoen addressed a memorandum to the cabinet entitled 'Apartheid at universities'. He said the government had been brought under increasing public scrutiny to 'provide separate educational facilities for non-whites at universities'.[12] In December 1953 a commission, chaired by Dr J.E. Holloway, was appointed to look into the financial feasibility of providing separate university facilities for non-Europeans. Supporters of educational segregation, including UNISA, the University of Pretoria, Potchefstroom University, SABRA and the NAD, presented their cases. Werner Eiselen, the father of Bantu Education, who had been appointed secretary for Native Affairs in 1951, gave the most dramatic testimony. He envisioned three separate 'Bantu university institutions', divided along ethnic lines and under the control of UNISA as 'an ultimate ideal'.[13] With the presentation by Eiselen and others to the Holloway Commission, the notion of university education along ethnic lines was given credence for the first time.

In making his report in February 1955, Holloway shunned the call to build new separate institutions, saying it was neither practical nor financially wise.

Yet Beale writes that 'the balance of power in the cabinet changed from moderate to hard-line support for apartheid' in the months before the report was released. And Minister of Native Affairs Hendrik Verwoerd rejected the Holloway report, telling the cabinet that 'where the Bantu are concerned, I find the whole approach of the Commission is wrong and as a consequence I cannot identify myself with its recommendations'.[14] In November 1955, ignoring the recommendations of the Holloway Commission, the government announced the formation of a committee to look into the application of apartheid at the universities.[15] It became increasingly obvious that the government viewed separate universities as vehicles of social control, and would fight to make sure they were established. Verwoerd recommended a system similar to that presented to the Holloway Commission by Eiselen. And, as Beale writes, owing to the shift in power within the NP in favour of the hard-liners, when articulated by Verwoerd, the policy, for the first time, seemed likely to be implemented.[16]

Indeed, in March 1957, Viljoen introduced into parliament the first draft of what was then termed the 'Separate University Education Bill'. It called for the establishment of university colleges for black students, the transfer of Fort Hare and Natal Medical School to the government, and declared the open universities (in most cases) off limits to blacks. Fort Harians and other opponents of the bill were granted a brief reprieve when Professor Dennis Cowen of UCT discovered a constitutional flaw in the bill. Because it dealt with matters of public policy and private interests, the bill was declared 'hybrid' and the NP was forced to withdraw it. However, the technicality did not delay matters for long as the bill was quickly replaced with another, which omitted reference to Fort Hare and the non-European medical school. A second, separate bill dealing with Fort Hare that proceeded through parliament independently was also drawn up.

In May 1957, the bill was placed before a select committee in parliament. The committee recommended 119 changes to the bill, the most significant of which was to establish separate segregated advisory councils and senates. The name of the bill was changed to the Extension of University Education Bill. At Fort Hare, despite inevitable differences among personalities from time to time, the Council and Senate, consisting of both Africans and Europeans, had always operated successfully. Yet the government paid no attention to Fort Hare's history. It saw itself as trustee to Africans in the Bantustans, assuming control of their lives until the day that they were 'civilised' enough to control themselves. Referring to the 'present state of immaturity of the non-European groups', which rendered them 'unable to finance, staff, and control a university college of their own', the commission sought to bring the senates and councils in line with the new roles outlined by the separate development of Bantu Authorities.[17]

The government's justification for the establishment of separate universities illuminates its reasons for ignoring Holloway's conviction that establishing the facilities was not economically feasible. Introducing the revised non-hybrid bill in the House of Assembly, Viljoen outlined the context of the government's university policy, voicing concern over the growing African political opposition, particularly, 'the numerous defiance campaigns ... amongst the non-white population groups'.[18] Beale writes that in the late 1950s 'the failure of the government to dispel the threat of African political mobilisation, and the exacerbation of the conditions that fed that mobilisation led increasingly to political manipulation of the ideas of ethnicity'.[19]

Fort Hare in particular was viewed as a threat to government policy. The minister of Bantu education felt that the students were being indoctrinated, and the government felt the students were 'being turned into agitators'.[20] It therefore sought to curb what it called the 'smouldering and undesirable ideological elements' emanating from Alice.[21] Speaking at the second reading of the Fort Hare Transfer Bill in Parliament, the minister of Bantu Education said that the government had to control Fort Hare, because it had not only refused to practise apartheid, but directly opposed it and destroyed the means the government had created to apply it.[22] 'Minister Maree said that the trouble with Fort Hare was that it produced "black Englishmen". What he presumably wants to produce in his "Bantu Colleges" are "loyal Bantu" loyal to the scourge of apartheid', the December 1959 ANC report said.[23]

Abolishing the open universities was a key component of the government's plan. 'We do not want non-white students in the same university as the young European students of today who are the leaders of tomorrow,' said Verwoerd. 'We do not want Europeans to become so accustomed to the Native that they feel there is no difference between them and the Natives.'[24] The Commission on the Separate University Bill wrote, 'The existing open universities will give the students a background which does not fit in with their national character and will give them an alien and contemptuous attitude towards their own culture.' In making their case against the open universities, the government spoke of their danger to the Bantustan policy:

> The majority of non-Europeans who received their university education
> at the European universities have not been prepared to use their talents

in the service and development of their own people. They have, on the contrary, sought a livelihood in European-oriented communities.

The commission acknowledged that the main purpose of the university colleges was to provide for the growth of the Bantustans: 'Without their own university colleges the development of the Bantu areas and indeed of the whole project of Bantu development … would be an impossible task.'[25]

In its final form, the Extension of University Education Bill provided the minister of Bantu Education in the NAD with immense powers over Fort Hare and the other proposed ethnic colleges. In addition to appointing senate, council and advisory body members, faculty at the new institutions were to be civil servants under his control. Lecturers were regarded as state employees to be dealt with at the discretion of the minister. The state assumed the power to conduct inquiries into the political leanings of students and staff in order to 'protect the developing ethnic groups against irresponsible political agitation'.[26] Furthermore, in an attempt to lessen the threat of African political organisation in urban areas, the new campuses were to be situated in the 'native reserves', physically removing some of the more highly educated people from the cities.[27]

Most importantly, as Beale writes, 'Putting African university education directly under the control of the Department of Bantu Education increased the opportunities available for the government to manipulate the political cultures of the university colleges.'[28] From 15 May to 12 June 1959, a select committee of parliament debated the Fort Hare Transfer Bill and pronouncements by its members during the proceedings outline the role envisioned for the new colleges. One minister said: 'The colleges must prevent a spirit of equality arising.' Another said they 'will destruct the disastrous influences of liberalism which is using the university as a breeding place'. It was also proclaimed that the colleges were necessary to 'prevent evil influences infiltrating' and that students of the colleges must 'develop along healthy lines from the bottom up'.[29] Z.K. Matthews wrote that the proposed structure of the colleges was 'frightening' in that,

> All members of council will have to be pro-Government and Senate will be subject to a discipline code which will convert them into automatons. 'Do what you are told, eat sleep and be merry!' will be the obvious motto for such a staff.[30]

Outsize effort for a comma

'So the bombshell has fallen,' wrote Z.K. Matthews on 14 March 1957. In Johannesburg facing treason charges, [31] Matthews kept abreast of the news about university apartheid, and the subject dominated letters to his wife, Frieda, in Alice. On reading the terms of the university apartheid bill, he wrote: 'Verwoerd seems determined to get everything African under him.' Three days later, he wrote to his wife: 'I feel that the Bill is even worse than we had anticipated. Every single freedom usually associated with Universities will be gone.' Yet Matthews was not paralysed by the shocking nature of the bill. As soon as he was aware of its contents, he began to formulate opposition. [32]

Separate universities were topics at numerous senate meetings, even before the terms of the bill were announced. Z.K. Matthews writes: 'The question of the future of Fort Hare was exercising the minds of members of the academic staff,' beginning in 1955. [33] On 11 June 1956, the Senate issued a resolution: 'The best interests of the College would be served by the retention of its present relationship with the Department of Education, Arts and Science and that the college should continue to accept students on the same basis as before.' [34] Shortly afterwards, Matthews was arrested on charges of treason. Professor M.H. Giffen, head of the Botany Department, became acting principal whenever Matthews was unavailable due to the trial. Yet the official response to the bill at Fort Hare did not skip a beat.

Shortly after the provisions of the initial Separate University Education Bill were announced, the Executive Committee of the Governing Council met to draft its response. 'The executive committee … has read with dismay the proposals for [Fort Hare's] future development. The college is in fact to be reduced from the status of an autonomous university institution to a branch of the civil service.' [35] While the other ethnic universities were to be created, Fort Hare, as it had been known, was to be destroyed. Throughout their opposition to the bill, the Fort Hare administration emphasised this point. They pointed to the 1947 Brookes Commission Report, which had said that the future of Fort Hare should be that of an independent institution, viewing the bill as an attack on Fort Hare's progress:

> Fort Hare has forty years of experience and development behind it. During that long period it has progressed from High School to full university college and has gained many of the rights and privileges of self government proper to a university. Under the proposed bill all these rights and privileges are to be abrogated, the traditions of the

college lost, and its future made entirely dependent on the will of the minister.[36]

From the outset of debate over the bill, the prospect of government interference in educational decisions upset the authorities at Fort Hare. On 16 October 1957, the Council and Senate of Fort Hare presented written evidence to the government charging that '[t]he first necessity for any satisfactory functioning of any institution which claims to be a university is autonomy, the power to work out its own salvation free of political pressures.'[37] Council and Senate felt the bill gave excessive and unparalleled powers to the minister and that there were no academic or logical grounds for changing control of the college. They saw a danger in the unchecked authority of the minister, writing: 'A principal answerable only to the minister may at times be tempted to soft-pedal academic interests in favour of current political policies.'[38]

Meanwhile, conservative and 'middle group' staff members who felt the 1955 closure of the college had impacted the government's decision to control Fort Hare briefly sidetracked the opposition. The group, which included Donovan Williams, had 'become increasingly concerned about lack of action on recommendations of the "Duminy Commission", designed to set Fort Hare's house in order'. It drew up a 'Memorandum Relative to the Future of the College', which focused on rules and regulations largely pertaining to student discipline, and lengthy Senate debates ensued. According to Williams, there was consensus among staff that the government was keeping a watchful eye on Fort Hare and that it was necessary to 'show a good face in public'. [39]

That this discussion was an issue – with university apartheid legislation gaining steam in parliament – shows just how out of touch some of the administration remained with the political situation outside Fort Hare. The memorandum was unacceptable to certain liberal members of Senate who 'did not believe that the closure of 1955 and its aftermath had anything to do with Government intentions to take over Fort Hare'.[40] Indeed, the university apartheid legislation was much bigger than Fort Hare. It was part of the apartheid government's far broader efforts to curb African political activity and promote separate development. To blame separate university legislation on the 1955 takeover is historically short-sighted and ignores the government's larger plans for entrenching Afrikaner power.

In 1958, Professor H.R. Burrows, who had been chairman of the Economics Department at the University of Natal for 20 years, was named principal. Opposition to the university apartheid bills increased during his tenure. The Senate submitted a memorandum to the commission on the Separate

University Education Bill, and was later invited to present oral evidence. The memorandum attacked state control of the proposed university colleges, questioning whether the government's stated intention to eventually turn management of the colleges over to the non-European community was genuine. 'From top to bottom the government of the College is not to be in the hands of the non-European community,' stated the memorandum.[41] On 10 January 1958, Burrows, Matthews and Professor D.Z. de Villiers presented oral evidence to the Separate Universities Commission. The Fort Hare Lecturers Association also stated its case, saying that for a university to function properly, it must 'have the power to decide upon its own policies and organise its own affairs. In particular, a university must be free from external party political pressures.' The Lecturers Association called for academic freedom to be guaranteed, and for no changes in the manner of appointment of council and senate. They condemned the proposal to introduce differential salary scales based on race. [42]

The proposal for dual senates and councils divided along racial lines particularly upset staff at Fort Hare. Williams calls the pre-university apartheid structure 'thoroughly acceptable' to everyone involved. 'Diversity of political opinion and principles was divisive; race was not ...The mere thought of a discriminatory, dual senate system, with one body for the Whites and another for the Blacks ... touched everyone in the quick.'[43]

Staff members march through the streets of Alice to protest against the
proposed takeover of Fort Hare, 1958

On 25 July 1958, the college sent a memorandum to the minister of Education, Arts and Sciences and the minister of Native Affairs, requesting that they receive a delegation from Fort Hare. The government replied that it regretted it would not do any good to discuss the situation, because Fort Hare had already voiced its objections before the commission.[44] This was the government's normal reaction. It paid little attention to the opposition to the proposed bills, which centred on deputations and memorandums of protest. There was at least one march of staff and students through Alice, but this, and all other protest, was largely ignored. Though many staff would choose to leave the university once the legislation had been passed, there is no evidence that a boycott was ever discussed at this stage. Sipo Makalima says the government response to the protest was negligible: 'They allowed the change from no comma to have a comma in … their arguments.'[45]

We want the car and the fuel

At an emergency mass meeting on 27 October 1956, students rejected a proposal merely to discuss the government's proposed action, and voted instead 'that a conference of all students be called at which would be decided various ways and means of opposing segregation in Universities. Such a Conference must be called by Fort Hare with no collaboration with NUSAS'. [46]

A delegation to Parliament including Z.K. Matthews (third from left), Principal H.R. Burrows (sixth from left) and Dr Alexander Kerr (seventh from left) was not able to sway the government to abandon its separate universities plan, 1959

Yet just over a year later, in March 1957, the Fort Hare students voted unanimously to rejoin NUSAS so that the university apartheid bills could be fought from a united standpoint. The anti-liberal sentiment of the early 1950s was put on hold as the students recognised they would need all the help they could get in fighting against the government's proposed policy. Also, by 1959, owing largely to student reaction against the perverse separate university legislation, a discernible shift occurred within NUSAS. The group's liberals – who had long pushed for the organisation to focus more on national issues than student matters – prevailed, and NUSAS fervently petitioned and demonstrated against the legislation.[47]

In a press statement, SRC president Makiwane said the situation had changed since 1952 and that the Separate Universities Bill had shown the need for cooperation between all bodies sincerely opposed to university apartheid.[48] In much the same way that the ANC had joined forces with left-wing groups earlier in the decade, re-affiliation to NUSAS was seen as a political move, enlisting the support of white students against university apartheid. Throughout the late 1950s, opposition to the university apartheid bills dominated SRC activity and led to frequent mass meetings of students.

Ironically, it was the government onslaught that brought the students and college authorities closer together. From Johannesburg, Z.K. Matthews wrote: 'I am pleased that Ambrose Makiwane and company are going to Cape Town and will probably come up here later. The SRC seems to be doing very well this year.'[49] It would have seemed impossible just a few years earlier that the principal would compliment the president of the SRC. And praise by the SRC for the administration would have been even more unlikely. 'Professor Z.K. ... he was very helpful,' says Makiwane. 'We were using his car and petrol ... sometimes when we wanted the car, we had no money. We'd tell [his wife, Frieda] we want the car and the fuel.'[50] Indeed, in the face of the government onslaught, the administration appreciated the SRC's militancy and even supported its activities.

For the first time in the college's history, students and staff protested in unison as solidarity against a common enemy replaced the anger towards the authorities of earlier in the decade. The government took note of the improved relations between students and staff. In March 1957, plainclothes policemen offered students up to £10 for information on whether staff or student leaders had attempted to incite resistance to the Separate Education Bill.[51] In 1958, despite the police interference, Makiwane led a group of approximately 300 students and staff through the streets of Alice to protest against the acts. Isaac

Mabindisa recalls the march as being dignified, with staff in academic dress walking at the front of the procession.[52]

Relations between staff and students did hit a stumbling block in 1958, but the will to fight against the taking of Fort Hare eventually won out. Makiwane led Fort Hare student opposition to university apartheid, representing the college on a delegation to parliament, and authoring many of the memorandums issued by the SRC against the legislation. One statement he wrote on the findings of the Separate University Bill Commission caused trouble. Makiwane wrote:

> The commission's so-called conviction 'that the placing of the Bantu University Colleges under the control of the Native Affairs Department will make for better and more rapid development' is unacceptable because it makes for better and more rapid development towards the degradation, mental regimentation, and slavery, and aims at making the student mind mere pulp that can be manipulated to suit the whims and fancies of a fatal ideology.[53]

Then followed what Williams describes as 'several statements of conviction, delivered with evangelical fervour'. Among them was the following:

> We wish to warn the architects of University Apartheid and the whole country that while the architects of University Apartheid cherish the illusion that this corruption will obtain at Non-White Universities the same corruption will eventually strangle the throats of the entire population of South Africa.

The memorandum was sent to the press without the required Senate approval, touching off a heated debate. Burrows felt its nature was 'such that even Jabavu School children would not be proud of it', and noted the language was 'obviously not written by an English-speaking person'.[54] Leslie Blackwell, a law professor who had spent 27 years in parliament, considered the statement libellous.[55]

The SRC responded that they 'did not aim at style or marks in an examination, but were expressing their feelings unequivocally'. An incensed Blackwell tore into Makiwane, asking him whether he was a 'czar, whether the SRC executive did not realise they were only "BOYS", unskilled, unexperienced [sic], whereas he had spent 27 years in parliament'.[56] SRC members were threatened with expulsion, but they eventually put aside their differences with the administration in an effort to present a united front against the legislation. The students issued a revised memorandum and, ironically, Blackwell became a liaison to the SRC in their efforts to articulate legal opinion against the separate university legislation.

On 14 October 1958, a revised draft of the memorandum condemned 'in the strongest possible terms, the Separate University Education Bill'. The students particularly found fault with the divisive nature of the proposed colleges:

> Why, we ask, can Fort Hare not be taken as a living illustration of the stability we should have in the country without a coerced system of regimented existence. Anyone who pays a visit to the College … cannot escape the fact that University life at Fort Hare is a complete negation of the commission's allegations and misrepresentations about the potentialities of the non-European people as members of a multi-racial South Africa.

Makiwane and his colleagues proclaimed the government was overlooking that

> [t]he non-European students do not regulate their student relationships on ethnical considerations. On the contrary, they gain considerably in the ultimate field of human relations by having a common student life, with common aspirations, in an atmosphere where they benefit mutually from the variety of their different, but not antagonistic, backgrounds.

The statement refers to a campus visit by the Separate University Bill Commission in which the commissioners were 'impressed by the harmonious relations between staff members of all races, between the students of various backgrounds, and between staff and students'.[57]

The final memorandum was ready for the press by early November, with strong language curiously similar to that of the first one. It stated that only Africans could determine 'what form of education they want, not the stooge-chiefs of an imposed racialist government policy'. Seemingly with reference to the historic *Brown vs. Board of Education* decision in the United States the students vowed to fight the 'hypocritical theory of "separate but equal"' university institutions.[58]

◆◆◆◆◆

Andrew Masondo calls Makiwane a charismatic leader, but adds: 'I also had the feeling that he was a bully. He's the type of leader you'd want if you were fighting. You wouldn't want him to be your leader when you are strategising.'[59] As president of the SRC during the fight against university apartheid, Makiwane had to do a bit of both, making enemies, but simultaneously earning respect as a strong political leader. He arrived at Fort Hare in 1955 at the age of 34, older than most students, full of life experience, and primed to assume a leadership role in the political struggle on campus. Beard wrote: 'Never did he hesitate to say what was on his mind, and he made a habit of criticising university policy and the actions of the authorities whenever they did not come up to his expectations.'[60]

Makiwane was born on 29 November 1921 in the rural Transkei, where both of his parents were teachers and his father also worked as a peasant farmer. Although his father was not politically active, Makiwane's mother became one of the rural area organisers for the ANC shortly after it was founded in 1912. Makiwane remembers becoming politically aware through her involvement. The provincial ANC frequently met in his home and he recalls, as a child, earning a kind of informal membership in the organisation 'before I even enrolled, because I used to be sent on errands for the movement'. He says: 'I became aware through the meetings there at home. I began to know that something was wrong. And I got interested.'[61]

Makiwane's first political activity was at Clarkebury, a mission school in the Engcobo district of the Transkei: 'When I went to school, I knew already about these injustices and I used to react accordingly when anything reactionary was done by authorities.' Makiwane led a variety of protests against the missionary authorities. 'We resented them ... opening our letters ... they would discover that some are in love.' He also rebelled against the religion that permeated the school: 'You had to make confessions. And I refused. I said no. There are no gods. I can't confess my sins to them.' School authorities eventually expelled Makiwane from Clarkebury over his leadership in protests against poorly prepared food. 'I refused to be punished, rejected corporal punishment outright. And they expelled me.'[62]

Makiwane moved to Johannesburg in 1939, where his political involvement heightened. He joined the YL, which was founded in 1944. He also joined the SACP. Makiwane did matriculation studies privately, while working to save for further education. He was secretary of the Laundry Workers' Union and the Rope and Canvas Workers' Union, and an organiser for the South African Clothing Workers' Union, participating in strikes. Makiwane also became increasingly involved with the ANC as a member of the Orlando and Pimville branches.[63]

In 1951 he moved on to Adams College in Natal, where he enrolled in a teaching course. After finishing at Adams, Makiwane worked as a teacher during the onset of Bantu Education. Once again, politics took centre stage, and once again Makiwane was expelled. This time, it was for campaigning against Bantu Education and Bantu Authorities.

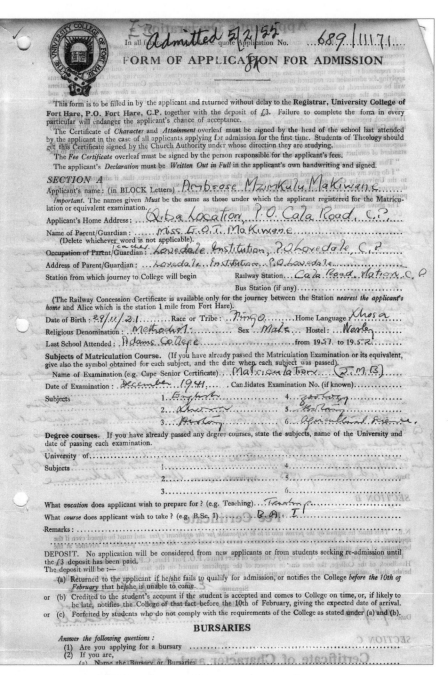

Ambrose Makiwane's Fort Hare application

Thus, when Makiwane finally arrived in Alice in 1955 at the age of 34, his political outlook had long been formed. His influence on the campus in the late 1950s is unquestionable. In 1958, he exhibited the organising skills he had developed in Johannesburg, leading a nurses' strike at Lovedale Hospital in protest against the dismissal of an African nurse. As Beard notes, 'no move was made by the nurses without prior consultation with the SRC executive committee'.[64] The students provided food and blankets to the nurses, upsetting the administration, which felt any outside political student activity would draw the government's ire. Fort Hare turned a blind eye when Makiwane was arrested for aiding the illegal strike, upsetting the SRC president, who had hoped the university would come to his support.[65] The YL was also active in 1959, organising a boycott of potatoes in the dining hall in solidarity with the ANC's nationwide campaign against prison labour practices on potato farms. This action might also be viewed as a gesture of defiance against the government's apartheid education bills.[66]

Govender speaks of the 'ANC of Makiwane', and says that Makiwane (called 'Gumbo' by the students after his clan name) was an 'outstanding figure during this time'. He remembers Gumbo as a 'tall, bearded man' with 'his own style'.[67] Matsepe-Casaburri says that Makiwane's debating prowess 'stands out … in a manner that you had never really heard people engage in debates'.[68] Makiwane says the student body was 'absolutely moved' by the attempted takeover, and opposition dominated the pages of *The Fort Harian* student publication.[69] Calling the proposed new Fort Hare a 'Bantu College tied to the apron strings of the minister of Native Affairs', one student wrote, 'These bush colleges are definitely to be established to produce intellectual yes men and to impede the pursuit of truth.'[70] Another wrote: 'The principle underlying the segregation is compatible with the aim of Bantu Education; to prepare the non-White for the society he has to serve, that is, the tribal society.'[71]

♦♦♦♦♦

It was not only the Fort Hare campus that was in revolt. Lovedale had fought its own battle against Bantu Education in the mid 1950s and the institution became involved in the struggle at Fort Hare. Isaac Mabindisa, a Lovedale student from 1956–1958, thus felt Makiwane's influence even before arriving at Fort Hare.

Mabindisa was born in Healdtown in 1940 and grew up in Port Alfred, where both of his parents were teachers. Although his parents sympathised with the ANC, neither of them was politically active. His father served on local advisory boards, but, because he was a civil servant, was not allowed to participate openly in politics. After primary school in Port Alfred, Mabindisa went to St Matthew's College, a mission school near Keiskammahoek. Growing up in Port Alfred, Mabindisa remembers reading, with interest, copies of Hansard that were sent to his father detailing the parliamentary debates. The Defiance Campaign, which was active in his hometown, also had an impact: 'Every Sunday we used to listen to these political speeches and the experiences of people who had come out of jail. So my education in politics began that way.'[72]

In 1955, the government took over St Matthew's, and declared it a girls' school. Mabindisa received another political lesson. He was forced to move to Lovedale, which was reserved for boys under the Bantu Education scheme. 'One of the things that the government wanted to do was to dismantle missionary education because they felt the type of education we got was preparing us to join the elite of the country and would make us envious of the European life,' he says.[73] At Lovedale, Mabindisa began reading *New Age* and *Torch* and, influenced by Makiwane, he joined the YL.

Sigqibo Dwane (1963–1964), a student at Lovedale from 1955–1959, says that Makiwane played a powerful role as an educator:

> We did not have meetings at Lovedale but we went across to Fort Hare to meetings with … Ambrose Makiwane, who was our teacher. We sat at his feet. Thabo [Mbeki] was in the group. And we would go to his room and be lectured to by Ambrose. And then on other occasions, we would go to public meetings, which were held under a twisted African tree and listen, discussing and learning from [him].[74]

Along with Thabo Mbeki and Chris Hani, Mabindisa was party to these sessions.[75] Thus, when he arrived at Fort Hare in 1959, even though Makiwane had graduated, Mabindisa was well prepared to join the fight against the separate university bills.

◆◆◆◆◆

Government attempts to repress Africans created more intense ideological responses among Africans generally and students in particular. Many, like Makiwane, embraced Marxism, while others rejected class analysis and propounded a race-based African nationalism. Within the ANC a rupture between these tendencies occurred in 1958, and the following year some of the nationalists (who called themselves 'Africanists') founded the PAC. At Fort Hare, this split was mirrored in student politics, though a united opposition to separate universities rendered the divide far less important on campus than it was at national level.

Chris Hani (lying on ground seventh from right) lounges in Freedom Square with his classmates, including Isaac Mabindisa (second from right on ground), around 1959

Marumo Moerane was a member of the student body affected by the events surrounding the government takeover. He arrived at Fort Hare in 1959 at the age of 17, politically conscious, but not active. Moerane, the son of M.T. Moerane, an ANC leader, knew of the tumultuous racial situation in South Africa from around 1949, when his father spoke out against the anti-Indian riots in Durban: 'I was only seven then, but I have a vivid memory of that time.' Having grown up in an intensely political family, Moerane, at the age of 10, was prepared to participate actively in the Defiance Campaign: 'I'm told by my mother and father that I wanted to go and join the campaign and present myself for arrest, go and sit on a park bench reserved for Europeans, as they were then called, go to playgrounds, and use the swings reserved for white kids.'[76]

In 1955, Moerane entered St Joseph's College, a Roman Catholic mission high school in Natal, to do his junior certificate. 'There were no political meetings,' he says. 'We were very good boys and girls who did things by the rules. It was a very regimented society … perfect silence in the evenings, study rooms where you are monitored.' Without political organisations or forums for discussion, Moerane didn't become active while at St Joseph's. 'From study hall you go to your rooms and sleep until the bell rings. So there was no time to engage in any political discussion. There were no youth leagues or anything of the sort.'[77]

That would all change when Moerane arrived at Fort Hare in 1959, a year of heightened political activity on campus. 'Fifty-nine is when the PAC was born,' he says. 'That's when the government took over Fort Hare from the old regime … The changes were dramatic.' Moerane recalls being intrigued by the level of fervour in the debate and discussion on campus. 'Seretse Choabi used to speak and introduce every speech of his with the phrase "according to Karl Marx". He used to speak until he frothed at the mouth.'[78] Moerane, like many of the other students, was drawn into active campus politics by the heated atmosphere on campus. 'When I got to Fort Hare, it was really the first time in my life that I attended political meetings,' he says. Influenced by some friends in his hostel, Moerane joined the PAC branch at Fort Hare. He says that he was also influenced to join the PAC by his father.

> Within the ANC you had a nationalist faction i.e. an Africanist faction and a Marxist faction. My father was not a Marxist. He was an African Nationalist. He influenced me. So when there was a question of making a choice between what I viewed as Marxist-Leninist ideology and pan-Africanist ideology, I opted for the pan-Africanist ideology.[79]

Moerane describes participating in gatherings of the Fort Hare PAC branch as educational: 'We used to hold meetings on Sundays in the bush. It was really a question of studying literature about pan-Africanism, holding discussion groups. No qualitative action … It was an eye-opener. I was politically conscious before, but not in an organised sense.'[80]

Non-political politics

The emergence of the PAC, which would lead to the 1960 Sharpeville emergency, was overshadowed at Fort Hare, however, by the crisis posed by the state takeover. Opposition to university apartheid came from the entire English-speaking university community in South Africa. Both individually through university SRCs and collectively through NUSAS, English-speaking students all over South Africa fought against separate universities. Opposition to the proposed policy dominated NUSAS activity in the 1950s, with presidents Ernie Wentzel and then John Shingler instrumental in leading the opposition. In 1957, Wentzel said the proposed institutions were 'unworthy of the name university'.[81]

The SRCs at UCT and Wits organised processions incorporating academic staff to protest against the acts. In a statement, the SRC at UCT declared the government 'was not establishing new university colleges for non-Europeans. Rather it was setting up institutions to be used for the indoctrination of non-European students in order to produce men and women incapable of rising about a predetermined level in society.'[82] In September 1956 at a meeting of 1 300 students at Wits, only 51 voted for the compulsory introduction of apartheid. At UCT in October, a similar meeting produced a vote of 1 114 to 15 in favour of full university autonomy.[83]

Authorities at institutions such as UCT, Rhodes and Wits also protested. The chancellor of UCT said the bill 'flouted the principles of true university education'. Dr Thomas Alty, the principal of Rhodes, organised a protest at the Grahamstown campus. In his speech at the rally he said that the protest was not political, and that universities are specialised institutions with the privilege of freedom from external control. He said that they should never be dragged into political battles. The principal from Wits made a similar statement, provoking this response from Z.K. Matthews:

> The great joke is that when the principal addressed the crowd, he stressed the point that the demonstration was entirely 'non-political'. So afraid people are of the word 'political' that even when they are demonstrating against a political measure they have to say they are non-political.[84]

Indeed, Alty could not help but speak in political terms, despite his best efforts. He called proposals for the new colleges completely unsatisfactory:

> We find ourselves in a unique position in which it is proposed to force through Parliament measures which are apparently not actively desired by any university, which are opposed by responsible opinion in all the universities concerned, and which are condemned in no uncertain terms by the whole university world of the West.[85]

The Marxist TLSA took a more overtly political stance against the legislation. In a statement issued in November 1959, the TLSA characterised the 'rigid control and regimentation of students and teaching staff' as the worst features of the proposed tribal colleges. Assuming an avowedly political position, the TLSA said that any teacher who accepted an appointment in the new colleges 'will do so in the full knowledge of the nefarious part they will have to play in the indoctrination of the Non-white students'. Calling on teachers to refuse appointments to these tribal colleges, the TLSA compared the schools with the 'co-ordinated universities of the Nazi regime of Hitler's Germany'.[86]

Others that spoke out against separate universities included the Natal Indian Congress, the Anglican Bishop and Catholic Archbishop of Pretoria, and the South African Institute of Race Relations.[87]

Impending doom

Despite the combined efforts of the opposition forces, time and again their words fell on deaf ears. University apartheid was an integral part of Verwoerd's Bantustan policy and the government intended to gain control of Fort Hare, regardless of the level of resistance. Frieda Matthews wrote: 'Absolutely no notice was taken of the protests.'[88] Though protest continued until the very end, by 1959 there was little hope within the opposition that their action would have any effect. An air of imminent disaster permeated the Fort Hare campus. 'In the rooms where lectures met, there was talk of impending doom, there was talk of what was going to happen,' says Herby Govinden.[89] De Villiers explained: 'Over us has been hanging this guillotine. We feel like the French aristocrats. We are on the way, but we have not yet reached the guillotine.'[90]

The last inter-racial council at Fort Hare, including alumnus Wycliffe Tsotsi (top, third from right) Z.K. Matthews (top, far right) and Alexander Kerr (seated, fourth from left)

The government did not assume control of Fort Hare until 1 January 1960, but the effects of the forthcoming takeover began to affect the college well before that time. For three years, opposition to the government dominated university life. Education did not. Discussion of the forthcoming takeover preoccupied Council, Senate and SRC meetings as the energies and emotions of the staff and students were concentrated on saving the college. Though classes continued without overt interruption, college life was affected in other ways.

In 1956, Z.K. Matthews, as acting principal, petitioned the Department of Education for a government grant to fund new departments, faculty and buildings. The government responded that the application was to be put on hold and would stand for consideration by the NAD. This was the new climate within which Fort Hare operated. The university was unable to obtain funds to establish a Department of Bantu Languages, for pharmacy courses, for improvements to the Department of Education or for the construction of buildings. 'Fort Hare has been severely handicapped during the last few years,' wrote Burrows in 1959. 'Development in many fields has been officially checked "owing to impending changes".'[91] In 1955, by way of Universities Act No 61, Fort Hare was granted full university status, placing it in a position of equality with other tertiary institutions with respect to government grants. But the threat of government intervention usurped Fort Hare's new-found status, leading to a state of uncertainty that severely hindered college life.

The designation of Matthews merely as acting principal marked the first sign that Fort Hare could no longer operate as an independent entity. The country's most distinguished African intellectual and a member of the Fort Hare faculty since 1936, he was clearly the best person for the job. Yet in an era of heated debate over separate universities, Matthews obviously had one qualification that was not viewed as a positive: his long association with the ANC. As one government nominee on the Council explained:

> Matthews served in a temporary capacity as Acting Principal to the complete satisfaction of the Council, but it was made clear to the Council or Council acted on the assumption, that the appointment of a Black Principal at Fort Hare would not carry the approval of the Government. Fort Hare was already under heavy fire and some were afraid lest it be closed down by the Government. To appoint as Principal Z.K., who was known to be persona-non-grata with the Government, was perhaps felt by some members of Council to be provocative.[92]

Govender, a first-year student in 1956, watched as Matthews was sidelined. 'Here is a great man, loved by his people, immaculate in manners, unimpeachable in terms of his thinking … Burrows was brought in, a man who couldn't match his stature or experience.'[93] Once in place, the new principal was forced to spend his entire tenure consumed by the takeover.[94]

The spirit that led to the sidelining of Matthews was evident again in 1958. Govan Mbeki wrote: 'And now the English-speaking teachers whom the nationalists suspect of being opposed to the debasement of education are thrown out of work to starve or surrender.'[95] At the end of 1958, a memorandum was sent to each member of staff explaining that a bill would be introduced to transfer Fort Hare to the government. Each was asked to cross out whichever of three choices was not applicable – that he favoured the bill; was opposed to it; or was noncommittal – and return their answers to the State Department. Some 10 months later, the first stage of the purification campaign was begun when eight leading members of the college staff were dismissed.[96]

Frieda Matthews writes that government officials came to campus to issue the dismissals: 'The atmosphere was tense as one by one the staff filed into the room which represented the Nationalist's guillotine for the week.'[97] Eight of the more liberal staff members had their services terminated from 31 December 1959 without explanation. They were the registrar Sir Fulque Agnew, his wife, geography lecturer Swanzie Agnew, botany lecturer G.F. Israelstam, English professor F.H. Rand, history professor Donovan Williams, law professor Leslie Blackwell, philosophy and politics lecturer Terence Beard and chief librarian J. Hutton. The purge was clearly political. 'They were very wise at that stage, the Nationalist government,' says Tootla. 'They took away the people they thought would be a problem and those were the people teaching us. It's like digging out the roots. The plant won't survive.'[98]

The dismissal of Williams, one of the more conservative staff members, shows how far the government was willing to go to control the new Fort Hare. There was 'puzzlement' at Fort Hare as to why Williams, who was not close to the students and 'kept to himself', was included in the dismissals. But in the sensitive discipline of history, the Nationalists were looking for someone who could teach the subject along their lines. Many years later, Cragg summed up the government's reasoning in an interview with Williams: 'They wanted a good Nat teaching History because it's such a vital subject in politics.'[99]

Blackwell wrote: 'The council invited me to remain as a professor of law for the year 1960 and I would have been glad to do so. But the government … has decided otherwise; and I will not be remaining.'[100] Frieda Matthews wrote that the Agnews were fired because they were vocal critics of government policy and frequently entertained Africans in their home.[101] Explaining the mass dismissals, the minister of Bantu Education said: 'I will not permit a penny of any funds of which I have control to be paid to any persons in those institutions who are known to be sabotaging the government's policy of apartheid.'[102] The Senate of Fort Hare issued a statement recording 'its extreme regret at the action of the minister of Bantu Education in disregarding normal university procedure by arbitrarily terminating the services of eight members of the academic and administrative staff'. The Governing Council said that the dismissals came without any prior notification and that it wished to dissociate itself 'entirely from this very unusual academic procedure on the part of the government'.[103]

Terence Beard, one of eight staff members fired when the government took over the university, is given a cigarette box by student Peter Mopp at a farewell event, 1959

In addition to the eight staff members forced out, Burrows was informed his 'services would not be retained'.[104] Many whose jobs were spared by the minister chose to resign and others who had applied for posts withdrew their applications. Some successful applicants for vacant posts refused to take up their appointments when they learned of Fort Hare's perilous future. From 1957 through to June 1959, 23 staff members left Fort Hare. By the end of June, there were 14 vacancies on a permanent staff of 44.[105] In July, only one staff member remained to teach 147 students three science courses.[106] Commenting on the mass resignations, Blackwell wrote: 'If one of its professors were to say or do one-tenth of what his colleagues in a European university may freely say or do – but possibly in the wrong direction – then a three months notice of dismissal, signed by an official, may be the result.'[107]

By 23 September, all members of staff were informed whether they would have jobs the next year. None of the African staff members was dismissed, but many resigned of their own accord, including education professor D.G.S. Mtimkulu, Bantu languages professor C.L.S. Nyembezi, and Z.K. Matthews. Marumo Moerane says there was a great deal of debate on campus as to whether the African members of staff should resign. 'That was the burning issue in 1959. The student body felt the lecturers should resign.'[108] The notion of whether to boycott colonial/state institutions or participate in them gets played out over and over again throughout South African history. With the emergence of the PAC and its orthodox nationalism in 1959, it should not be surprising that students felt the lecturers should resign. In 1959, 75 per cent of the staff either resigned or were dismissed. Twenty-five members of staff remained, comprising three categories of thought: those who agreed with the government legislation; those who could not afford to leave for personal reasons; and those who wanted to 'reduce the effects of the change in control'.[109]

The resignation of Z.K. Matthews illustrates the ruthless nature of the government takeover. The NP promised that those who were dismissed would receive all their pension benefits. And indeed, the eight European members of staff that were let go by 23 September received all of their benefits plus a bonus for the inconvenience.[110] Their African colleagues were not as lucky. 'The pension issue was very cleverly and diabolically manipulated' by the NP, wrote Frieda Matthews. 'Everyone on the staff knew that Enemy Number One of the Nationalist government was my husband and expected that he would be the only one … to be told to leave.'[111] Fully expecting to be fired, the 58-year-old Z.K. Matthews made plans to take his benefits and move to Bechuanaland (now Botswana) to open a legal practice. He walked into his interview certain of his fate:

> It was the longest interview as he was given in no uncertain terms the
> conditions for his re-appointment … Amongst these were that he would
> be expected to resign from the ANC and take no part in political activity.
> He would have to cooperate fully with all that was embodied in the new
> Tribal University Legislation. He was in fact to become an ordinary
> civil servant, ready to do his master's bidding at all times … To say we
> were shocked is to put it mildly … so sure were we of dismissal.[112]

The NP knew Matthews would not agree to their terms, that refusing to fire
him would hurt more than a dismissal. Matthews was mindful of the financial
loss associated with leaving Fort Hare, but there was never any doubt as to
whether he would depart. However, he would not give up his pension without
a fight. On 26 October, Matthews wrote to Burrows saying the passage of the
Fort Hare Transfer Act had 'so radically altered' the terms and conditions of
his employment that if he was to resign, this could not 'possibly be regarded as
voluntary resignation'. He asked Burrows to do anything possible to help him
avoid 'serious financial loss'.[113] Burrows forwarded Matthews's request to
the executive committee of the Governing Council, which recommended that
members of staff who, 'for reasons of conscience, resign … should be paid
pension benefits on the same basis as those members of staff whose services
were terminated by the minister of Bantu Education'.[114] Yet the minister of
Bantu Education did not accept the council's recommendation and there was
little else Burrows could do. On 30 October 1959, Matthews submitted his
resignation to the secretary of Bantu Education, forfeiting his entire pension.

> After giving this offer of continued employment very careful
> consideration I regret to say that I find myself unable to accept the offer
> and have therefore decided to notify you of my resignation … with
> effect as from December 31, 1959.[115]

He wrote to Fulque Agnew, the registrar, saying: 'I shall always treasure the
happy memories I have of my association for many years with the Governing
Council, the Senate, the Staff and the students of Fort Hare.'[116] In his final
address at Fort Hare, he said: 'It will be impossible for me to learn to be part
of a new Fort Hare, so much have I been a part of old Fort Hare.'[117]

Matthews broke ties with the institution he had known since he arrived as a
matriculation student in 1919.[118] He became the school's first graduate in 1924
and joined its staff in 1936, serving as lecturer, professor, head of department
and acting principal. Yet in spite of Matthews' long association with Fort Hare,
Joe Matthews claims that the decision to leave the college did not affect his

father emotionally. 'There were no such things as emotional this and that in his make up. He was an intensely intellectual person who always thought why he did something.' Thus, despite losing his pension and leaving the institution he had been associated with for 25 years, Z.K. Matthews left Fort Hare with peace of mind. 'He just decided to resign, to make it quite clear,' says Joe. His father's decision inspired others:

> A lot of people followed his example in the teaching profession. They said look here if he can do it, then we who are younger, we can do it. So a lot of Fort Hare graduates all over the country really decided to pull out of Bantu Education schools after his example.[119]

The senior Matthews wrote, 'during the period when I had to make this decision, which I knew would cost me my pension rights when I was within two years of retirement, not a single one of my friends offered me any advice one way or the other. I had to wrestle with my own conscience.' Matthews was 'amused' when he read newspaper reports that the minister of Bantu Education had made a statement, saying that the ANC had compelled him to resign. 'The decision was entirely my own. It was only after I had taken the irrevocable step and made the announcement at a public gathering at Fort Hare that I began to receive congratulatory telegrams and letters from those who felt I had lived up to their expectations.'[120]

The funeral

On 25 September 1959, the secretary of Bantu Education wrote to Burrows, informing him of the new rules governing admission to Fort Hare for the 1960 school year. 'It should be noted that as far as Indian and Coloured students are concerned and Bantu of ethnic groups other than Xhosa, these can only be admitted if no facilities are available elsewhere.'[121] Yet like a terminally ill person who gets his house in order as the end nears, Fort Hare had already begun to prepare for its death. Burrows and the Fort Hare administrators knew this letter was coming. In expectation of the imposed restrictions, the authorities admitted extra students in 1959. Rather than turn away more than 100 qualified applicants, three emergency huts were built and a staff house was converted into a hostel.[122] This small but symbolic gesture resulted in record numbers of Indian and coloured students studying at Fort Hare in 1959, and ensured that the multi-racial student body at Fort Hare would live on for the first few years of the 1960s.

The class of 1959

Dr Edgar Brookes speaks to graduating students, 1959

Yet in the wake of mass dismissals and resignations, the brief extension of the life of multi-racial Fort Hare provided little respite to the college community. A new council was appointed, consisting almost entirely of supporters of the government's policy. Burrows was informed that Dr Johannes Jurgens Ross, a University of the Orange Free State law professor, would replace him. Fort Hare continued to prepare for its own funeral. After more than four years of protest, the community turned inward, seeking to soothe itself with memories of the institution before government interference.

The Senate assigned Williams the task of surveying university records and depositing a representative sample of documents at Rhodes for safekeeping.[123] A souvenir issue of the *Fort Harian* was published, full of students' remembrances of Fort Hare, spanning many generations. The last page resembles a tombstone. It says, 'R.I.P, 1916–1959.'[124] Z.K. Matthews, Alexander Kerr and others prepared eulogies as the entire community gathered on 28 October 1959 for an academic assembly to mark the end of the university as a free institution. The ceremony was not open to the public, but Shingler quotes one of South Africa's leading political correspondents: 'The report of the farewell ceremony at Fort Hare was one of the saddest things I have ever read.'[125] Details of the speeches, including Matthews's admonition that 'South Africa will come to disaster' if the people of different races cannot learn to live together, can be found in a souvenir booklet produced by the university to mark the occasion.[126] Visitors to Fort Hare will find a plaque on Livingstone Hall, near Freedom Square, a testament of the assembly, that reads:

> The University College of Fort Hare, in deep gratitude to all who between 1905 and 1959 founded, maintained and administered this college at Fort Hare and in remembrance of all who between 1916 and 1959 taught and studied here in association with the University of South Africa and Rhodes University.

I wish to express sincerely my warm thanks to the following :—
Mr. G. R. Moodley, B. Sc. Mr. A. Ntanga. (Photographer). and
Mr. C. Manona (Photographer),
Your Services are greatly appreciated.   *Editor.*

R. I. P.
Born : 1916

End of Chapter :   1959

EPITAPH

Here lies a growing nation's pride,
Principles, ideals, traditions die—
Icy injustice in full stride—
A memory now doth Fort Hare lie.
Indelible shall her work for ever be,
An " Alma Mater " to us all was she.

Autographs   *Editor*

The *Fort Harian* student publication marks the end of an era

Notes

1   Z.K. Matthews, letter to H.R. Burrows, 26 October 1959, Z.K. Matthews file, Fort Hare Papers.
2   Karis and Carter, volume 3, *Challenge and Violence, 1953–1964,* 286.
3   *Ibid.,* 464.
4   Peter Calvocoressi, *South Africa and World Opinion* (London: Oxford University Press, 1961), 45.
5   Beale, 'Apartheid and University Education', 146.
6   'Extension of University Education Bill', Fort Hare Papers.
7   Beale, 'Apartheid and university education', 19.
8   *Ibid.,* 2.
9   Karis and Gerhart, From Protest to Challenge, volume 5, *Nadir and Resurgence, 1964–1979,* 90.
10 Apartheid government control of Lovedale, a school that had educated many Fort Harians, created uneasiness at Fort Hare. Later in the 1950s, Williams notes that university staff looked towards the deterioration of Lovedale as a sign of what was to come at Fort Hare. Williams, *A History,* 454.
11 Williams, *A History*, 161.
12 Beale, 'Apartheid and university education', 96.
13 *Ibid.*, 100.
14 *Ibid.*, 105 .
15 'New move for student apartheid', *Cape Times,* 7 November 1955.
16 Beale, 'Apartheid and university education', 107.
17 *Ibid.*, 134.
18 *Ibid.*, 114.
19 *Ibid.*, 142.
20 Council Minutes, 1959, Fort Hare Papers.
21 Mary Beale, 'The task of Fort Hare in terms of the Transkei and Ciskei: Educational policy at Fort Hare in the 1960s', *Perspectives in Education*, 12, 1 (1990), 42.
22 John Shingler, 'Crack heard round the world: Leave Fort Hare alone – Away with indoctrination,' *Student: The International Student Magazine* (1959),18, Cory Library Alexander Kerr Collection, PR 4228.
23 Karis and Carter, volume 3, *Challenge and Violence, 1953–1964,* 464.
24 Shingler, 'Crack heard round the world', 18.
25 'Extracts from Report of the Commission on the Separate University Education Bill', Fort Hare Papers, 2.
26 'Extension of University Education Bill Memorandum', 25 August 1958, Fort Hare Papers.
27 Beale, 'Apartheid and university education', 100.
28 *Ibid.*, 146.
29 H.R. Burrows and Z.K. Matthews, *A Short Pictorial History of the University College of Fort Hare, 1916–1959* (Alice: Lovedale Press, 1961), 42.
30 Matthews, *Freedom for My People,* 122.
31 Following the adoption of the Freedom Charter at the Congress of the People in Kliptown in 1955, the police arrested 155 people and charged them with treason. The trial dragged on and finally ended in 1961 with the acquittal of all accused, owing to lack of evidence of revolutionary intent.

32 Matthews, *Freedom for My People,* 121–122.
33 Z.K. Matthews, 'The University College of Fort Hare', *South African Outlook,* 1 April 1957 (Alice), 57–78, 61.
34 Matthews, 'The University College of Fort Hare'.
35 Minutes of Executive Committee of Governing Council, 26 March 1957, Fort Hare Papers.
36 *Ibid.*
37 'Additional Evidence by Fort Hare to the Commission', Fort Hare Papers, 8 January 1958.
38 *Ibid.*
39 Williams, *A History,* 315–316.
40 *Ibid.,* 316. Williams believes the effort was led by either Terence Beard or Beda warden Archdeacon H.P. Rolfe, who was a favourite of the students and a noted liberal on the staff.
41 'Memorandum on Extension of University Education Bill,' 25 August 1958, Fort Hare Papers.
42 'Summary of Evidence before Commission by Fort Hare Lecturers Association', April 1956–November 1957, Fort Hare Papers.
43 Williams, *A History,* 456. Williams pays detailed attention to the differences in political opinion among staff members at Fort Hare, writing that the students developed four groups to categorise them: conservative, middle, liberal and beyond liberal. Williams writes that he himself avoided categorisation because he never 'got closer' to the students, but that some suspected his sympathies might be 'nearer' to those of the National Party. Despite the labels, nearly all staff – even the conservatives – rallied against university apartheid: Williams, *A History,* 88.
44 Burrows and Matthews, *A Short Pictorial History,* 35.
45 Makalima, interview.
46 'Letter to Senate,' 30 October 1956, Fort Hare Papers.
47 Karis and Gerhart, From Protest to Challenge, volume 5, *Nadir and Resurgence, 1964–1979,* 66.
48 'Fort Hare decides to rejoin NUSAS', *Natal Mercury,* 25 March 1957. Inter-racial cooperation had been formally adopted by the ANC at the 1955 Congress of the People. It is possible the ANC's newly formed multi-racial alliances impacted the Fort Hare students' decision to re-affiliate with NUSAS.
49 Matthews, *Freedom for My People,* 136.
50 Makiwane, interview.
51 'Police interference at Fort Hare alleged', *The Star,* 19 March 1957.
52 Mabindisa, interview.
53 Ambrose Makiwane, 'SRC Statement re: Findings of Commission of Enquiry,' 21 August 1958, SRC and Other Committees, Fort Hare Papers.
54 A local primary school.
55 Williams, *A History,* 421–423.
56 *Ibid.,* 423.
57 'Memorandum,' 14 October 1958, Fort Hare Papers.
58 Williams, *A History,* 437.
59 Masondo, interview.
60 Beard, 'Background to student activities', 168.
61 Makiwane, interview.

62 *Ibid.*

63 *Ibid.*

64 Beard, 'Background to student activities', 169. The strike eventually lost its edge as the nurses' solidarity began to fade. The SRC responded by banning all nurses from the campus, leading to disputes among the students. For a gender analysis of this strike, see Anne Kelk Mager, *Gender and the Making of a South African Bantustan: A Social History of the Ciskei 1945–1959* (Cape Town: David Philip, 1999).

65 Williams, *A History,* 400.

66 *Ibid.*, 511.

67 Govender, interview.

68 Matsepe-Casaburri, interview.

69 Makiwane, interview.

70 M. Swana, *Fort Harian*, 1959, Howard Pim Library, 29.

71 Asher L. Ntanga, *Fort Harian*, 1959, Howard Pim Library, 30.

72 Mabindisa, interview.

73 *Ibid.*

74 Sigqibo Dwane, interview.

75 After studying at Lovedale, Thabo Mbeki went into exile and did not attend Fort Hare.

76 Moerane, interview.

77 *Ibid.*

78 Choabi studied politics and philosophy at Fort Hare until his arrest for ANC activities in 1964. From 1964–1967 he served a prison term on Robben Island. Upon his release, he was placed under house arrest. He left South Africa in 1968 to study philosophy at Magdalen College, Oxford, after which he taught in Nigeria. Choabi then returned to London to head the Luthuli Foundation, where he worked until 1988, when he was transferred to Lusaka to become secretary of education. He died in 1991.

79 Moerane, interview.

80 *Ibid.*

81 *Daily Dispatch,* 15 March 1957.

82 *Ibid.*

83 *Eastern Province Herald*, 28 November 1956, quoted in Beale, 'Apartheid and university education', 121.

84 Matthews, *Remembrances,* 142.

85 Dr Thomas Alty, 'Address to meeting of protest against university bills', 4 April 1959, Cory Library, Alexander Kerr Collection, PR4123.

86 Teacher's League of South Africa, 'Statement on university apartheid', 20 November 1959, Cory Library, Alexander Kerr Collection, PR4204.

87 Beale, 'Apartheid and university education', 120.

88 Matthews, *Remembrances,* 63.

89 Govinden, interview.

90 Williams, *A History,* 462.

91 Burrows, 'Fort Hare History', Howard Pim Library, Box 2, Serial 17.

92 Unsigned, Fort Hare Papers.

93 Govender, interview. Willams notes that Burrows had introduced himself to the students by saying, 'Should there be anyone hoping to become a youthful politician, would you please wait until you have completed your studies before setting out to put the world right.' His arrival on campus was greeted by student notices on bulletin boards reading, 'Burrows, go home!' Professor James Davidson a student favourite, said the signs were

placed to emphasise that the time was ripe for a black principal. Williams, *A History,* 360.

94   *Souvenir Fort Harian*, 1959, 40.

95   Govan Mbeki, *Souvenir Fort Harian*, 1959, 17.

96   Shingler, 'Crack heard round the world', 18; for more on the 1950s at Fort Hare and specifically for information on staff dismissals in the wake of the government takeover, see Donovan Williams's work based on his experiences, and the personal papers he accumulated, while on the staff at Fort Hare.

97   Matthews, *Remembrances*, 71.

98   Tootla, interview.

99   Williams, *A History,* 529.

100 Leslie Blackwell, *Souvenir Fort Harian*, 1959, 11.

101 Matthews, *Remembrances*, 70.

102 Shingler, 'Crack heard round the world', 18.

103 Burrows and Matthews, *A Short Pictorial History,* 45.

104 Shingler, 'Crack heard round the world', 18.

105 *Cape Times,* 23 June 1959, Cory Library, PR4095.

106 Burrows and Matthews, *A Short Pictorial History*, 44.

107 Leslie Blackwell, 'Alice, Where Art Thou?', 4.

108 Moerane, interview.

109 Burrows and Matthews, *A Short Pictorial History,* 46. Williams, *A History,* 498.

110 Matthews, *Remembrances*, 71.

111 *Ibid.*, 70.

112 *Ibid.*, 71.

113 Z.K. Matthews, letter to H.R. Burrows, 26 October, 1959, Z.K. Matthews File, Fort Hare Papers.

114 'Minutes of Governing Council Executive Committee', 20 November 1959, Fort Hare Papers.

115 Z.K. Matthews, letter to Secretary of Bantu Education, 30 October 1959, Z.K. Matthews File, Fort Hare Papers.

116 Z.K. Matthews, letter to Registrar Fulque Agnew, 11 November 1959, Z.K. Matthews File, Fort Hare Papers.

117 See footnote 126.

118 In 1979, Frieda Matthews wrote to the then rector of Fort Hare, J.M. de Wet, saying that she was no longer able to work and asking if he could reinstate her husband's pension. De Wet replied that the issue was not in his hands, Z.K. Matthews file, Fort Hare Papers.

119 Matthews, interview.

120 Matthews, *Freedom for My People,* 197.

121 Minister of Bantu Education, letter to H.R. Burrows, 25 September 1959, Fort Hare Papers.

122 Burrows and Matthews, *A Short Pictorial History,* 32.

123 Minutes of the Governing Council, 26 November 1959, Fort Hare Papers.

124 *Souvenir Fort Harian*, back page.

125 Shingler, 'Crack heard round the world', 17.

126 I could not locate one of these booklets, *University College of Fort Hare. Final Ceremony of 1959. 28 October 1959* (Fort Hare, Cape Province, South Africa), but an account also appears in *South African Outlook,* 89 (1064), I (December 1959), 180–187. An excerpt from Matthews's speech is in Matthews, *Freedom for My People.*

Birth of a Bush College: The Onset of Apartheid at Fort Hare

The [government-appointed rectors to the tribal institutes] will not
be the heads of educational institutions, but superintendents of brain
washing camps. Instead of having docile tribalised students to deal
with they will have to handle a hotbed of insurgents.
NUSAS president John Shingler[1]

Welcoming the regime

Ivy Matsepe-Casaburri remembers waking up on the morning of 23 October 1959 to find

> flags up and flagpoles cut, things written on top of Stewart Hall, the library ... And posters and lampoons all over the place, very methodically done, with precision. And there was not a single student around you who knew how that happened ... It was quite clear that there had been those who had been organised to do this, did it well, and nobody talked.[2]

Having lost the battle to keep their school free from government interference, the energies of Fort Hare students would shift towards expressing their dissatisfaction with the new, apartheid-appointed regime that ran the university. And, on the occasion of a campus visit by the newly appointed government rector, Johannes Jurgens Ross, the new registrar, H.G. du Preez, and the head of UNISA, Professor S. Pauw, the students offered a preview of what was to come. When the three came to address the students, they were greeted with banners bearing the slogans, 'We don't want fascists here', 'Leave Fort Hare alone – away with indoctrination' and 'Ross verwag mofilkheid' (Ross expect trouble).[3]

The attacks on the new administrators did not stop with words. Professor Pauw's car was vandalised and students pelted Du Preez with eggs and tomatoes. Herby Govinden, a young lecturer at the time, says: 'We gave them a pretty rough time. So they got a taste of what they were coming into.'[4] G.S. Tootla says: 'Oh God! … Du Preez got a hiding from us. He was messed up from head to toe.'[5] Williams cites Professor O.F. Raum's account of events, saying that certain staff members who staunchly opposed the bills took delight in the protest, 'milling around with the students … enjoying themselves immensely'.[6]

The skull and crossbones replaced the South African flag during the new administrators' visit, 1959

Students gather to greet the new administrators, 1959

Students let incoming Principal J.J. Ross know what they think of the onset of university apartheid, 1959

Students have a message for the incoming government-backed administrators

The 1960s brought unprecedented conflict at Fort Hare. In an era when opposition to apartheid was generally muted throughout the country after the Sharpeville massacre, protest against the authorities at Fort Hare served to politicise what would otherwise have been a silenced student body. With political organisations forced underground by government ban, the opposition at Fort Hare was waged primarily by a leaderless student body that ultimately refused to elect an SRC, and was forbidden by the authorities to cooperate with NUSAS. As the government attempted to reconfigure Fort Hare in the mould of a tribal university, the students responded with fervour. Faced with an inferior quality of education compared with pre-1960 Fort Hare and an increasingly draconian administration, Fort Hare students attended the university college – a 'bush college' to them – in a permanent state of protest.

Whereas previous administrations had faced the students' growing sense of nationalism, the difficulty on campus in the 1960s was of a different nature. While the missionary administrators never truly understood the students' political strivings, their stance against political activity was grounded in a liberal view of change. Kerr and Dent tried to crush student activism but, as Joe Matthews says, they were not politicians.[7] They felt the students would achieve equality through education and not militancy. In the 1960s, however, the tension was over a very different matter: the imposition of government policy. The rectors were clearly present to carry out the wishes of the National Party government. The 1961 Report of the Liaison Committee looking into the causes of student unrest concluded that the protest was 'connected with the concrete government policy and with the present political situation'.[8]

Students returned to campus in 1960 uneasy about their future as participants in an apartheid government institution. 'If we could first know where we are and whither we are tending, we could better judge what to do and how to do it,' noted Seretse Choabi, quoting Abraham Lincoln, in an SRC presidential address to the student body in March 1960.[9] Choabi astutely outlined the students' predicament. It would be more than 12 years before students considered walking out of the university in protest. In 1960, the goal was to find a way to reconcile personal political beliefs with the reality of the campus situation. Choabi said:

> We are well aware that Fort Hare is now a Government institution, and consequently, its continued existence depends on the acceptance by all of Government policy; or at least there should be no deliberate attempt to undermine this policy …It should therefore be clear to us all that whatever our individual aspirations and beliefs are, we have to be careful when and how we express them.[10]

PRICE : 2/-

October 1960

FORTHARIAN

WHAT DOES THE FUTURE HOLD?

The cover of the *Fort Harian* student publication wonders what the future under government control will look like

In reality, Choabi's speech may have been the only attempt to placate the new authorities. Ntombi Dwane says,

> We went to Fort Hare because you had to get a tertiary education and if you were going to get it, that was the university for you. And you were not going to sit and boycott your own development. But you were not going to cooperate with the regime. It was called REGIME, REGIME, right through. You were not going to cooperate with the regime; you were not going to play the game according to their rules.[11]

Terence Beard (centre) with one of his brightest students, Seretse Choabi (right), who served a prison term on Robben Island from 1964–1967 for ANC activities

Protest in the 1960s was directly related to the government takeover of Fort Hare. Minor grievances such as food took a back seat to the broader issue of government control of student experiences. 'The administration was there to push the policy of the government and then in that way it became a target,' says Ntombi Dwane. 'Each time they acted against a student, the whole university rose.' When Matsepe-Casaburri awoke to find the campus covered with slogans, it was clear the new objects of the students' protest were to be the representatives of government policy on campus, namely the administration. Matsepe-Casaburri describes the successful beginnings of the protest:

The skull and crossbones was right in the centre of the flagpole that used to house the South African flag between three buildings – the library, Stewart, and Henderson. And they had also oiled the pole so nobody could go up this pole at all. And the frustration of the rector [Ross] was just, to me, I guess it set in one's mind that you can outwit them. You don't have to succumb; you can do things and make it uncomfortable.[12]

The Afrikaners are coming

From 1960, the government sought to transform Fort Hare from a campus of agitators to one that produced docile students ready to fall in line with its Bantustan policy. The primary goal of the separate, ethnically divided universities was to promote political quiescence. To achieve its aim of recasting Fort Hare as a tribal university, the administration fundamentally altered the social and educational structure of the college. Most importantly, as Beale writes,

> The successful introduction of the new policy required a sympathetic staff ... to clear the staff of hostile elements ... and to substitute academics and administrators with whom the task of transforming Fort Hare into a Bantu Education institution could be trusted.[13]

The purge of the so-called liberal staff, coupled with the ensuing mass resignations, marked the first step in the process. Appointing their replacements – crucial to the government intervention at Fort Hare – came next. The Fort Hare Transfer Act assigned wide-ranging authority to the rector, and the minister of Bantu Education chose Ross to wield these extensive powers. Described as an 'ideologue' by Beale,[14] Ross believed that separate university education provided the only 'real opportunity for the full blossoming of human dignity'.[15] He was a perfect choice to carry out government policy on campus. An experienced administrator and educator, he exhibited an interest in the development of government policy, serving on the editorial board of the *Journal of Racial Affairs*. He served as inspector of native education in the Orange Free State from 1928, earning the post of chief inspector in 1942. In 1954, he moved on to the University of the Orange Free State, where he taught law. In 1955, he was appointed professor of public law, serving in that post until he left for Fort Hare in 1960.

Rector J.J. Ross

The rector, of course, needed like-minded administrators and staff to work with him. H.G. du Preez, from the NAD, was appointed registrar. Large numbers of academics trained at Afrikaans-medium universities joined Ross and Du Preez. Even before the takeover, with government interference imminent, the staff composition began to change. 'With the impending takeover, the Afrikaners were coming in,' says Logan Naidoo. 'The late '50s, people from universities, particularly the Free State University, were coming in. They could hardly speak any English.'[16] After the 1959 mass exodus, 23 vacant posts were available. Instead of advertising them, the Department of Bantu Education filled the positions internally.[17] With political control usurping education as the primary purpose of the university college, sympathy with the government became the main criterion for appointment to the Fort Hare staff. Tootla recalls: 'They got lecturers from Afrikaans universities who couldn't speak English. I know in my biology class we had a guy who couldn't say a word of English and he lectured to us.'[18] Selby Baqwa (1969–1973) says:

> You'd find … people who had been brought up truly in the Afrikaner tradition … then ready for work. And then they'd realise they can't speak English. … And they'd get posts anyway. And you'd find a person could hardly articulate himself. But what could you do? This is how it was.[19]

A clear trend in staffing policy developed in the 1960s, with blacks and English-speaking whites appointed at a bare minimum. With the exodus of pre-1960 staff, the government made 21 appointments for the 1960 school year: 15 were Afrikaner by name. Moreover, of the new appointments to the governing council, 13 were Afrikaans-speaking, one was an English-speaking white, and none were African.[20] Beale writes, 'The new regime's strategy was to appoint their own men, some of them recent graduates, invariably from the Afrikaans-medium universities, and promote them rapidly.'[21] The approach was two-pronged. First, staff loyal to the NP would alter the academic atmosphere at Fort Hare; second, control of the tribal universities – there would eventually be five – gave the NP a handy pool of patronage jobs to dispense to the less competent graduates of its expanding system of Afrikaans-medium white universities.

By 1962, almost 60 per cent of the Fort Hare staff had been educated at Afrikaans-medium universities. Two years later, nearly three quarters of the staff had received their training at such institutions. Excluding the sciences and focusing solely on the more politically oriented humanities departments, more than 80 per cent of the staff in 1964 were graduates of Afrikaans-medium universities. From 1960 to 1969, blacks on the lecturing staff fell to 19 per cent from 35 per cent.[22] Very few blacks held senior positions. Sizwe Satyo ('68–'71) says, 'It was a real Afrikaner university, only that the student body was black.'[23] Moerane says that the 'face of the regime was presented to us in the form of these lecturers from Stellenbosch, Potchefstroom and Pretoria'.[24]

Nkosinathi Gwala writes that government reproduced the intellectual environment of Afrikaans-medium universities at Fort Hare, with students receiving the same type of ideological training given at these universities. Calling Fort Hare and the other tribal colleges 'extensions of Afrikaans universities', Gwala implies that the staffing policies served to alter the intellectual atmosphere on the ethnic campuses.[25]

With a sympathetic staff and council in place, the NP went about altering the educational experience of the students at Fort Hare. Administrators manipulated the curriculum to ensure that black students did not advance beyond prescribed bounds in society. Ross felt it necessary to adopt the curriculum to a 'Xhosa character' and that it be taught in a 'Xhosa way'. To him, that meant adapting 'more effectively and more adequately both the contents of its curricula and the methods of presentation to the needs and cultural background from which the Bantu student comes and to which he will return'.[26] The latter part of the statement, 'to which he will return', was crucial. As Burrows predicted shortly before the takeover, the purpose of tribal Fort Hare was to 'equip Xhosa people for a life of sophisticated, modernised tribalism'.[27]

This new, overtly political view of Fort Hare as a vehicle to promote tribalism stands in sharp contrast to the university under missionary control.

Speaking generally of pre-1960 staff members, Joe Matthews said they 'had no particular political viewpoint except that they were working in a black university and were trying to prove that blacks were as good as anybody when it came to education'.[28] The missionaries, Matthews said, thought all politics was 'nonsense' and felt equality would be achieved through education. 'The big thing is to be educated,' he said of their philosophy.[29]

Under protest

In practice, Ross's politically induced new vision of black education lowered academic standards at Fort Hare, creating what Beale calls a conservative and positivist intellectual atmosphere.[30] Pedagogical methods fitted the new government approach. In the History Department, English-speaking staff members were dismissed and a new syllabus was 'designed to leave the student without any meaningful understanding of the historical processes surrounding the subjugation of the black people'.[31] Native administration replaced a previous favourite course of the students, public administration. 'At one time I had hoped to do an honour's degree in history or public administration,' says Stanley Mabizela ('58–'61). 'But once Bantu Education was introduced in Fort Hare in 1960 I gave it up.'[32] Balintulo writes that the new subject was interpreted 'from the angle of the White man's mission of spreading Western civilisation and the necessity of discriminatory laws'.[33]

Lecturers subjected students to an uncritical and far from rigorous intellectual environment. Sigqibo Dwane says that the students were treated as 'glorified high school children'.[34] Satyo recalls:

> The quality of education was very bad ... We were undereducated because it was notes, notes, notes. The lecturer would walk in there, stand in front of you and say 'Where did we stop yesterday?' and continue reading, while we were just taking down notes. No discussion, no input from our side whatsoever ... I still have copies of some of those notes here where sentences were incomplete because the guy was talking so fast you couldn't cope.[35]

In the new world of Afrikaner educators at Fort Hare, students often chose major subjects based on who was teaching the courses. 'Things were so bad that you decided which subjects you were going to do on the basis of who was running the department,' says Satyo. 'If it was a monster, you'd say I'm not going to do that subject.' Satyo originally planned to major in English and history. However, after one year of history, he decided to change paths.

> The English professor was very unpleasant and the history professor
> was also very unpleasant. So I felt that I wasn't going to have two
> unpleasant professors. I was not going to do well. I decided I was going
> to do ... Xhosa because the professor there was a black person and he
> was very pleasant. [36]

Selby Baqwa remembers a private law lecturer, Mr de Haan, who would say,
'I have a class of 49 fools, imbeciles, nincompoops. I don't care if you don't
do your work. My salary doesn't go 1 cent down, nor does it go 1 cent up.'[37] In
an anonymous letter to De Haan, a student called him 'one of the intimidating
lecturers'. The letter goes on: 'Your chances of calling me a Bantu are extinct
... Your coming here was not altruistic but to get a cheap platform where to
propagate your cheap sub-intellectual propaganda.'[38]

The spirit of student life went down along with the quality of the university's
academic life. 'We were really there under protest,' says Ntombi Dwane.
Students boycotted graduation ceremonies and refused to elect an SRC.
'Throughout the time I was at Fort Hare, we never really had a full student
life with an SRC, people campaigning for elections, rag. We did not have all
of those things,' Dwane adds.[39] The vibrancy of campus life that had been the
trademark of pre-1960 Fort Hare vanished. Consider Govender's description
of the pre-1960 graduation ceremonies:

> Graduation was always a dignified affair. The solemnity of the occasion
> always made a deep impression on me. The people who came were
> black mothers and fathers, grandfathers and grandmothers from the
> countryside and the rural areas. With tears in their eyes, they came to
> see their children graduate ... It was the only day the breakfast, lunch
> and supper were first class because parents were eating with us. The
> peas and the beans came out. The meat was so nice. The best food
> we ever ate was on graduation days because Magile had to put out his
> best.[40]

Sigqibo Dwane says that the students suffered because of the decline of the
multi-racial atmosphere. 'One felt that it wasn't the university it was before,
where one had people from other cultures and one was therefore learning from
people of different cultures. That caused a deprivation. We felt it.'[41]

The saving grace in terms of student life was the few staff members sympathetic
to the students' cause remaining in the wake of the takeover. Former Fort Hare
students Andrew Masondo and Herby Govinden lectured in the early 1960s
and became involved in the political life of the university. Long-time staff

members Professors James Davidson and A.S. Galloway and senior lecturer Gertrude Darroll also chose to remain to mitigate the effects of the takeover on the students. Davidson, called Davi by the students, taught physics devotedly, well beyond the takeover. Ntombi Dwane says, 'He actually stayed on as a missionary, as it were, to see to it that black students got the best that he could offer.' Davidson was not active in campus politics, but Dwane says he led by example:

> I don't know if he ever made a political comment, but he lived, he lived politics in the way he identified fully with students … inviting students to his house for dinners, for meals. He did that on a regular basis. So he really was revered, he was held in awe, he was loved.[42]

Though Professor Galloway had conservative political views, Jeff Baqwa calls him a 'marvellous person who assembled a team of brilliant scientists'. Baqwa says it was possible to learn in the sciences because the faculty had some people who were politically advanced.[43] Darroll, who taught English, is also spoken of highly by a number of students. Joe Matthews says she 'taught all of us how to pronounce English correctly … especially the chaps from the North like [Robert] Mugabe … If you listen to them, she's the one responsible for getting their accents to be more reasonable.'[44] Ntombi Dwane says that Darroll refused a professorship after the takeover, telling the authorities that she had not stayed on after the exodus of lecturers for honours of that nature. Darroll remained to 'teach English to African students'.[45] Darroll refused to accept notices from the registrar in Afrikaans, saying that if he could not send them in English, he should 'try Xhosa'.[46]

Yet while the few compassionate staff members made life slightly more pleasant for the students, there was little the likes of Darroll and Davidson could do to stem the government barrage. Course offerings were expanded, but only because black students could petition for admission to white schools if courses were not available at Fort Hare. The broad course offerings were part of a vaguely defined idea of providing a skill base for the Bantustans, but this component of the university college strategy was never thoroughly conceptualised.[47] Extensions to the college between 1962 and 1966 included an administrative block and a science block.[48] Though new departments were created and buildings constructed, real educational opportunities were not. Beale writes: 'The administrators were themselves so unclear about what skills the institution was trying to transmit that it is difficult to establish whether they set any tangible goals … The task of defining these goals was secondary to the political imperative of segregation.'[49]

In addition to interfering with the educational development of African students, control of the political atmosphere at Fort Hare was a key component of the government's scheme. Speaking in 1959 in favour of the transfer of Fort Hare, a minister in parliament said, 'We should ensure, having placed our foot on the path of separate development, that intermingling should be systematically stopped in South Africa, and that is the reason why Fort Hare should be fitted into a new milieu and a new pattern, and that is why the transfer is essential.'[50] By 1964, it was evident that the element of ethnic segregation, key to their strategy, was working. In 1959, a year before the government takeover, 38 per cent of the student body of 489 at Fort Hare was of Xhosa origin. The rest of the diverse student populace consisted of 14 per cent each Indian and coloured, 9 per cent each Sotho and Tswana, 6 per cent Zulu, 3 per cent Swazi and 7 per cent from outside South Africa. By 1964, there were only 3 Indians and 5 coloureds in a student body of 272. Four years later, there were no Indians and just one coloured theology student. By 1969, a total of 83 per cent of the student body described themselves as Xhosa. [51] Coupled with the influx of Afrikaans-educated academics, the ethnic transformation of the Fort Hare student body moved the college further away from its multi-racial roots, bringing it into line with the government's vision of the Bantustan.

Yet the government plan went well beyond demographics. Not only did it dictate the ethnicity of the students admitted to Fort Hare, but it also controlled their socialisation once on campus. The government was trying to erase the mores of pre-1960 Fort Hare, sparing no effort to quell the politically charged atmosphere reminiscent of the university's independent days. As soon as he arrived, Ross had a telephone line installed in his office as a direct link to the local police station.[52] Early in 1960, the minister of Bantu Education sent a letter to Ross, directing new students to be separated from students who were registered in 1959, both in the hostels and in the dining halls.[53] The administration also sought to curb the influence of the remaining staff who were sympathetic to the students' cause. In 1965 Ross suspended Curnick Ndamse for criticising university apartheid in one of his lectures. Ndamse apparently said, 'The white man has never had a firmer grip on the control of educational affairs of Africans.' Ross regarded his words as 'a serious breach of discipline'.[54]

When the administration could not silence the students on its own, officials sought help from the security police. Rev. G.C. Oosthuizen, who served as a liaison between the students and administration, says that from 1961 students increasingly complained of the disturbing amount of Special Branch activity at Fort Hare. He says the students felt the presence of the Special Branch on the campus indicated that the rector required it to maintain discipline.[55] Stanley Levenstein, a NUSAS delegate from Stellenbosch University, said that 'there were many instances of constant vigilance over the students, and they were known to be watched by spies and informers'.[56] Sigqibo Dwane says,

> The government had planted spies on the campus to watch what was going on. So one had to be very careful. Even with the reading material, it was sort of handed from one person to another very surreptitiously. You took it and put it inside your pocket and then went to your room and locked your door to read it.[57]

Satyo says students would often take a break from late-night political discussion to relieve themselves, with trees outside Wesley House serving as bathrooms:

> You stand under the trees; you come across the policeman; you never come back. It became so dangerous that no one was allowed to walk out alone. So you had to go in twos or go on threes, the third one standing not far from the tree to see what happens because the police were really, really, middle of the night, 12 midnight, 1 a.m., you'd find those guys out there.[58]

When pressed about the presence of the security police on campus, Ross said that he had never called them in, but that 'it doesn't preclude that from being a possibility'. Ross also said that the police did not fall under his jurisdiction. 'I am in no position to interfere with them if they, for any reasons of their own, feel it is necessary to carry out investigations or to be on the campus. It is not within my power to interfere and I do not intend to do so.'[59] In 1966 Justice Moloto (1966–1968) organised a petition in protest against the police presence on campus. Ross said the students had not been given permission to discuss the police and removed the petition from campus notice boards.[60] In response, Moloto and others wrote to the minister of Bantu Education, informing him that students had been harassed and taken into custody, without provocation, by members of the South African Police Force. [61] The minister replied that students at Fort Hare were afforded the same protection and security 'guaranteed to all law abiding citizens'.[62] Up to 20 students were refused readmission to Fort Hare for 1967, including many leaders of the agitation against the police presence.[63]

Staff members were also constantly under watch and perpetually in fear of dismissal. The legislation establishing separate universities stipulated that a lecturer would be guilty of misconduct if he committed or permitted acts prejudicial to the administration or government; commented publicly on the administration or government; joined a political organisation; or partook in political activity.[64] Writing in the *Fort Harian* student magazine just before the government takeover, a student predicted that these restrictions would mean that 'distinguished scholars, both white and non-white, who differ with the government's policy cannot hope to be appointed on the staff'.[65] These words proved on the mark in 1960. In October, geography lecturer Nicol Childs resigned after being harassed by the security police. With the full knowledge of Professor Ross, Childs had been stopped and searched on the road and his mail and telephone conversations had been monitored. Ross said that Childs was targeted because of his 'close association with the students'.[66]

Herby Govinden, who returned to Fort Hare as a lecturer in 1960, says that in the early 1960s a young lecturer was caught with 'subversive material' and fired. Govinden, who had not been active during his student days in the 1940s, joined the Unity Movement as a lecturer. He says,

> We had meetings in what was called the bachelors' quarters, where the younger lecturers were housed. We had the Special Branch keeping an eye on us ... I was later called by the Special Branch and detained for half a day. They wanted to know what my political affiliations were. What did I think of the students at Fort Hare? What did I think of other lecturers? And I didn't [say anything]. I kept mum.

Govinden says the security police were omnipresent:

> They were looking in at us from the sports field. They were lurking around the bachelors' quarters. They had informers amongst the students who were asked to listen to what we said during lectures. What we did over weekends, who visited us, where we went during our spare times, what kind of relationships we had with students. Were we calling them to meetings? They were always very suspicious of us.[67]

The relationship between the university authorities and the police can be seen clearly in a 1962 incident when security police detained Rhodes economics lecturers Trevor Bell and M.B. Dagut, who had come to Fort Hare to provide extra tutoring to the students. The two lecturers were told they had no right to be on the Fort Hare campus. The *Sunday Times* reported that as Bell was chatting with a student, the student pointed to a car and said, 'There goes the Special Branch.' Indeed, the registrar had telephoned the police and alerted them to the presence of the two men. NUSAS president Adrian Leftwich condemned the authorities' action, saying, 'Political police and university officials are clearly working hand in glove.'[68] In a statement released to the press, the Fort Hare students said they 'wanted the public to know that conditions at Fort Hare were not what they used to be in the old days'.[69]

In addition to sympathetic black and white staff having their every move watched, black faculty members were excluded from university policy-making bodies, paid less, and promoted at slower rates than whites.[70] Black staff members could join an advisory council, but it had no power and the students felt it was made up of sell-outs. 'I don't think it was an effective body,' says Govinden. 'It was just a token.'[71]

Differential salary scales were a fundamental component of the separate universities. Proposing lower salaries for black staff, a minister said in Parliament:

> My policy will be that there must be a difference between the salary scales of white and non-White … staff. The salary scales of whites have always been determined in accordance with the salary structure of the White community and similarly the salary structure for non-White … staff ought to be determined in accordance with the salary structure applicable to corresponding posts within the Bantu community.[72]

African lecturers resented differential salary scales. Masondo says:

> I was a lecturer. There was a chap who was with me at Wits. Now I did my honours in one year. He did his honours in two years. When he came back, he got a post in Afrikaans … But you see, his salary, where his salary started, mine stopped. But status was the same. Only because I was black. That was a bit of a problem for me.[73]

Before the onset of university apartheid, racial discrimination in salaries at Fort Hare did not exist. When university salaries across the country were raised in the late 1950s, the Department of Education refused to subsidise increases for non-white staff, but Fort Hare Council used its own funds to bring African salaries into line with the new standards. After 1959, the new, all-white, government-appointed Senate would not do the same. 'I was chosen along with Ndamse to address the Senate … made up of whites … on this whole matter of salary scales,' says Govinden.[74] The Senate response was lukewarm. Its statement reads: 'Senate, whilst it cannot associate itself entirely with the manner in which the plea is motivated … nevertheless supports consideration of progressively narrowing the gap between the salary scales of European and non-European staff.'[75]

S.P.

D.F. Coetzee.

34861 x 64.

DEPARTMENT OF BANTU EDUCATION:
PRIVATE BAG 212,
PRETORIA.

Mrs. A.M.L. Masondo,
6962 White City,
P.O. Jabavu,
JOHANNESBURG.

24 12 1959

Greetings,

    I have pleasure in informing you that the Honourable the Minister of Bantu Education has approved of your appointment at the University College of Fort Hare, as indicated below:-

Rank:	Lecturer in Mathematics.
Classification:	State Post.
Commencing salary:	£810.
Salary Scale:	£810x20-900x40-1060.
Date of Effect:	Date of assumption of duty.

    The appointment is on twelve months' probation and subject to the provisions of the University of Fort Hare Transfer Act, 1959 (Act No. 64 of 1959) and the regulations promulgated thereunder and further subject to the submission by you of a satisfactory health certificate on the attached form Z.3 which must be completed by a district surgeon after you have filled out the declaration at the top of the form. The certificate must be returned to this office as soon as possible.

    Kindly inform me immediately (by telegraph) whether you accept the appointment on the abovementioned conditions and the earliest possible date on which you will be able to assume duty. It will be expected of you to be available as from the 15th of February, 1960 to assist with the necessary organisation and other preparatory arrangements.

    A seperate communication will be addressed to you in regard to your admission to membership of the Union Pension Fund.

    In connection with the payment of your transfer expenses to Alice please refer to the annexure hereto.

Greetings,

V. M. STEWART.

SECRETARY FOR BANTU EDUCATION.

The Registrar,
University College of Fort Hare.

    Copy for your information. Kindly report Masondo's date of assumption of duty.

Andrew Masondo was unhappy that the salary in this appointment letter was less than that earned by his white colleagues

Govinden and Ndamse were not convinced of the Senate's bona fides. Ndamse said the term 'progressive narrowing of the gap' was 'of small effect, since there had in fact already been a progressive increase in non-European scales'.[76] And Govinden wanted to know exactly what was objectionable in the motivation by the non-European staff. The Senate replied, 'If non-Europeans asked for too much, their case would be weakened instead of strengthened.'[77]

The past will not be observed

The authorities felt that limiting contact between Fort Hare students and NUSAS was crucial to their plan of segregation and to their control of the university college. Shortly after opening under government control, the issue of NUSAS sparked a pitched battle between the students and administration, leading to the dissolution of the SRC. Speaking at a meeting of students shortly after Fort Hare opened in 1960, SRC president Seretse Choabi said:

> Great changes have taken place at Fort Hare, and we find ourselves part of an entirely new Fort Hare … As you all know, Fort Hare has for many years been affiliated to NUSAS. The position under the new management is that this cannot be allowed to continue.[78]

On Wednesday morning, 7 September 1960, NUSAS president John Shingler and two other officers arrived, unannounced, at the rector's office at Fort Hare. Ross said that the NUSAS representatives 'presented themselves without an appointment and in spite of the fact that NUSAS very well knows that affiliation of this Institution with that body has ended'.[79] The three presented Ross with letters from UCT, Rhodes and Natal, protesting against the proscription of NUSAS on the Fort Hare campus. Together with the Fort Hare SRC, the NUSAS delegates met with Ross to discuss the banning of the organisation. Ross grew offended at the tone of the meeting, charging that the students 'took the opportunity of criticising government policy generally, and especially its policy in regard to separate development and the institution of separate universities'.[80] In the course of the SRC/NUSAS meeting with Ross, a note was passed under the door signed by 60 students asking for Shingler to address them at a mass meeting that evening. When Ross refused to grant permission for such a meeting, the students took matters into their own hands. That night, the NUSAS representatives met with Fort Hare students in Alice, assuring them of their organisation's sympathy and support.

Ross's refusal to grant permission for the mass meeting of students sparked a controversy. Before 1960, the SRC constitution provided the students with the power to call for mass meetings. If enough students were moved to call for a meeting, the principal would invariably agree to it. Although there was at least one instance prior to 1960 when the principal refused to grant students' request for a mass meeting, students generally assumed the SRC constitution gave them the right to call such gatherings. Under the new regime, however, the old SRC constitution held little weight. The students requested a meeting with Ross to discuss the powers of the SRC and the possibility of drawing up a new constitution. At an emergency mass meeting on 8 September, the students resolved:

> Whereas it was with the understanding that the SRC would function as in the past and it has become abundantly clear that this is not the case, we feel that we have been deceived and consequently request that the Rector meets the students to explain the constitutional structure of the SRC.[81]

Ross agreed to meet the SRC. He said, 'I then explained to the SRC that they had to accept the position that under the new regime all arrangements made in the past would obviously not be observed.'[82] In constant contact with the minister of Bantu Education throughout the disagreement, Ross told the SRC that the principal, not the students, had the power to convene mass meetings.[83]

At the same time, discontent boiled over in the dining halls, where the wardens assuming control over meals replaced the tradition of the SRC presiding. The students viewed this as another example of the new administration flouting the authority of the 1959 SRC constitution. Throughout September, they interrupted meals with foot-stamping and mysterious blackouts. The clash between students and the authorities reached its climax when a student threw a knife, nearly injuring Professor M.O.M. Seboni, who was despised as a pawn of the apartheid regime.

After the knife-throwing incident the executive committee of Senate forced all students to sign a declaration pledging good conduct. Any student refusing to sign would be expelled. Moerane says:

> Meetings were held. I remember one particular day where meetings were held the whole day. There was division in the middle. The question was to sign or not to sign. Some senior students could see their futures going down the drain. Some had received telegrams from home saying that they dare not return.[84]

Masondo remembers: 'People were strong. I remember one girl, she was saying they shouldn't sign. Then Choabi said, if we don't sign, then we don't leave this place, even if the police come. And this woman asked, "Do police also arrest women?"'[85] Eventually most students signed, but they were not putting their names to a peace accord with the administration.

The students remained unhappy that they were not operating under the 1959 constitution. At a mass meeting on 18 September, they resolved to request that the rector present them with a new written constitution by Monday 19 September at 1 p.m. When Ross refused, the students dissolved the SRC in protest. Ross responded by saying that he was no longer willing to work with the students, and that they, 'by their action, deprived themselves of the means of being heard in connection with redrafting [the constitution.]' Ross cut off SRC constitution negotiations for the remainder of the year, and forbade the students to hold further mass meetings.[86]

Meanwhile, Shingler and Ross continued to spar over the banning of NUSAS from campus. In a letter to Ross, Shingler wrote, 'I urge you to retract your proscription of NUSAS upon the campus of Fort Hare before you do irreparable harm to our generation of South African students.'[87] Ross replied, 'I am no longer prepared to have any further negotiations with your organisation … Kindly also note that your presence, or that of any of your officials, on our campus, will in future be considered trespassing and will be dealt with accordingly.'[88] Thus, by the beginning of October, Ross had completely cut off the lines of communication with his own student body and with NUSAS. Over the next year, relations worsened. In February 1961, the students wrote to Ross:

> Since the dissolution of our SRC last year a state of impasse and uncertainty has set in. … There can be no happy relations between the students and the college authorities unless a solution has been found for this undesirable and unconducive atmosphere … Cooperation cannot be achieved until the students have a recognised representative council.[89]

However, the students never managed to meet with Ross on the issue of the SRC and they eventually abandoned those efforts.

Throughout the period of unrest, the students were worried about more than just the SRC constitution. They were concerned with what it stood for, namely independent Fort Hare. Moerane says, 'There was a school of thought which said, rather destroy Fort Hare because these people have come to impose new values and new ethos, new politics, Bantustan politics. Many of the students felt that was something to be resisted.'[90] In the middle of the disagreement, a new organisation was launched on campus, called the *Force Publique*.[91] Its policy statement reads,

> The aim of the Force Publique is to prevent the University College of Fort Hare from being turned into a tribal college in spirit and to demonstrate this to the world ... The Force Publique wants to restore once more the solidarity that has existed in the past.[92]

Though the influence of the *Force Publique* was minimal, its founding is telling. The reference to the old Fort Hare in its policy statement shows that although the students may have been fighting for a constitution on the surface, on the lower frequencies, the struggle was for much more.

Here is this dog

'I joined the liberation struggle very early,' says Stanley Mabizela (1958–1961). 'I think I must have been about 12 years of age when I first joined the ANC Youth League.' Mabizela, whose parents were not politically active, first became involved in politics when he was sent to school in Port Elizabeth. One of his earliest recollections of the racial strife in South Africa is of an incident in Port Elizabeth:

> Sometimes you'd be walking on the pavement and whites would come in the opposite direction and if you don't get off the pavement, you could be kicked to pieces. You could be boxed. I remember at one time I was boxed in PE. My eardrum was blown up and people had to take me to the hospital for treatment.

Mabizela stayed with an aunt whose entire family was involved with the ANC. 'Those are the people who took me to the ANC,' he says. The atmosphere in Port Elizabeth, a hotbed of the ANC, intrigued the young Mabizela, and he frequented evening meetings and Sunday rallies. Mabizela was kicked out of the Mariazel Mission School in the Transkei for ANC political activity, but his activism at Fort Hare in 1961 resulted in an even more memorable expulsion.[93]

By 1961, just over a year into the Ross regime, confrontation coloured all interaction between the authorities and students at Fort Hare. The expulsion of Stanley Mabizela that year shows the extent to which the relationship between the two had deteriorated. The trouble began after a meeting of the Advisory

Council on 13 April 1961, when Mabizela was charged with insulting one of its members, former Fort Hare student Kaiser Matanzima. [94] Matanzima, in a letter to Ross, wrote,

> This student shouting at the top of his voice, first said to some of his colleagues, '*Kuzele apha zii nyhwagi*' [This place is full of dogs, sell-outs]. Then while I was looking at him, he came past me and Mr. Mzamane and uttered words in a manner intended that I should hear them '*Nantsi le nywhagi uMatanzima*' [Here is this dog, sell-out, Matanzima] ... I take a very serious view of the conduct of this student and I appeal to you that in light of my status not only at your college but in South Africa as a whole, very strong disciplinary action should be taken.[95]

In a statement to Ross, Mabizela related a different sequence of events. He wrote,

> I deny I directed the words mentioned to Mr. Matanzima. There were a number of students standing about and they were discussing the presence of the Advisory Council at the College. We were discussing whether they were serving a useful purpose at all. We saw Mr. Mabude [Sol Mabude, the head of the Advisory Council] and went to him and expressed our feeling towards him about the Advisory Council ... I told Mr. Mabude that the Advisory Council and the Tribal Authorities were useless and sell-outs.[96]

Ross responded that the Advisory Council was in a position of authority, and thus Mabizela's conduct constituted gross insubordination. 'I had no option but to demand from him to leave the institution within 24 hours.'[97]

In reality, it appears that neither Mabizela's nor Matanzima's account accurately reflects what happened that April afternoon. Interviews with Mabizela, some of his classmates and Andrew Masondo, who was a lecturer on campus at the time, paint a different picture. Mabizela says,

> I was seeing Matanzima for the first time in my life. I was very near him, because I wanted to see the man, wanted to see his face ... And then somebody from behind us, there were many of us, but I was in the front, somebody behind us says, '*Nanzi le nja nyaghi uMatanzima.*' 'Here is this dog, sellout, Kaiser Matanzima.' Well, when the man was speaking behind me I could tell who it is. Because it is somebody I had known for a long time ... The person who made that statement was a chap called Griffiths Mxenge (1957–1961). And I was together with Griffiths at Newell High School ... Of course when this remark was made by Griffiths Mxenge, many people laughed and agreed with him.

> But strange enough … it was said that it was me who said Matanzima is
> a sellout and I was expelled from Fort Hare by the principal.[98]

The administration singled out Mabizela because of his political activity. He
was consistently a thorn in the administration's side, and the incident with
Matanzima provided a chance to rid the campus of one of its main political
agitators. Additionally, Professor M.O.M. Seboni had a hand in fingering
Mabizela as the student who offended Matanzima. Mabizela says, 'Seboni
hated me. He even expelled me from Beda hostel.'[99] Masondo describes Seboni
as 'the administration's man', and it is likely that Seboni blamed Mabizela to
spite him.[100]

Yet Mabizela's role as a campus leader meant that the administration could
not get rid of him so easily. 'The moment Ross expelled me, every student
stopped school. Not only the students went on strike, but the domestic workers
stopped cooking for the people there. Everything came to a standstill.' The
students called Mabizela to a meeting, asking him to comment on the situation.
Mabizela says,

> So I said, I want to tell you all here as you are looking at me that I
> know who said those words, but I will never tell anyone of you who
> it is, who he is. I will never give you his name. I will never give his
> name to anybody. I am not a sell-out. Gee whiz, they just stood up and
> applauded.[101]

Tixie Mabizela, his girlfriend at the time of the incident and later Mabizela's
wife, says: 'I said "Did you do it?" and he said, "No, I did not do it and I'm
not going to tell you who did it." So I said "Why are you not going to tell?"
He said, "Because the other student is a lightweight. Nobody will do this for
him. But for me, they will do it and it will work." And this is exactly how it
happened.'[102]

Mabizela knew the students would fight his expulsion tooth and nail. To him,
accepting the blame was, in and of itself, a political act. Not only would it save
Mxenge from certain expulsion, but it would also serve to rally the students in
protest against the administration. Andrew Masondo describes what happened:
'I'm going towards my office and I meet Sizakele Sigxashe [1958–1961]. And
Sigxashe says to me, "They've expelled Mabizela"… I meet Chris Hani. I
said to Chris, "I'm going to organise the black staff. You go and organise the
students."'[103] Ntombi Dwane says, 'We went to mass meetings and we were
told that we were going to storm the rector's office.'[104] Led by Choabi and

Hani, among others, the students marched into Ross's office. In a report at a special Senate meeting, Ross stated:

> One of the students directed himself to me and told me that the students had come to demand that Mabizela be reinstated, that they had not come to argue about the matter, and that they came with a plain and simple demand; that they were tired of my dictatorial dealings with students and they demanded the reinstatement of Mabizela … I thereupon told the students … I was not prepared to concede to a demand.[105]

Immediately after the students left Ross's office, 13 members of the non-European staff, led by Andrew Masondo, walked into Ross's office, upset that they had not been consulted about the expulsion. Ross said, 'They informed me they were perturbed about the unrest among the students as a result of Mabizela's expulsion.'[106] Masondo says:

> Professor Ross tells us, reads all these powers, because according to the Transfer Act, the rector had immense powers. So ultimately I said to him, look, you can't expel that person … I said to him, the rector must, yes, he's given such powers, but it is supposed that he'll use them responsibly or else it would just be destroying and building nothing …[107]

At the request of some African staff members, Ross referred the Mabizela case to a liaison committee, which recommended Mabizela be reinstated. He was subsequently allowed to continue as a student. More revealing, however, are the committee's comments on the atmosphere leading to the Mabizela unrest. 'No matter how we reason,' reported the committee, 'the fact remains that the students consider him another victim of political circumstances.'[108] The committee viewed the unrest as a symbol of the deteriorating relationship between the students and authorities that had plagued the college since the takeover:

> It is a fact that there was trouble in the past. But the present difficulty is of a completely different nature … There is no contact whatsoever between the authorities of the College and the student body. This fact is a source of constant friction, suspicion and distrust. It is the cause of the explosive atmosphere that constantly hangs over the college.[109]

The Mabizela unrest stemmed directly from the events surrounding the onset of government control at Fort Hare. As Mabizela put it, 'We were not going to play nicey-nicey with [Ross] because we knew that he is a member of the NP.'[110]

♦♦♦♦♦

Ntombi Dwane remembers the Mabizela expulsion as her initiation into politics. Examining her first few months on campus shows how the events surrounding the new regime at Fort Hare politicised the student body. Dwane arrived at Fort Hare in 1961, a year after the takeover by the NP, and found a Fort Hare far different from the one she would have encountered had she been there a few years earlier. Dwane was born in 1942 at the foot of the Drakensberg in the Mount Fletcher District of the Transkei, where her father was the headmaster of a primary school and her mother, who had done industrial education up to Standard 6, was a housewife, caring for Dwane and her six sisters. Dwane's parents were both heavily involved in church work, and thus religion, not politics, dominated her childhood. She attended primary school in the Transkei town of Etyeni, where her family moved after her father's death in 1951.

Dwane studied towards her junior certificate at Cicirha, near Umtata, before moving on to Shawbury, near Qumbu, for high school. At Cicirha, she says there was an emphasis on evangelism and trying to convert pupils to Christianity, while at Shawbury students had much more freedom. 'We were left most of the time on our own. There were a lot of debates.' Dwane remembers a history teacher, Mr Mayekiso, who was openly political. 'He actually introduced us to politics. It was the time of 1959, 1960. The time of Ngquza Hill.'[111] Sharpeville happened in March when we were in Standard 10 … He would go away and he would bring newspapers. And not only would he bring a newspaper, but he would talk about it.' Dwane says that Mayekiso, who came from Pondoland, would tell his students about the uprising in the area. 'He opened our eyes. He was able to weave things into the teaching of English and history.' At the same time, a classmate's boyfriend who worked for *New Age* would bring the newspaper to campus. 'We'd hide it in desks and we'd discuss it,' Dwane says. 'But we were afraid. We didn't quite know what would happen to us.'[112]

Shortly after her arrival at Fort Hare, Dwane remembers descending on Ross's office to defend Mabizela. 'You went as part of the crowd. We were going to march *en bloc,* that was the first time I heard that phrase, into the rector's office and demand the reinstatement of Stanley Mabizela.' Though her eyes were opened during her time at Shawbury, Fort Hare presented a completely different experience: 'You got to Fort Hare … and you find a boiling pot, and then you are thrown to the middle of it. While we were not as students in high school conscious so much of repression, you just knew when you got to Fort Hare that here, it's bad.'[113]

Hani was an integral part of generating the heat that boiled the pot and Dwane recalls how he gently nudged her towards politics:

> I remember he made a joke against me. I was sitting in the library and reading … I've always taken a very active interest in religion, church, worship and all that …And uChris Hani, I think it was before I joined the ANC, so one afternoon I was sitting in the library reading, uChris Hani came to this section of the library where I was, which was not Latin or English, which were his subjects … So I was sitting alone on this particular afternoon and reading. And uChris Hani, I think he just made a beeline for me. I think Chris Hani was sort of saying to me the time has come for you to get involved … And uChris Hani came and stood behind me and made as if he was getting a book out. Of course he was not getting any book out. He didn't do science. And then he said, softly, but clearly for me to hear, 'Man shall not live by the Bible alone, but also by politics.' And then he walked away. Well, by that time I think I was about to join the ANC anyway, so I did.[114]

Dwane recalls that right after the Mabizela incident, the students responded to a call by the ANC for a national stay-away to protest against the withdrawal of South Africa from the Commonwealth by boycotting classes:[115] 'We had to tell the mamas who worked in the kitchens and the tatas who did the grounds to go away for three days.' The students painted slogans on building facades to protest against the establishment of the Republic of South Africa. Dwane remembers that intense political education accompanied the stay-away: 'At Eluk we had quite a lot of political teachings to orient us new people, juniors, to the situation. I remember Manto Tshabalala-Msimang walking around with a button with Chief Luthuli's head. And I remember her saying "*Ndiya sebenza*". I am working. I am working for the country.'[116]

Still reeling from the students' victory in the Mabizela case, the administration reacted strongly to the boycott of classes. Senate declared, 'The entire action by the students must be considered a wilful and deliberate defiance of authority.'[117] At the end of the three days, Ross closed down the college. 'We were all expelled,' says Dwane. 'We were given 48 hours in which to pack our clothes and go.'[118]

Going underground

The coming of apartheid to Fort Hare coincided with a shift in political tactics by the liberation movements nationwide. On 8 April 1960, in the wake of the Sharpeville Massacre, government declared the ANC and PAC illegal organisations. Through the Suppression of Communism Act, membership in either organisation was made a crime. Increasingly, the work of the liberation movements, particularly the ANC, shifted underground. In October 1960, led by Nelson Mandela, the strategy of armed struggle was adopted and MK was launched in December 1961. Many of the leaders went into exile, including Oliver Tambo.

At Fort Hare, a parallel shift occurred. Still without an SRC to articulate their grievances and desires, the students turned to the national political structures for direction. Particularly in the Eastern Cape, the spirit behind the M-Plan lived on in the early 1960s, with Fort Hare serving as a vital component of the underground structure.[119] Isaac Mabindisa says:

> We decided at that time … to follow the M-Plan, that is the Mandela Plan. We wouldn't meet in big groups, but in small groups. We would divide ourselves into cells. It really became difficult now, divided into cells, to influence the non-political students because we knew that we were watched all the time.[120]

Thus, the vibrant political atmosphere of the 1950s, with open discussion dominating campus life, was replaced by one of secretive meetings. 'Oppression was now very, very clear and one started to become aware of *impimpis*, talk about informers and so on, the special branch,' says Dwane.[121] Mabindisa comments:

> There was the special branch assigned to the town. Some of them were very cruel people. I remember one called Hattingh, I'm sure you'll hear many stories of that man … But what we didn't know was that the government had infiltrated these cells, spies were also in the cells, the ANC Youth League cells that were operating at Fort Hare. And this became clear later on when many students who belonged to the ANC were arrested at Fort Hare round about 1963–1964.[122]

Isaac Mabindisa receives his degree, 1962

Dwane attended meetings secretly:

I was in Doreen [Gumede's] cell. There was a hierarchy and your own connection was with your leader, your cell leader … There were about four of us in our cell … We'd have political discussions … We've got to do this now, we've got to go and scatter pamphlets, try and recruit a person, try and get somebody interested … I took my orders from Doreen.[123]

Isaac Mabindisa and his parents at his graduation, 1962

Isaac Mabindisa, Chris Hani and Leslie Xinwa, 1962

Sigqibo Dwane adds, 'It was all anonymous. You only knew people in your own cells. You didn't know about people in other cells in the same organisation.'[124] Masondo says that he worked underground at Fort Hare, along with Chris Hani, under the direction of Govan Mbeki:

> Chris and I, '61, we go to Ntselemanzi. The police are combing the area and we wanted to put leaflets. Govan [Mbeki] has asked us to do that, to mobilise people for that area. So the two of us go to Ntselemanzi. The police are combing the area. We move behind the police, as they are going that way, we are putting leaflets in the houses.[125]

Mabizela says: 'When I was at Fort Hare, I was already part of the ANC underground in the Eastern Cape. I was operating at Fort Hare and sometimes [elsewhere] in the Eastern Cape. Sometimes I used to be sent to Cape Town. Govan Mbeki would send me.'[126]

The government introduced measures such as the 90-Day Detention Act and the 180-Day Detention Act. When arrests began to take place throughout the country, students at Fort Hare were not immune. 'Students started getting detained,' says Dwane. 'We had to organise food and run to the court room, we were afraid of course, during free periods. Some people would stay away from a lecture to take food; some of us were organised to collect food; and others would take it to the students who were standing trial.'[127]

On 11 July 1963, a dry cleaning van pulled into the driveway at Liliesleaf Farm in Rivonia, the headquarters of the MK high command. Police officers emerged from the van and found 12 men sitting around a table, engaged in discussion. They searched the farm and confiscated hundreds of documents. The entire high command of MK were detained under the new 90-Day Detention Act.[128] Charged with high treason, they faced possible death sentences. In the wake of the Rivonia Trial, with detentions around the country increasing, many political activists began to leave the country. With leaders such as Govan Mbeki (on trial for high treason) and Andrew Masondo (arrested for sabotage in 1963) out of commission and others in exile, activism at Fort Hare began to drop off. Masondo says:

> One day I went with my unit to sabotage the pylons, but by this time, the police were preparing to ban me. And on the day we acted, they were there at my house. And when I came back, they arrested me for that. Then I went to Robben Island. I was arrested on 3 March '63. I was ultimately sentenced to 12 years on 22 April.[129]

Three days after his arrest, Masondo was suspended from his lecturing duties at Fort Hare.

Dwane says the increased vigilance of the government hurt Fort Hare students. 'In 1963 quite a lot of people just left the university. There was actually a break in leadership at that time … The ANC instructed them to go into exile.'[130] 'People just disappeared. I remember some people, we read about them in the newspapers and we saw, that's so and so, although she's got her back to the camera, who left the university, went into exile.'[131] Manto Tshabalala-Msimang was studying for her BSc when, according to Dwane, 'she just disappeared'.[132]

S.P.

J.J. du Plessis.
x 329.

Mr. A.M.L. Masondo,
c/o University College of Fort Hare.   26. 9. 1963

Mr. Masondo,

In terms of Section 30 (1)(f) of the University College
of Fort Hare Transfer Act, 1959, (Act No.64 of 1959),
you are hereby informed that it has been decided in accor-
dance with the provisions of Section 18(21)(e) of the
Public Service Act, 1957 (Act No. 54 of 1957), to terminate
your services with effect from the 6th of March, 1963.

Yours faithfully,

R. J. VELDSMAN.

SECRETARY FOR BANTU EDUCATION.
The Rector,
University College of Fort Hare,
P.O. FORT HARE.
Copy for your information and transmission of the attached
letter to Mr. Masondo.

SECRETARY FOR BANTU EDUCATION.

JJDUP/RJ.

12.9.63.

Naar Sen. Hutting
oorhandig.

23/10/63.

After his arrest, Andrew Masondo lost his job at Fort Hare

The Broederbond arrives

From 1964 to 1968, activism at Fort Hare was quieted. With ANC leaders either in jail or in exile and no SRC to speak of, the campus was far from the hive of political activity it had been in previous years. Barney Pityana, a first-year student in 1966 who had participated in Fort Hare politics while a student at Lovedale from 1960 to 1964, says things had changed. 'This was a different Fort Hare I was coming to. The radical edge of the university had gone.' With the traditional means of organising blocked by the government, the main vehicles for political expression in the mid 1960s were denominational societies. Campus religious groups linked with the nearby Federal Theological Seminary (Fedsem) provided the students with a forum to assert themselves politically. Lecturers at Fedsem – including Desmond Tutu – served as chaplains to the denominational societies.[133]

A political rebirth of sorts began towards the middle of 1968 when Ross retired and the government named Johannes Marthinus de Wet to replace him. The selection of De Wet, like that of Ross before him, was a calculated move on the part of the Department of Bantu Education. Oosthuizen remembers that De Wet was a member of the Broederbond, and calls him a 'Nazi type'.[134] De Wet came to Fort Hare from Potchefstroom University, where he taught mathematics and headed the Department of Statistics. His résumé provided no hint of any interest in African education, other than his service on the all-white Fort Hare Council from 1960.[135] From the outset, the appointment of De Wet re-energised the students at Fort Hare, who resented the Broederbond influence filtering into their university.

With French and American students in revolt abroad, Fort Hare students made their own news by boycotting De Wet's installation ceremony. 'We were protesting against the Broederbond capturing of the university,' says Stofile. 'We didn't want him. We wanted him gone.'[136] Pityana adds, 'Blaar Coetzee came to speak. We protested the whole installation. In fact, we made a whole lot of noise around it to try to flood it out.'[137] Satyo says:

Rector J.M. de Wet

Coetzee was one of the terrible ministers in the cabinet of John Vorster
… Everybody was just shouting Blaar! Blaar! Blaar! Blaar! And
they were very, very angry about that because Afrikaners and their
supremacy, if a person of authority like a cabinet minister to be shouted
at by non-voters, to them that was very insulting, demeaning.[138]

Pityana says that the boycott was a success, with all students staying away.
'We wanted to make it very clear to De Wet that he was not welcome at Fort
Hare. In fact, I don't think De Wet ever forgave us for that.'[139]

◆◆◆◆◆

De Wet's authoritarian and condescending approach sensitised students who
entered Fort Hare with varying levels of political awareness. Sizwe Satyo,
born in Lady Frere in 1948, arrived in Alice a relative political novice. He
was aware of the situation facing blacks in the country, but had never assumed
the role of activist. One of his earliest political memories is of South Africa
becoming a republic in 1961: 'All our primary schools were supplied with
miniature flags and badges, and the teachers were supposed to hand over
those things to us. But because the teachers were very much politicised, what
they did was not to give any flags to any pupil.' His parents were not openly
political, but Satyo says: 'Because the political parties were banned, there was
that tacit knowledge that everybody belonged to a political party.' Satyo grew
up under Bantu Education, but at the time was not aware what it meant. 'We all
knew that we were attending BC schools. You knew that in your address you
must write Mount Arthur, BC School. It was only later in life when you knew
BC school means Bantu Community School.'[140] Satyo arrived at Fort Hare
just in time to greet De Wet. He studied under Ross for one semester, with the
boycott of De Wet's installation marking his first open political involvement.

The unrest surrounding De Wet's appointment continued well beyond the
rector's unceremonious greeting. In fact, the appointment of De Wet had the
students clamouring for their old nemesis, Ross. '[Ross] was regarded as far
more open-minded than De Wet,' says Satyo. 'Even if Ross was not going to
do what you were asking from him, at least he would give you a hearing, and
then would just not give you what you asked for. De Wet didn't want anybody
to go and discuss anything with him.'[141] Barney Pityana adds, '[Ross] didn't
present himself like De Wet, as a kind of die-hard ideologue of the regime.'[142]
Though their relationship with Ross had been far from rosy, the coming of
De Wet sparked even worse interaction between the students and their rector.
'Soon after De Wet came, things changed completely,' says Satyo. 'It was very

clear that there was going to be a strike.'[143] And indeed, in the second half of 1968, there was a protracted battle between the students and De Wet that led to the closure of the university and the expulsion of 21 alleged ringleaders.

The unrest in 1968 was partly a continuation of the earlier SRC dispute. Since the SRC had disbanded in the early days of the Ross regime, there had been no representative body on campus. The students were determined that no SRC should be formed for two reasons. First, they feared the administration would use the SRC to identify and victimise student leaders. Second, they were afraid that the SRC would disintegrate into a body collaborating with the administration. In March 1968 a student poll was taken on the prospect of forming an SRC. One student, on his ballot, called it an ARC or 'administration representative council'.[144] Pityana says the students vowed never to form an SRC as long as De Wet was the rector because they did not want him there and weren't going to collaborate with him in any manner.[145]

The tension surrounding the installation of De Wet grew as the year moved on. The presence of the security police and informers angered the students. 'We know that the campus is overrun with police informers, that the Security Branch and the police know what is being said and done there at all times,' said one student.[146] Problems began late in August 1968 when Professor John Marshall of Johns Hopkins University in the United States delivered a lecture on Namibia, then South-West Africa, justifying its colonial subjugation by South Africa. Students at Fort Hare were offended by his analysis and vociferously denounced the professor.[147] Around the same time, the students presented De Wet with a petition detailing grievances and proposing certain changes. The petition arose out of a University Christian Movement (UCM) mission to Fort Hare led by Bantu Steve Biko, a Natal medical student. According to Pityana, the mission aimed to assess the situation at Fort Hare and find a way to activate students by forming a UCM branch at the university. Biko told the students they held responsibility for the whole university, 'including the people that are working, underpaid and treated like slaves'.[148] The students were convinced, but De Wet denied permission for UCM to exist at Fort Hare, on the grounds that it contained 'a liberal element that would mislead the students'.[149] However, the petition that arose out of Biko's mission continued the momentum of dissent that had begun with the boycott of De Wet's installation.

The students were also angry with what they felt was the unjust treatment of 17 students, who had been singled out by the rector after political slogans such as 'We do not want Potch boere scum', 'Fort Hare not rubbish bin for Potchefstroom scum', 'Fort Hare for Africans not for Afrikaners', and 'Vorster is identical to Hitler' were scrawled on the university library and the Great Hall.[150] Ignoring their plea to be brought before a disciplinary committee, De Wet warned these students they would be responsible for any future trouble that might occur at the university. Additionally the security police, whom the students felt were in communication with De Wet, questioned some or all of the 17. [151]

In general, students alleged that De Wet acted arbitrarily and treated them like schoolchildren.[152] The rector's refusal to permit students to hold a variety concert to raise funds for charity, his banning of mass meetings, and the proscription of UCM further angered them.[153] When the students tried to organise a 'Hunger Week' to aid children in Alice, the rector told them to 'go and study. You will help your people when you have graduated and left Fort Hare.'[154] The students felt that under Ross there would have been no difficulty in organising the events they had planned.

When the students asked De Wet to meet them to discuss the newly imposed restrictions on student social activities, the rector asked to meet a delegation from the student body. Pityana says that the students refused for fear that De Wet would victimise the group. They wanted him to address the entire student body. When De Wet refused, the students concluded he had ignored their petition. 'We then decided to march on the administration,' says Pityana.[155] Day after day of sit-ins followed, with classes suspended for an entire week. Administrators warned students they would be ordered to leave campus if they continued with their action.[156] De Wet continued to insist that he was prepared to meet 'a small delegation from the students', but that his offer would expire after 3 p.m. on 5 September. The students continued to respond that they were 'a leaderless group'. They sent a memo to De Wet, stating that,

> The students maintain that they are not prepared to send a delegation.
> They do not want time until 3 p.m. because they have already decided.
> They say that democracy means that the Rector should appear before
> the students. They do not want to listen to a delegate from the Rector,
> but to the Rector himself.[157]

Eventually, efforts by a student delegation to negotiate with De Wet came to naught and the administration announced that the campus was to be closed. At 2 p.m. on 6 September, with the students refusing to leave campus, the police were called in. A few minutes after three o'clock, at least 10 police vans with six police dogs and 30 policemen equipped with tear gas and riot gear arrived on the scene.[158] As students sat in front of the administration block singing 'We shall overcome' and '*Nkosi sikelel iAfrika*', police removed them in small groups, watched them pack, and loaded them on buses that took them to the railway station in Alice.[159] As they were taken away, the students chanted, 'Justice will prevail'.[160] More than 400 of the 453 enrolled students left campus, including 350 who had been suspended.[161]

Both during and after the disturbances, the students vehemently denied De Wet's allegations that the strike stemmed from the agitation of a select group of leaders. They issued a statement to the press: 'It was a spontaneous demonstration with no leaders and no links with communism, foreign groups, Nusas or any other body. The demonstration was due to oppressive conditions on the campus and the interrogation of 17 students by the Security Branch.'[162]

The students' worst fears were realised when the administration singled out the alleged 'ringleaders' of the strike and expelled them. Twenty-one were 'sent down', including Pityana, Kenneth Rachidi, Justice Moloto and Peter Vundla. All other students were allowed back after agreeing to abide by stringent new rules. Writing to De Wet, the Right Reverend Gordon Tindall, Bishop of Grahamstown, said:

> In fact, precisely what the students most feared and guarded against in their protest has happened – the victimisation of a small minority who are labelled and condemned as agitators. Is this not why the students refused to send a delegation – because of what happened to the 17 earlier and what they feared would happen to such a delegation?[163]

Following pressure at a meeting to discuss the unrest with parents, the 'ringleaders' were allowed to write their final examinations, but they were not readmitted as full students of the university. Some of the leaders chose not to write. Pityana says:

> I personally took the view that it would be wrong to take the final exam when we were not on campus because part of our struggle was to not be expelled. And for us to accept the lesser of the two things was not acceptable. So I never wrote … I never graduated from Fort Hare.[164]

The struggle against the administration continued throughout the remainder of 1968. In late October, students were again caught painting slogans on campus buildings. Seven students were charged with malicious injury to property for scrawling such phrases as 'Go home, scum,' 'Why turn Fort Hare into police camp', 'Away with Nazis,' and 'Stamp out police informers, or else.'[165] All told, the protests of 1968 bore little fruit. Karis and Gerhart wrote, 'Somewhere in the potential repertoire of resistance tactics there were ways to shift the balance in favour of blacks, but students had yet to discover them. Before imagining wider change, black students first needed to find ways of mobilising the resources within their own ranks.'[166] This mobilisation would occur with the emergence of SASO.

BA bush college

In 1970, the government repealed the Fort Hare Transfer Act. Yet the annulment of the act did not result from the decade of student protest against Ross, De Wet and Bantu Education. Rather, it flowed directly from the government's strategy to transform Fort Hare into a Bantustan university. The Fort Hare Act of 1969, which granted full university status to the University College of Fort Hare, replaced the Fort Hare Transfer Act. Long a constituent college of various other 'white' institutions, Fort Hare was finally given the chance to issue its own degrees and move along on its own path of development. Its name was officially changed from the University College of Fort Hare to the University of Fort Hare.

However, in 1970, in the era of university apartheid, the onset of autonomy, a long-sought-after goal for the entire university community, was not a cause for celebration, at least not for the students of Fort Hare. While the administration planned a gala braai complete with fireworks, the students were not in a mood to rejoice. Despite government proclamations that the act signified greater academic independence for Fort Hare, the students agreed with the United Party's chief spokesperson, P.A. Moore, who said that the minister of Bantu Education had not divested himself of any authority over Fort Hare, but proposed to get more control than before.[167] They saw the granting of autonomy as the cheapening of their degrees, the 'ghettoisation' of their education.[168] They feared Fort Hare's autonomy would mean a drop in academic standards, the increasing use of Afrikaans as a medium of instruction and that their degrees would not be recognised.[169] They viewed the government's act as the continuation of the apartheid policy to curb the critical and independent thinking for which Fort Hare had become known and to replace it with a curriculum in line with the policy of separate development. They agreed with Helen Suzman when she argued in the House of Assembly that autonomy would mean the government would 'decide what should be taught, who should be taught and who should teach'.[170]

To the authorities at Fort Hare, autonomy was an achievement to celebrate. They commissioned a commemorative book to mark the occasion and planned festivities that included sports, fireworks, a braai, art exhibitions, exhibitions of science apparatus, the graduation ceremony, a dinner for white guests, a separate dinner for non-white guests, and the laying of a foundation stone for the new agriculture building. Invitations were sent to the prime minister of South Africa and the minister of Bantu Education. De Wet described the celebrations as a 'resounding success', although the majority of the student body chose not to participate.[171]

To the authorities, independence marked a 'milestone' in Fort Hare's history. Autonomy placed Fort Hare in a position to 'adapt both the content of its curricula, and the methods of presentation more effectively and more adequately to the needs of the people it serves'.[172] Former rector Ross felt that autonomy 'made it possible for Fort Hare to meet the specific needs and demands of the specific community which it is called upon to serve in a greater measure'.[173] And De Wet wrote, 'the future responsibility of Fort Hare is to train the Xhosa students in even greater measure so that they may pass on the benefit of their education by rendering service to their fellow countrymen in the most effective manner'.[174] Indeed, independence was just one more piece of the government's plan to make Fort Hare into an institution to serve the Xhosa-speaking Transkei and Ciskei homelands.

To the students, independence marked a low point in Fort Hare's history. They viewed autonomy as just one more step along the path towards making their education useless. Moerane comments: 'What they taught at UNISA, they taught to everybody, to whites and blacks and Indians and coloureds. Now they were going to be taught a particular Fort Hare curriculum which they associated with Bantustans. That's why they resisted that.'[175] Satyo says:

> The students were dead against that because they felt that it was part of a general plan to ghettoise black education … UNISA was regarded as quite a prestigious university so to have a degree from UNISA not from these other colleges … it was regarded as prestigious to have behind your name B.A. UNISA rather than B.A. Bush College.[176]

Thus, while the government celebrated what was viewed as the crowning achievement of the separate university system, the students, once again, protested. Makhenkesi Stofile, says:

> We boycotted the autonomous celebrations. I don't know how many cattle were slaughtered, but we just stayed away. It was a feasting time for the peasants. They came from Ntselemanzi, Gqumashe and all those

villages. The workers and non-workers, they just came and consumed the meat and whatever was there. We bought all the bread from town and we shared our own bread and we didn't participate. But the celebrations went ahead without us.[177]

The few students who participated in the festivities did so because the administration had timed them to coincide with graduation. Thus, students who turned out for graduation seemed to be in support of the celebrations. Yet Satyo says that even students who attended graduation were not in support of autonomy, and symbolically protested against the short-changing of their education by refusing to wear the graduation gowns of the autonomous Fort Hare: 'Students went specifically to buy UNISA gowns and went to the graduation.'[178]

The independence celebrations provided the authorities at Fort Hare and the government with the opportunity to take stock of the decade-old separate university system. They liked what they saw. De Wet wrote: 'The new status actually crowns the success of the ten-year period since the transfer of Fort Hare to the Department of Bantu Education.' He pointed to the increased enrolment of African students throughout the country as evidence that the system of separate universities was working. In 1959, when Fort Hare took in students of all the population groups, the total enrolment was 489. By 15 May 1970, Fort Hare was home to 615 students and combined enrolment at the five bush colleges totalled 4 668. To De Wet, the tenfold increase in student numbers over ten years was 'made possible by the founding of these [separate] universities'. He estimated that autonomy would allow Fort Hare to increase its student numbers to 1 500–2 000 by 1975.[179]

Yet the system was working in terms of numerical expansion only. While the creation of separate universities made university education available to more black students, Beale writes that the policy of university apartheid had a contradictory effect. It increased the access of black students to university education, but simultaneously lowered the quality of the education provided.[180] 'The government was methodically, but often clumsily pursuing its strategy for breeding a compliant future leadership class, programmed to play a cooperative role in maintaining social order.'[181]

Draconian administrations continually quarrelled with the students. Lecturers were hired who sometimes could not speak English. Uncritical styles of rote instruction were introduced. Departments were reconfigured in alignment with government philosophy. Yet while the state's policy sought to quell political opposition by promoting ethnic identification, the nation's bush colleges erupted in the 1970s with a new brand of nationalism, the ideology of black consciousness. By the early 1970s, it became apparent that university segregation was producing 'hothouse conditions' for the growth of a new spirit of resistance. '[The] approach was scientific, but the chemistry went badly wrong.'[182]

Notes

1   Shingler, 'Crack heard round the world', 18.
2   Matsepe-Casaburri, interview.
3   Shingler, 'Crack heard round the world', 18.
4   Govinden, interview.
5   Tootla, interview.
6   Williams, *A History*, 551.
7   Matthews, interview.
8   'Report of Liaison Committee', 5 January 1961, Fort Hare Papers, 2.
9   Seretse Choabi, 'Presidential address, March 1960', *Fort Harian*, April 1960, Howard Pim Library.
10   *Ibid.*
11   Ntombi Dwane, interview.
12   Matsepe-Casaburri, interview.
13   Beale, 'Task of Fort Hare', 43.
14   *Ibid.*
15   Lin Menge, 'Narrow path to higher learning', *Rand Daily Mail*, 1 July 1968.
16   Naidoo, interview.
17   Beale, 'Task of Fort Hare', 45.
18   Tootla, interview.
19   Selby Baqwa, interview, Pretoria, 15 July 1999.
20   Williams, *A History*, 518.
21   Beale, 'Task of Fort Hare', 45.
22   *Ibid.*, 44–45.
23   Sizwe Satyo, interview.
24   Moerane, interview.
25   Nkosinathi Gwala, 'State control, student politics and black universities', in W. Cobett and R. Cohen, (eds), *Popular Struggles in South Africa* (London: Africa World Press, 1988), 170.
26   P. Duminy, 'A tribute to Professor John Jurgens Ross' (June 1968), 2, Fort Hare Papers.
27   Burrows, 'Fort Hare History', Box 2, Serial 17, Howard Pim Library.
28   Matthews, interview.
29   *Ibid.*
30   Beale, 'Apartheid and university education', 145.
31   M. Balintulo, 'The black universities in South Africa', in J. Rex (ed.), *Apartheid and Social Research* (Paris: Unesco Press, 1981), 150.
32   Stanley Mabizela, interview, Cape Town, 19 April 1999.
33   Beale, 'Task of Fort Hare', 46.
34   Sigqibo Dwane, interview.
35   Satyo, interview.

36 *Ibid.*
37 Selby Baqwa, interview.
38 'Letter written to one of the intimidating lecturers, to De Haan', unsigned, Fort Hare Papers.
39 Ntombi Dwane, interview.
40 V.R. Govender, interview.
41 Sigqibo Dwane, interview.
42 Ntombi Dwane, interview.
43 Jeff Baqwa, interview.
44 Joe Matthews, interview.
45 Ntombi Dwane, interview.
46 Williams, *A* History, 559.
47 Beale, 'Task of Fort Hare', 47.
48 Menge, 'Narrow path to higher learning'.
49 Beale, 'Task of Fort Hare', 47.
50 Fort Hare facts and fiction, Fort Hare Papers, 8.
51 Student Statistics, 1964–1969, Fort Hare Papers.
52 Williams, *A History,* 557.
53 Minutes, 24 February 1960, Fort Hare Papers.
54 Beale, 'Task of Fort Hare', 44
55 Oosthuizen, interview; Minutes, 9 May 1961, Fort Hare Papers.
56 'Victimisation at Fort Hare alleged', *Cape Times*, 14 July 1965.
57 Sigqibo Dwane, interview.
58 Satyo, interview.
59 Minutes, 9 May 1961, Fort Hare Papers.
60 Minutes, 19 May 1960, Fort Hare Papers.
61 Justice Moloto et al., Letter to Minister of Bantu Education, Student Unrest, 17 August 1966, Fort Hare Papers.
62 Minister of Bantu Education, letter to Justice Moloto et al., Student Unrest, 11 November 1966, Fort Hare Papers.
63 'Fort Hare refuses some students re-admission', *Eastern Province Herald*, 24 February 1967.
64 Shingler, 'Crack heard round the world', 18.
65 *Fort Harian*, 1959, Howard Pim Library, 30.
66 Beale, 'Task of Fort Hare', 43.
67 Govinden, interview.
68 *Sunday Times,* 21 October 1962.
69 *Pretoria News*, 16 October 1962.
70 Karis and Gerhart, volume 5, *Nadir and Resurgence, 1964–1979,* 91.
71 Govinden, interview.
72 'Fort Hare facts and fiction', 1 July 1959, Fort Hare Papers.
73 Masondo, interview.
74 Govinden, interview.
75 Minutes, 11 September 1962, Fort Hare Papers.
76 Minutes of Advisory Senate, 9 October 1962, Fort Hare Papers.
77 *Ibid.*
78 Choabi, Presidential address, 5.
79 Senate Minutes, 12 September 1960, Fort Hare Papers.

80 *Ibid.*
81 'Emergency Mass Meeting Resolution', 8 September 1960, Student Unrest, Fort Hare Papers.
82 Senate Minutes, 12 September 1960, Fort Hare Papers.
83 *Ibid.*
84 Moerane, interview.
85 Masondo, interview.
86 Senate Minutes, 18 September 1960, Fort Hare Papers.
87 John Shingler, letter to J.J. Ross, 21 September 1960, Fort Hare Papers.
88 J.J. Ross, letter to John Shingler, 3 October 1960, Fort Hare Papers.
89 Stanley Mabizela, Sizakele Sigxashe, Seretse Choabi, Petition to Ross, 27 February 1961, Student Unrest, Fort Hare Papers.
90 Moerane, interview.
91 The context of the name *Force Publique* is revealing. *Force Publique* was the Belgian, and then independent Congolese Security Force, in the Congo. Following the precipitate granting of independence to Congo by Belgium on 30 June 1960, *Force Publique* soldiers staged a mutiny against its Belgian officers. At the very least, the naming of the new organisation on campus shows that the students were aware of events elsewhere in the continent. It is likely that the students equated the situation in the Congo with their own in South Africa, particularly in the wake of the takeover.
92 *Force Publique* statement, 15 September 1960, Fort Hare Papers.
93 Mabizela, interview.
94 Matanzima was appointed by the government as paramount chief of Emigrant Thembuland. Believing that Verwoerd's policy of separate development was in the best interests of his people, he became head of the Transkei government in 1963 and led his country to 'independence' in 1976. He later became Transkei president. Authoritarian in manner, he was despised by many blacks as a collaborator.
95 Kaiser Matanzima, letter to J.J. Ross, 13 April 1961, Mabizela File, Fort Hare Papers.
96 'Minutes of Meeting between Mabizela and Ross with Registrar present', 28 April 1961, Mabizela File, Fort Hare Papers.
97 *Ibid.*
98 Mabizela, interview.
99 *Ibid.*
100 Masondo, interview.
101 Mabizela, interview.
102 Tixie Mabizela, interview with Stanley Mabizela.
103 Masondo, interview.
104 Ntombi Dwane, interview.
105 Minutes of Special Meeting of Senate, 1 May 1961, Fort Hare Papers.
106 *Ibid.*
107 Masondo, interview.
108 'Report of Liaison Committee Mabizela Dispute', 1 May 1961, Fort Hare Papers.
109 *Ibid.*
110 Mabizela, interview.
111 The most serious clash of the Pondoland revolt (1960–1961) took place on 6 June 1960 in a valley adjoining Ngquza Hill, between Bizana and Lusikisiki in the Transkei. Africans had met there to discuss grievances against the government-imposed Bantu Authorities system. Two police aircraft and a helicopter dropped tear-gas and smoke bombs on the

crowd, and police vehicles approached from two directions. The Africans raised a white flag to show that their meeting was a peaceful one, but police suddenly emerged from the bushes and fired into the crowd, killing 11. Subsequent rebellion led to the declaration of a state of emergency and the execution of 23 people. In 1997, the Truth and Reconciliation Commission exhumed those bodies from graves in Pretoria and reburied them in the former Transkei.

112 Ntombi Dwane, interview.

113 *Ibid.*

114 *Ibid.*

115 From 31 May 1961, when it became a republic, South Africa ceased to be a member of the Commonwealth.

116 Ntombi Dwane, interview.

117 Minutes of Senate Meeting, 3 June 1961, Fort Hare Papers.

118 Ntombi Dwane, interview.

119 The M-Plan, named after Mandela, was initiated in 1952 so the ANC would be prepared to operate underground, in small groups known as cells, if necessary.

120 Mabindisa, interview.

121 Ntombi Dwane, interview.

122 Mabindisa, interview.

123 Ntombi Dwane, interview.

124 Sigqibo Dwane, interview.

125 Masondo, interview.

126 Mabizela, interview.

127 Ntombi Dwane, interview.

128 Mandela, *Long Walk to Freedom*, 305.

129 Masondo, interview.

130 Ntombi Dwane, interview.

131 *Ibid.*

132 *Ibid.*

133 Barney Pityana, interview, Grahamstown, July 1999.

134 Oosthuizen, interview.

135 *Ibid.*

136 Makhenkesi Arnold Stofile, interview, Bisho, 22 March 1999.

137 Pityana, interview.

138 Satyo, interview.

139 Pityana, interview.

140 Satyo, interview.

141 *Ibid.*

142 Barney Pityana, interview.

143 Satyo, interview.

144 SRC File, 4 March 1968, Fort Hare Papers.

145 Pityana, interview.

146 'Fort Hare students hit at denial of freedom', *East London Daily Dispatch*, 10 September 1968.

147 Mokubung Nkomo, *Student Culture and Activism in Black South African Universities* (Connecticut: Greenwood, 1984), 147.

148 Lindy Wilson, 'Steve Biko: A life', in Pityana, Ramphele, Mpumlwana and Wilson, *Bounds of Possibility* (Cape Town: David Philip, 1991), 24.

149 'Fort Hare students hit at denial of freedom.' UCM was founded in 1967 by liberal white clergymen responding to the disillusionment of a younger generation with outmoded religious forms and traditions. Over the next two years, branches cropped up on 30 campuses across the country. For more, see Karis and Gerhart, volume 5, *Nadir and Resurgence, 1964–1979,* 72–75.

150 'Quarter of students left at college', *Rand Daily Mail,* 9 September 1968.

151 'Bishop delivers protest letter to De Wet', *East London Daily Dispatch,* 10 October 1968.

152 'Police, dogs clear campus: Sitters at Fort Hare sent home', *Rand Daily Mail,* 7 September 1968.

153 'Fort Hare crisis is mounting,' *East London Daily Dispatch,* 9 September 1968.

154 'Fort Hare students hit at denial of freedom', *East London Daily Dispatch,* 10 September 1968.

155 Pityana, interview.

156 Minutes of Senate, 29 August 1968, Fort Hare Papers.

157 Minutes of Senate, 5 September 1968, Fort Hare Papers.

158 'Fort Hare situation serious', *Natal Daily News,* 9 September 1968.

159 'Police, dogs clear campus: Sitters at Fort Hare sent home', *Rand Daily Mail,* 7 September 1968.

160 'Defiance at Fort Hare: Chanting marchers are sent home', *The Star,* 7 September 1968.

161 'Fort Hare crisis is mounting', *East London Daily Dispatch,* 9 September 1968; 'Fort Hare situation serious', *Natal Daily News,* 9 September 1968.

162 'Expelled students deny leading Fort Hare demonstration,' *Rand Daily Mail,* 13 March 1969.

163 'Bishop delivers protest letter to De Wet', Howard Pim Library Press Clippings, date and publication not known.

164 Pityana, interview.

165 'Students told they were misguided,' *East London Daily Dispatch,* 20 November 1968.

166 Karis and Gerhart, From Protest to Challenge, volume 5, *Nadir and Resurgence, 1964– 1979,* 93.

167 'More power for college', *Natal Witness,* 7 March 1969.

168 Satyo, interview.

169 'Boycott at Fort Hare was protest at autonomy', *Rand Daily Mail,* 10 June 1970.

170 'Suzman in clash on Fort Hare', *Rand Daily Mail,* 14 March 1969.

171 'Boycott at Fort Hare was protest at autonomy', *Rand Daily Mail,* 10 June 1970.

172 J.M. de Wet, *Fort Hare Autonomy* (Alice: Fort Hare University Press, 1970), 15.

173 De Wet, *Fort Hare Autonomy,* 73.

174 De Wet, *Fort Hare Autonomy,* 36.

175 Moerane, interview.

176 Satyo, interview.

177 Stofile, interview.

178 Satyo, interview.

179 De Wet, *Fort Hare Autonomy,* 36.

180 Beale, 'Apartheid and University Education', 4.

181 Karis and Gerhart, volume 5, *Nadir and Resurgence, 1964–1979,* 90.

182 *Ibid.*

5

Countering Separate Universities:
Fort Hare and SASO

I want to kill SASO.
Johannes Marthinus de Wet, Fort Hare Rector[1]

A widening of scale: The traditional Fort Hare fades away

The onset of university apartheid, the arrival of J.M. de Wet, and the granting of autonomy stamped out any lingering remnants of the traditional Fort Hare. Barney Pityana makes frequent mention of this 'traditional' or 'historic' Fort Hare.[2] This institution, from the 1930s, produced a spirit of fraternity and resistance among its students that reached a crescendo with the protests against the introduction of university apartheid. By 1973, the Fort Hare that Pityana speaks of – that of the Mbekis, Mdlaloses and Govenders – was a relic of the past. Indeed, as the protest surrounding the introduction of university apartheid died down, the third-rate system of black higher education was expanding, and Fort Hare, thrust into this environment, no longer occupied the unique place in the South African landscape that it had in earlier years. The centre of gravity had shifted, and though political activity at Fort Hare lived on, the situation at the university more closely reflected that of the rest of the country.

Events at Fort Hare in the late 1960s and early 1970s take on greater meaning when viewed in the context of this fading Fort Hare tradition. Protest at the university before and immediately after the takeover was aimed at preserving Fort Hare's distinctive culture of resistance. It failed. Yet student political activity at Fort Hare did not stop after 1960. In the new situation, opposition to government policy continued, but as part of a wider movement. As the NP consolidated its vision of black university education and seemingly stifled the student resistance that it viewed in large part as a product of the old Fort Hare, a new stream of activism emerged.

Indeed, the expropriation of Fort Hare failed to produce the docile and isolated group of students desired by the government. Although the segregated black university colleges sought to curb political activism, they spawned the experiences and created the conditions for black consciousness to develop. With black students growing increasingly disillusioned with the white-dominated NUSAS, the South African Students' Organisation (SASO) was founded at a conference at Turfloop in July 1969. 'By the late 1960s, black youth could no longer accept white leadership and political representation in matters that affected them and the rest of their community.'[3] Under the leadership of Biko, SASO emerged to fill the political vacuum resulting from the banning of the PAC and ANC in 1960.

When viewed in comparison with protest of earlier times, it becomes evident that the Fort Hare of the late 1960s and 1970s shared a great deal with the four other bush colleges and with black South Africa as a whole. Fort Hare continued to be an important player in the nationwide resistance to apartheid, but it was no longer unique. Pityana says: 'As far as real support behind SASO, Turfloop and Ngoye were probably much better [than Fort Hare].'[4] With the introduction of university apartheid, the government succeeded in cutting off the head of the monster they considered Fort Hare to have become. However, further monsters soon emerged at Fort Hare and throughout the country, and the authorities found themselves confronted not just with one institution in revolt, but with many. Students at the bush colleges, previously unconnected with one another, began to establish contact.[5] While Fort Hare's importance declined in the overall picture, SASO ushered in a new, broader phase of resistance that reached beyond the Alice campus.

Yet even though its students were now part of a broader movement, memories of Fort Hare's uniqueness continued to reverberate. A residual difference between Fort Hare in the 1970s and institutions such as the universities of the North and Zululand did exist. Pityana says:

> We were always conscious during our generation of ... resisting the Fort Hare that was being constructed by Bantu education. We had a vision of being part of the historic Fort Hare. Really that is what defined the resistance we were part of ... The issues were about trying to preserve a tradition. Other institutions elsewhere didn't have a tradition to preserve.[6]

Thenjiwe Mtintso comments that the continuum of resistance separated Fort Hare from the other bush colleges:

> Here is an institution that had been there all along. It produced the Mandelas, the Sobukwes; it had a rich history ... It was not like these others ... And even when you get admitted to Fort Hare, there is this pride that you are admitted at Fort Hare, senior to all other institutions ... We were following the generation of the Pityanas and when they got in they were following another generation of the Mbekis. So you see generation after generation, you would get in there and say, here are the role models. At Turfloop, Tiro was the role model and ... prior to that, it has no history. But Fort Hare had this history. And when I got there I knew that Barney [Pityana] had been on strike. And you knew the kind of leadership that had been at Fort Hare before.

Selby Baqwa agrees that even if it was no longer unique, Fort Harians still drew inspiration from the university's past.

> It was still a bush college but it was better. The Zululands and the Turfloops were a much more transparent creation of the system ... a sham. I don't know what you call it, a superiority complex, even when it [Fort Hare] became a bush college, you still felt, if you've been to the Fort, you've been to the place. Even if the prestige or aura is more historical than real.[7]

Initially, the Fort Hare authorities, taking the government's cue, did not view SASO as an outgrowth of the Fort Hare tradition of protest. In the early days of SASO, the government heaped praise on the organisation, believing it signified that black students had finally acquiesced in separate institutions. 'Because it was a black students' organisation, the system was happy,' says Selby Baqwa. 'They said, yes, now the students have realised that they have to form their own organisations. Because NUSAS was a pain in the side of the system. It had become a nuisance.'[8] Pityana says: 'We were quoted in Fort Hare by National Party politicians as the new thing around that is going to put the liberals in their place.'[9]

Die Burger applauded the 'new spirit' that had 'taken root among some non-whites in South Africa', noting that its expression of black South Africans' 'desire to determine their future themselves as people in their own right ... fits in well with the objectives of our relations policy'.[10]

Believing that SASO showed the separate university system was working, the government initially provided running space for the organisation to develop. SASO leaders strategically took advantage of this initial label of legitimacy to build up an organisational base on the five bush college campuses. At Fort Hare, the administration even sponsored the local SASO branch, giving it the same financial support afforded to other campus societies. Following the government's lead, De Wet allowed SASO representatives to canvass on campus and hold open political meetings. However, as Selby Baqwa says, the official line on SASO reversed rather quickly: 'And sooner than later, though, they realised this is a Frankenstein monster. When we started making speeches about the system and what these universities themselves were standing for, then the honeymoon ended.'[11]

The abaKaringes and the abaThembus

SASO membership nationwide increased rapidly in 1970 and 1971. Since there was no SRC at Fort Hare, affiliation to the organisation was authorised by a majority decision at a meeting of the student body, and by 1971 a branch was operating on campus. Although SASO did gain recognition from the students at Fort Hare, it was not without a fight. Sipho Buthelezi writes: 'There was an overriding fear amongst some students, especially those who had been associated with NUSAS, that any form of division in student rank along "racial lines" amounted to tacit conformity to the policy of apartheid.'[12] Pityana says that this reluctance to embrace SASO was particularly evident at Fort Hare: 'Fort Hare had a strong liberal tradition, which was a problem. I myself was part of that liberal tradition. The idea of being part of an exclusive organisation was very hard for the students in my time to understand.' Pityana also suggests that Fort Hare students' hesitancy to join SASO was possibly because the administration encouraged the group.

◆◆◆◆◆

Though Pityana eventually became president of SASO, he first had to reconcile membership of SASO with his past. Pityana's growth in the liberal tradition began in New Brighton, Port Elizabeth, an ANC stronghold. Though neither of his parents was politically active, Pityana says that growing up in New Brighton, he could not avoid ANC politics. At the age of 15, he was sent to Lovedale, where his involvement with the ANC increased. 'When you go to Lovedale, you just have to be immersed in it. We were very close to what was happening at Fort Hare. And the people at Fort Hare were very much involved in the politics of Lovedale.'

Pityana recalls going the short distance from Lovedale to Fort Hare for political classes in the early 1960s when the debate over the banning of NUSAS from campus was taking place. At the time, NUSAS carried significant weight on the Fort Hare campus because it was an outspoken voice against the separate university system. He suggests the students aspired to being part of NUSAS partly because it was banned on campus. 'The idea, the excitement, the adventure, the defiance, of really insisting on being part of that which the administration didn't want, conjured up the ideas that there must be something right and good about it.'[13]

Having grown up around Lovedale and Fort Hare, Pityana found it difficult to accept the validity of an exclusively black organisation: 'The appeal to black was very difficult to understand at the beginning.' Indeed, at the 1968 UCM conference in Stutterheim, where black students walked out of a multi-racial student organisation for the first time and formed a black caucus, Pityana was 'probably the only one who spoke against it'. He says that at the time, he had good relations with NUSAS and continued to participate in the organisation's activities. Late in 1968, Biko invited Pityana to a meeting of black students in Mariannhill, Natal. 'I didn't go because I wasn't convinced that it was the right way forward.'[14]

That same year, Pityana was expelled from Fort Hare. He slowly began to realise that what was needed 'was a qualitative and radical way of mobilising students'. Despite his concerns over the perceived racial structure of SASO, Pityana 'began to see that through SASO we were really going to be able to mobilise students in a way that we'd not been able to do before'. He came to terms with the idea that joining SASO did not mean leaving his ideological homes behind:

> I was the one who articulated the idea that we haven't broken from liberals, but we have actually formed a home for black students ... By being in SASO, we hadn't abandoned our political homes and SASO by its nature wasn't a substitute for the liberation organisations, but that SASO was an expression of a desire for black students to come together, to make a difference politically in their country at a time when nothing else was really taking place.[15]

In 1970, after a long, inward journey of questioning, Pityana attended his first SASO meeting, where he was elected president.

♦♦♦♦♦

Pityana's difficulties in becoming a SASO supporter were mirrored in the experiences of numerous other students at the time. They did not always result in a commitment to SASO. Makhenkesi Stofile also grew up in the liberal tradition, born and bred in the ANC. He was born in Adelaide in 1944, the eldest of seven boys. His mother worked as a domestic servant, and his father had various jobs, including one on a chicken farm. Stofile's family moved to Port Elizabeth in 1952, in time for him to witness the events surrounding the Defiance Campaign. 'When we got to PE in 1952 my parents were already involved full time as activists of the ANC. We went with them virtually every Saturday and Sunday to the meetings at the old T.C. White Hall.' Stofile remembers his father enlisting as a volunteer in the Defiance Campaign:

> When people got arrested … we had to be involved in one way or another. As youngsters, the ANC had these meal coupon arrangements at the time for people who were in detention. And so we had to go and get the coupons and go and get their bread, soup and milk from the shop … and distribute it amongst their families.

Makhenkesi Arnold Stofile, 1969

Politics became intertwined in Stofile's everyday existence. 'We got used to being sent around with messages, letters or pamphlets.'[16]

The anti-Bantu Education campaign also influenced Stofile, a primary school student at the time. 'It was nice, the singing, the anti-Bantu Education songs and saying we were not going to school on the first of April, the song went. We are not going to school on the first of April.' In 1956, Stofile's mother participated in the Women's Pass Campaign. 'We were old enough to have been with our mothers when they protested, when they marched,' he says 'We were introduced to politics by our parents. They are responsible.'[17]

In 1960, Stofile joined the African Students' Association (ASA), which was formed after the banning of the ANC. (PAC students had formed

ASUSA, the African Students' Union of South Africa.) His political activity continued in this forum when he finished Standard 6 and started working on a farm. 'It had become a way of life, being part of a political programme,' he says. After working for two years, Stofile enrolled at Newell High School, where he studied up to matriculation. While at Newell, he participated in ANC discussion groups led by Harry Njomba. 'He took us to the coast, Deal Party coast,' Stofile says.[18] 'We walked there and had picnics and had political discussions. We were able to learn about the history of our country and they took us through the paces of political thought.'[19]

After his Newell High School experience, Stofile went back to work, first as a hospital porter and then in various positions at a factory. In 1968, he arrived at Fort Hare, fully schooled in the ANC tradition. It had become increasingly clear to Stofile that he would dedicate himself to fighting for freedom. 'Either you are going to fight for it or you just have to remain in that problem. We got to know people who got arrested, people got killed, people got detained for nothing, people got house arrested and people got beaten up for nothing ... So that was the experience we grew up in, in song, in life, in death sometimes.'[20]

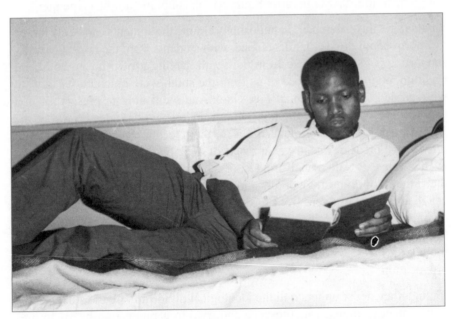

Makhenkesi Arnold Stofile studies during his first year, 1969

Having been schooled in the non-racial tradition of the ANC, Stofile could not accept what he thought to be SASO's racial foundation:

> It was a very serious challenge to those of us who came through the old tradition of the African Students' Association. We could not really buy this black consciousness thing. It sounded very funny. In fact, it sounded like negative, philosophies of reverse racism ... We thought it was a crazy, narrow, nationalistic organisation.

The ASA had a small following at Fort Hare. Stofile says, 'There was a unit. We had a discussion group on campus already. Those who sat in rooms to discuss the politics of the ANC, we could never join SASO. We never joined it until we left Fort Hare.'

Yet black consciousness spread in spite of the criticism it received from the likes of Stofile. 'Oh, it was the in-thing,' he says. 'It was the in-thing. Everybody – literally – supported SASO. We were a small minority, but a vocal minority. We spoke in each and every mass meeting and we said we're not going to join SASO because South Africa is not just for black people.'[21]

Pityana says the differences in philosophy among the students can be attributed to a north-south divide that developed, with students from the north generally supporting SASO and those from the south, having grown up in the liberal tradition, opposing it. 'Those of us from the south were much closer to what we regarded as the traditional Fort Hare. And we sought to preserve it in a way that the people from the north didn't understand.'[22] Indeed, most of the SASO supporters were products of the northern locations and townships, who arrived at Fort Hare mostly as a result of their own labour in factories and even in mines.[23] Called abaKaringes, or rebels, at Fort Hare, these were often the children of domestic workers and garden workers. The SASO detractors, called abaThembus, were from Eastern Cape families and were primarily the children of teachers, principals and nurses. Mtintso says that the abaKaringes felt the abaThembus were reactionary. Conversely the abaThembus felt the abaKaringes were irresponsible and would go on strike at the slightest provocation.[24]

Though they never understood the ideological divide among the students, the government recognised its presence and tried to capitalise on it. Authorities largely, and falsely, attributed unrest in the SASO era to the divided student body. They frequently pointed to 'sharp divisions amongst students' and an 'urban/homeland' rift, without understanding that the differences were well thought out and of an ideological nature.[25] The authorities presented the students as hopelessly divided and attributed the absence of an SRC to the notion that they could not get together to elect one. Senate minutes consistently refer to a cleavage in the student body. However, the more stark division was between the students and the authorities. By placing the emphasis on the students' differences, the authorities sought to remove themselves from the equation whenever the university erupted in protest. Events at the university prove that the student body could come together, across ideological lines, when provoked by the authorities. As in the pre-SASO days, the primary enemy was the second-rate system of separate universities.

SASO takes control

Having established a foothold at most of the black universities, teacher training colleges and seminaries, SASO launched an aggressive recruitment campaign at the beginning of the 1972 academic year. Organisers distributed some 4 000 SASO brochures and membership cards bearing the organisation's fist symbol to incoming students in February 1972.[26] That year witnessed escalating battles between the students and the administration. At the root of the disturbances was the government's system of separate universities. With a new, militant voice to articulate their grievances, student protest led by SASO swept across the campus and by the end of a tumultuous year it was estimated that over 60 per cent of Fort Hare students belonged to the organisation.[27]

The trouble at Fort Hare in 1972 dated back to the end of 1971, and once again, the SRC issue sparked the unrest. The Joint Hostel Committee, consisting of representatives from the various hostels, had assumed some of the roles of the non-existent SRC. When the committee approached De Wet on behalf of the student body to discuss a list of grievances, he said that the matters had nothing to do with hostel affairs and that the group had no right to bring these issues before him. De Wet wrote: 'The Joint Hostel Committee was really an ad hoc committee without a constitution, and its terms of reference were therefore limited to hostel matters of general interest to all the hostels and to the "approved fields" agreed to by the Rector.'[28] Feeling they had 'no real function to serve' the Joint Hostel Committee dissolved itself immediately.[29]

In April 1972, Vincent Gobodo (1969–1972) sought to revive the spirit behind the Joint Hostel Committee. He obtained permission from De Wet to hold a meeting to elect representatives to various campus committees. De Wet, anxious to get the body running again, said that he was mistakenly under the impression that Gobodo represented a revitalised Joint Hostel Committee. Following the Gobodo-led mass meeting, the students charged De Wet with trying to break the student body by a divide and rule strategy. They alleged that De Wet had granted permission to Gobodo to hold the meeting in an attempt to play one group of students against the other. When De Wet refused to address a mass meeting desired by both the abaKaringes and the abaThembus, hostility mounted against him.[30] The details surrounding this conflict over representation are murky. However, it is clear that the disagreement over the Joint Hostel Committee served as a launching pad for further action.

Around the same time that Fort Hare students were in turmoil over the position of the Joint Hostel Committee, events elsewhere in the country thrust the students into a broader context of activism. Conflict both within the student body and between the students and De Wet would have been enough to precipitate campus disturbances without any outside forces. But on 29 April 1972, Onkgopotse Ramothibi Abraham Tiro, president of the SRC at the University of the North at Turfloop, delivered a speech at the school's graduation ceremony that made a remarkable impact. He attacked the system of separate universities and warned the authorities that times were changing. He said that '[t]he magic of human achievement gives irrefutable proof that as soon as nationalism is awakened among the intelligentsia it becomes the vanguard in the struggle against alien rule'.[31] Tiro's speech shocked the university authorities, stepping 'far over the boundaries of official tolerance'.[32] Four days later, he was expelled from his post-graduate diploma course.

On 4 May, the day after Tiro's expulsion, students at Turfloop embarked on a lecture boycott and sit-in at the university's main hall in protest. The rector, Mr J.L. Boschoff, called the police onto campus. Officials closed down the university and expelled all 1 146 students.[33] The student action was not sanctioned by SASO, which had shied away from protest politics, instead focusing on building black strength through networks of organisation and communication. Nevertheless, once student anger boiled over, SASO assumed a leadership position.[34] An emergency SASO meeting, attended by 40 delegates from Fort Hare and other schools around the country, was held in Alice at Fedsem on 13 May to assess the Turfloop situation. Jeff Baqwa, who was at the meeting, says: 'After debating the importance of solidarity with Turfloop, Keith Mokoape ... moved the motion that everyone should go on strike and we should close up.'[35] The delegates issued the Alice Declaration, calling for 'all black students [to] force the Institutions/Universities to close down by boycotting lectures'.[36]

There were thus two forces at play. The Fort Hare students had their own problems in Alice. The Gobodo incident illustrates both the divisions within the student body and the rift between the students and the administration. But more importantly, there was the national issue, in the form of SASO's struggle against the bush colleges vociferously articulated in the wake of the Tiro expulsion. Fort Hare was now operating in the midst of a national revolutionary upsurge. The days of provincial squabbles due to stringent college regulation or the poor quality of food were over. The inquiry into the unrest at Fort Hare in 1972 concluded that, at this time, mid May 1972, a strike was inevitable. The commission wrote: 'It was but a step to organise, and stage, a protest at Fort Hare.'[37]

Indeed, in the wake of the Tiro expulsion and the Alice Declaration, it was clear that Fort Hare students were going to strike. May 1972 marked a period of intense activity at Fort Hare, with frequent meetings called to discuss possibilities for action. It appears the student body put aside their differences in expressing their support for the students of Turfloop despite the fact that Tiro was a SASO supporter. Stofile says,

> I was one of the most vociferous speakers in those mass meetings. So we supported that entirely. Tiro had been to Fort Hare the previous year in the … inter-varsity. And so it was ridiculous to have him chopped down like that. We were very sentimental and angry about what had happened to him. We could not find any justification for what Boschoff and his council had done. And we supported that 100 percent.[38]

Ultimately, students drew up a petition, unanimously accepted, outlining grievances with university life. These included complaints against the rector, lecturers, the administration of the university, police harassment on campus, facilities, sexual segregation in the dining halls and student fees. The students were particularly angry about the growing police presence. When SASO leader Strini Moodley came to speak on campus, a man who said, 'I am from the Special Branch and I demand your name and address' confronted him.[39] Before the Commission of Enquiry into the unrest De Wet admitted that he was in communication with the Special Branch:

> A White Special Branch man … he sometimes comes here to get information from the administration and I think they [the students] have noticed that. … So I asked Mr.- not to come again. If he wants something, phone us and we can let him have the information.[40]

In the petition, the students also expressed outrage against the encroachment of Afrikaans at the university, charging: 'It is distressing to note that Fort Hare is employing more and more Afrikaners into its lecturing and administration staff as if to employ them as watchdogs of the government policy to keep Fort Hare an exclusively Afrikaner institute, under disguise.' They bemoaned the lack of black representation on staff, noting that blacks comprised only 13 per cent of the academic staff and accounted for only one of the 30 university professors.[41] Most importantly, the students viewed De Wet as a mouthpiece of Pretoria. The *Daily Dispatch* labelled the unrest a 'direct confrontation between black students and white authority – the rector'.[42] The students' resolution reads: 'The major problem … seems to lie in the attitude and policy of the present government which – to the ordinary black student – dictates to more than guides the student; the method used is rather more dogmatic than persuasive, and instructive instead of consultative.'[43]

The students, still upset over De Wet's refusing to address them during the Gobodo incident, demanded that he meet with them immediately to discuss their memorandum. The petition reads: 'We demand to be addressed by [the] Rector and failing in which course, or in the event of any dissatisfaction with the address, to boycott lectures until we have been satisfactorily redressed.'[44] De Wet refused to speak at a mass meeting, but agreed to meet with a student delegation. This did not satisfy the students, who were intent on striking. Angry over De Wet's failure to address them and eager to display sympathy with the students of Turfloop, the Fort Hare students began a sit-in strike on 22 May with approximately 800 of the 900 students boycotting lectures. Carrying placards that read 'No redress, no lectures' and 'Rector don't dictate, negotiate', more than 500 students participated in the sit-in.[45]

It is unclear whether the incident at Turfloop impelled the students to draw up the list of grievances. The authorities seemed to think so, making repeated references to the fact that the student strike occurred just a week after the adoption of the Alice Declaration. The official commission of inquiry into the unrest, which was boycotted by the students, reported,

> SASO mounted a vigorous campaign against all administration in Black Universities; events at Turfloop escalated to many spheres, linked with Bantu Education; and Fort Hare had to stand up and be counted, regardless as to whether there were grounds or not for her taking action. … Something had to be done – even if it was token action – to place Fort Hare on the side of those who sympathised with the recent events at Turfloop, and to line her up with the decisions of SASO.[46]

At the same time, SASO refused to take the blame for the strike. In August, the Fort Hare branch wrote to De Wet saying that his failure to address the student grievances caused the strike, noting 'with regret that you, Mr. Rector, put the blame squarely on SASO's shoulders in the press statements you issued'.[47] SASO president Themba Sono blamed the strike on the Fort Hare administration and said that the Turfloop unrest was just 'the tip of an iceberg'.[48] He said, '[The students] are bitter because they interpret the authorities' action against them to be paternalistic and they resent being treated like children.'[49]

In analysing the 1972 unrest, the administration focused on unimportant details, rather than big questions. Instead of looking at the root of the problems – namely the system of separate universities – the authorities chose to blame SASO. They repeatedly referred to SASO as a 'pressure group,' and thus failed to legitimise the students' grievances. A SASO statement noted that this view 'insults the students' originality and intelligence. The Rector at Fort Hare must look at the part he is playing … and must question himself before making wild allegations at the organisation.'[50] In the world of the apartheid academic ideologues, the system was rarely, if ever, questioned. In labelling SASO the guilty party, the administration sought to absolve themselves from any blame for the deterioration of relations at Fort Hare.

To stay or not to stay

The strike drew to a close on 30 May with most students, except a group called 'hard-core' by De Wet, returning to classes on 1 June. But the resumption of classes did not mean that students and the administration were to coexist peacefully. A group of 23 students, spearheaded by SASO leaders Jerry Modisane and Jeff Baqwa, had begun to strategise about reconstituting an SRC. Selby Baqwa says: 'Some of us thought that maybe an SRC should be there … During the SASO era, other student bodies were able to access funds by which they were entitled to by virtue of the fact that they had an SRC. They were able to organise better.'[51] Jeff Baqwa says that following the strategy sessions, the SASO leaders called for a mass meeting to present their SRC proposal to the student body. He says,

> Each one of us, the 23, had a specific area of focus in terms of what you would address in your speech … And when all the people had spoken, we knew we had the house. And Kelly [Sesane, 1968–1971] and myself moved the motion. By that time it was easy. You could feel the electricity in the air. And when I finished speaking, they all stood up. It was very exciting times, actually, because you could feel the powers of change.[52]

Students adopted the motion with, according to Jeff Baqwa, 'a standing ovation'. The following morning, they presented the resolution calling for the institution of an SRC to De Wet. The rector, who had in the past had encouraged the students to form an SRC, said the students' demand was not acceptable because the result was not legitimate. 'The administration of the University refused to accept the resolution and blocked its implementation,' writes Baqwa, '[saying] … there had not been a quorum.'[53] Though there is no documentation to prove the point, it is probable that De Wet was afraid of a SASO-dominated SRC.

University documents make no mention of De Wet's refusal to accede to the SRC resolution. 'Anything that would be supported by [Jerry] Modisane or Jeff [Baqwa] would be unacceptable because it would be seen as strategy,' says Selby Baqwa. 'I knew it wouldn't be accepted because it would be seen as a vehicle for bringing revolution.'[54] Instead, the commission of enquiry into the unrest, made up of people appointed by and who participated in the apartheid government, stated: 'For the time being, and for a long time to come, the establishment of an SRC or anything purporting to be an SRC, must be written out, and consequently forgotten. There is no room for an SRC at Fort Hare and, for that matter, for anything resembling an SRC.'[55] The rapid and decisive about-face on the part of De Wet regarding the SRC was in large part due to the swift and powerful ascent of SASO to leadership amongst the students.

With their SRC proposal rejected, the students convened a meeting to discuss a way forward. On 7 June, the Fort Hare Students' Manifesto was issued, revealing explicitly, for the first time, the root causes of the disturbances. The manifesto, a document originating with SASO, was the students' attempt to capitalise upon the May unrest. Whereas the focus was previously on apparently isolated incidents, this new document sought to place the students' grievances within a broad framework. Jeff Baqwa writes that the 'campus conflict coincided with a national revolutionary upsurge'.[56] The commission of inquiry wrote: 'This manifesto brings to the fore, for the first time in this impasse, the whole broad and controversial issue of Government policy regarding University education for the Black people, Bantu Education and the whole gamut of politics, labour, racial issues, etc.'[57] Charging that all black institutions of higher learning 'are founded on an unjust political ideology of a White Racist Regime bent on annihilating all intellectual maturity of Black People in South Africa', the manifesto linked the widespread black student discontent to the system of separate universities.[58] In a clear reference to their disintegrating relationship with De Wet, particular mention was made of the 'unchecked powers vested upon the Rectors of the Tribal Universities'.[59]

The day after the Fort Hare Students' Manifesto was drafted, 42 students, including the entire SASO local committee, left the university voluntarily, refusing to give notice. Jerry Modisane, in an article in the SASO newsletter entitled *Why I Walked off Fort Hare in Protest,* analysed the causes of the 1972 unrest:

> That the education given by the white-racists to blacks is of an inferior calibre and thus not very useful to the eradication of black suffering is axiomatic. The big question is: What does one do about it? In the past there was argument to the effect that we Blacks have no alternative but to use what we are given and make the best of it. I would like to submit that there are more than one alternative: the walk-off from these tribal institutions of so-called higher learning ... At a tribal university one does not get real education ... I therefore submit that we must have nothing to do with this system. In fact we must pull out of these tribal universities and by doing so force the white racist politicians and educationists to change this system ... It is not so much us black people who need these tribal institutions ... It is actually the oppressor who needs them because they are ... their best weapon to keep us oppressed ... It is because I yearn for real black education that I reject tribal education.[60]

Selby Baqwa decided to stay at Fort Hare, even though his brother Jeff walked out. 'The realisation was that if you walk out of Fort Hare, Fort Hare is going to carry on like nothing happened.'[61] He comments on why his brother walked out:

> We went there because we realised together with our parents that we needed an education, whether it's Bantu Education and so on. Perhaps you'll go out and be a lawyer or be a teacher. If only they made it comfortable in terms of talking to you and trying to pretend at least to address your concerns, maybe trying to improve your food. I tell you, that regime would have lived longer. It's not as if you were anti-education. We saw these wrong things, but they actually forced you, for instance, Jeff and company walking out, because there was this impasse. Always, you were knocking yourself against the wall. And then it actually became a precarious thing for any self-respecting young black students to go to any of these institutions. Because it was totally impossible for you to last. You were not going to last. Sooner than later you were going to come up against this wall.[62]

Thus, the bush college system provoked what years of rigid missionary control could not: complete repudiation of a system to the point of nonparticipation. Students had held food boycotts and conducted mass meetings during missionary stewardship of the university, but that resistance always had its limits. It was directed against the missionaries, but at the same time, adhered to a more evolutionary view of change characteristic of the liberal tradition. Missionaries had taught the students that education and forbearance, not radicalism, would gradually lead to their acceptance by whites. But by the time Modisane and his colleagues left Fort Hare, the missionaries were long gone and it had become obvious that patience with an increasingly draconian system would not bring about equality.

Following the walkout of the Fort Hare 42, students seriously debated the issue of boycotting the bush colleges altogether. At the SASO General Student Council Meeting in July, Mokoape proposed a motion that SASO should withdraw from the campuses and urge all black students not to attend Bantu Education institutions. Lindy Wilson writes that Mokoape felt 'the stage was set for confrontation, and being part of these institutions compromised that'. Wilson says that Biko interjected with four main questions: 'As SASO, *were* they in fact operating within government institutions? Was there much to be achieved by students if they were not registered with universities? Would SASO be able to sustain political activity with a large number of students outside the campuses? What would happen to the remainder of students still at these universities?'[63] Biko saw SASO's presence at the universities as being more powerful than a potential boycott. Wilson writes: 'He had a vision of the potential impotence of students who, if they were no longer *students* in the struggle, would cease to have a base from which to operate.'[64] Shutting down the bush colleges was an attractive rallying cry, but in the end, Biko's even-handedness won out. With the absence of viable alternatives, organising at the bush colleges, not shutting them down, was more realistic.[65]

Take us all

Following the unrest in June 1972, those that remained at Fort Hare complained to De Wet that they could not concentrate on their studies and requested a cooling off period. The rector agreed to close the university a week early, moving forward the June vacation.[66] Yet it was going to take more than brief timeout to diffuse tension on campus. While the remainder of 1972 went off smoothly compared with the first half of the year, trouble began again early in 1973. By the end of the year, following more than six months of intermittent strikes, relations between the students and administration had deteriorated so dramatically that there was little hope for a resolution.

Following the 1972 sit-in strike, relations between SASO and De Wet grew increasingly strained. The rector was hurt by what he perceived as SASO's rejection of Fort Hare. In a letter to the SASO secretary late in 1972, he wrote: 'While SASO could have done wonderful work at University level on the black campuses, in my opinion they failed miserably. Its present leaders have far overstepped the limits of tolerance.' Pointing to the Alice Declaration and the article by Jerry Modisane in the SASO newsletter, De Wet concluded: 'Clearly some of your organisation's leaders are enemies of Fort Hare.'[67] Stating that he refused to subsidise Fort Hare's enemies, De Wet withdrew the financial support the university had previously given SASO.[68] By August, De Wet was so outraged at SASO that he forbade people expelled from other university colleges from entering the Fort Hare campus.[69] The SASO local committee report of July 1973 states that De Wet was trying to 'cripple' the organisation, and that he was 'generally keeping a Hawk's eye over the activities of SASO LOCAL and trying to intimidate [us].'[70] By 1973, the government started to crack down on SASO as well:

> The State, alarmed by the growth of student militancy and jarred by the sudden labour unrest[71] in early 1973, abandoned its earlier indifference to the Black Consciousness Movement, and in March, 1973 issued banning orders to eight key SASO and Black Community Program leaders.[72]

The first sign that De Wet's growing hostility to SASO would affect life at Fort Hare came in March 1973, when students were charged with holding an illegal meeting. More than 500 students attended the gathering at the sports field, called to discuss the banning of SASO leaders. Authorities charged Selby Baqwa and fellow SASO representative Pumzile Majeke with holding an illegal meeting on Fort Hare grounds and kept them in custody for about two weeks. A note in Majeke's student file reads: 'The charge is one of breach of regulation 8 in that at about 1400 hours on Sunday, 4th March, 1973, you held a meeting on the Fort Hare campus without previously obtaining permission therefor.'[73] A disciplinary hearing was held immediately and Baqwa and Majeke were found guilty of holding an illegal meeting.[74] The SASO report on the proceedings states, 'They subsequently appeared before the D.C. where the hearing was bulldozed, and in a matter of some 40 minutes, the defenceless were found guilty of "resisting and undermining authority".'[75] Baqwa and Majeke were each given a one-year suspended sentence.

The government's growing anti-SASO sentiment continued to colour events at Fort Hare throughout 1973. Though the year was full of many of the same clashes between students and administration that had occurred in past years, a new element of violence was introduced into the situation by the authorities. A special police branch in Alice, specifically set up to deal with Fort Hare, took centre stage in 1973.[76] The disturbances began with a boycott of lectures in protest against the Hogsback Rule, named after the road leading towards the Hogsback Mountains that marked the boundary between male and female residences. Students were not allowed to leave their side of the gender-defined barrier. In 1972, Vuyiso Qunta was caught in his Beda Hall room with a woman student. He was ordered to pay a fine of R20 and placed on probation.[77] The incident passed without much protest by the students. However, as Selby Baqwa says, the unrest of 1973 was a continuation of 1972 and, increasingly dissatisfied with the administration's refusal to negotiate with them, a similar case set off a battle between the students and the administration in 1973.[78]

The actions of Skhumbuzo Magongo, a 22-year-old third-year BA student from Port Elizabeth, renewed tensions in the winter of 1973. Magongo pleaded guilty to bringing a woman to his room and was rusticated. 'And of course the students said, no, nonsense, this Hogsback Rule again,' recalls Stofile. 'This thing is discriminatory.' With relations between students and administration having already deteriorated, the Hogsback incident set off a 'terrible strike' according to Stofile. 'Although it was so small a trigger, just this thing of a boy/girl sleeping in the room thing, it became a huge thing and it linked up with similar upheavals in other parts of the country … In fact emotionally it was a follow up ... to 1972 … of the Tiro Turfloop thing.'[79]

Upset over the suspension of their colleague, the students of Beda Hall sought the resignation of Mr. O.H.D. Makunga, the warden of the hostel, who had charged Magongo. They alleged that he persistently refused to cooperate with the students' House Committee and that he engaged in 'unnecessary nightly interference', walking into hostel rooms for 'no reason at all'.[80] A petition was drawn up and signed by 154 Beda Hall residents, demanding Makunga's resignation by 31 July. When the warden refused to resign, about 200 students held a demonstration in front of his home, which adjoined the hostel.[81] Claiming that the students had ransacked Makunga's home and threatened to hang him, De Wet called in the police, who arrived in nine vans and surrounded Beda Hall. Six students, deemed leaders of the protest, were arrested and the remaining students were rounded up and 19 were suspended.[82]

The Beda Hall suspensions set off a succession of troubles that never completely subsided in 1973. Describing the suspensions as 'unfair and unwarranted', a three-hour mass meeting of approximately 750 students decided to stage a walkout if all their 159 suspended colleagues were not reinstated.[83] Though the unrest began because of the students' unhappiness with Makunga, as events unfolded it became clear that their grievances had more to do with De Wet's obstinacy and the general oppressive campus environment. Hamilton Quambela, the Fort Hare chairman of SASO, said that the idea of a walkout stemmed from the students' 'frustration at being unable to negotiate or make realistic contact with the rector'.[84] A student from Cape Town told the *Natal Mercury* that Fort Hare had 'turned into a concentration camp. Police have access into our living quarters, we are treated like primary school children.'[85]

De Wet rejected the students' demand to reinstate the Beda students. Having exhausted 'all possible peaceful means' to meet the rector to discuss the fate of their suspended classmates, the students embarked on a large-scale stay-away from classes in the middle of August.[86] As the students boycotted lectures, a countrywide parent campaign called for the unconditional reinstatement of all students. By 20 August, 18 students had been readmitted and reinstatement applications were being considered for 34 others.[87]

Yet as students began to arrive back on campus, the situation remained threatening. Selby Baqwa says: 'Then we were ordered to come back, but there were conditions attached to us coming back. For instance ... you mustn't hold meetings without the rector's permission, you must not talk to the press.' These were conditions the students could not agree to. 'When we came back, the first thing we did was to call a meeting. Because we were saying, what kind of student body is it going to be, what are universities for, if you can't hold a meeting?'[88]

The gathering, called to discuss a strategy for the reinstatement of the entire Beda Hall contingent, ended in violence. Selby Baqwa says: 'We had this meeting which went into the night. And before we knew what was happening, the dogs and policemen were on us. I've got marks here where I was bitten by dogs.'[89] Mtintso remembers the meeting beginning in a peaceful manner:

> We were at the football stadium. We were having this meeting. Students were sitting there, very disciplined. And we were addressing them about now, we've waited for two weeks. There's no response. We've been on strike for two weeks. Should we now walk out of Fort Hare? ... And without any provocation we just saw the police coming. And we were quite young. And I think many students were very frightened. Very frightened. Just the sight of police and dogs. And they just let loose the dogs and the police with batons. Now those of us who were supposed to be in the leadership were forming this wall and we were saying to the students, if the police are going to arrest us, let them arrest us all. There was this slogan, Take Us All! Take Us All! So we were holding hands

that they must take all of us. But of course students just broke loose and
ran. And the more they ran, the more the dogs ran onto them.[90]

Five students were injured in the dog and baton charge, and five were
arrested. Amongst the arrested were Majeke and Selby Baqwa, prompting
student suspicion that the arrests were 'in line with the administration's hunt
for alleged instigators'.[91] However, the repression only fuelled the students'
fire. While De Wet took a hard line, prohibiting meetings, gatherings and
processions on campus, and promising 'drastic measures' for those breaking
his rules, a meeting of about 100 students in Freedom Square on 26 August
decided to continue with the boycott of lectures and stage a sit-in the next
day in protest against the arrests and detention of Baqwa, Majeke and Zolisa
Mdikane, a second-year BCom student. Though there was no police action at
this meeting, word of the students' resolution reached De Wet, prompting him
to call for reinforcements the following day. Increasingly, throughout 1973,
De Wet worked hand in hand with the police, bringing them onto campus
when he smelled trouble. On 27 August he said that he was 'obliged' to ask
the police to enter campus because there were 'certain students planning to
disrupt normal activities by boycotting lectures and preventing others from
attending lectures'.[92]

The police prevented the sit-in on 27 August, arriving on campus with six
vans at 07:00 a.m., but the situation had already spiralled out of control. The
next day, the rector issued an ultimatum to the students to return to lectures
or leave the university. Mayhem broke out. Newspaper reports of the events
of 28 August 1973 focus on a group of students who went into lecture rooms
and beat up fellow students with sticks and bricks. The reports allege that
the police were called onto campus to protect those who wished to return to
classes only after the students started the violence. Major H.C. Lerm, district
commandant of police at King William's Town, who commanded operations
on the campus, said: 'You will not believe the extent of the intimidation. They
have endangered the safety of those who continued to study. Agitators have
attacked those attending lectures with kieries and pounded us with stones.'[93]

In reality, the violence was likely to have been started by the police. First,
reporters were barred from campus because, according to Registrar H.
van Huysteen, the police 'were given a free hand and you know what can
happen'.[94] Thus, the newspaper accounts are based predominantly on police
reports. Second, student estimates put the number of students attending
lectures at about 40, leaving little room for the mass intimidation that
allegedly occurred.[95] It must also be remembered that just days before the

police had unleashed their dogs at an illegal student meeting. Reverend R.G. Brown, president of Fedsem suggests that the police provoked the unrest, stating that 'a police baton charge had again been made … on a group of students of the university who had gathered on the campus'.[96] Additionally, Mtintso remembers that Fort Hare students were 'not violent students' and that trouble started when De Wet brought in the police.[97]

Indeed, the newspaper accounts simplify the story to a point beyond recognition. The decision to strike was not, as the papers stated, taken by an angry mob of irrational students who 'worked themselves into a frenzy'.[98] Mtintso describes the thought and debate that resulted in the determination to boycott lectures. She says: 'So there was this strong feeling amongst the abaThembus that we should not go on strike. Even amongst the amaKaringes, we were all not just saying "Let's go on strike". I would sit down and think about the consequences. I'm on a bursary. What's going to happen to me and all those things.'[99]

Though the question of who started the violence on 28 August can be debated, the details of the violence and its aftermath are quite clear. The police arrived on campus and promptly hurled teargas canisters at and baton-charged a group of 300 students. The students dispersed, with many seeking sanctuary from the harassment of the police and dogs at Fedsem.[100] By late in the afternoon, 500 students had been rounded up by the police and detained in the Great Hall. Shortly thereafter, the students who had fled to the seminary returned and were ushered into the Great Hall.

All students who had been boycotting lectures were sent home as a result of the events of 28 August. A letter was handed to more than 400 students informing them: 'In view of criminal acts of violence committed by a large number of students on August 28 … it has been decided that all those who have been boycotting lectures must be removed from campus for the rest of the current year.'[101] More than 400 students were expelled for the remainder of the year and about 300 left campus voluntarily. As students were loaded onto buses and trains, it became obvious that the entire 1973 school year had disintegrated. 'The strike continued until the end of the year,' says Sigqibo Dwane, a chaplain to Anglican students at the time. 'I don't even know if they wrote exams.'[102] A senior staff member told the *Cape Argus*: 'The academic year has been completely disrupted … The vast majority of students will not now be admitted to examinations.'[103] Dwane says the various strikes 'went on for about six months. Students would go home and return and go home again. It went on.'[104]

Many students, mostly SASO leaders, left Fort Hare after 28 August. Selby Baqwa and Mtintso both abandoned their studies to work full time for SASO. At a final meeting on campus, the students decided they should inform their communities throughout South Africa about the unrest at Fort Hare and raise support for the unconditional reinstatement of all suspended students. 'After we got expelled, we met,' says Mtintso. 'And we said one of the first things we need to do is go country wide and explain to parents what has happened.'[105]

Ntombi Dwane, a former Fort Hare student who was a teacher at Lovedale and who lived adjacent to the Fort Hare campus, recalls the strikes in 1973 going on for a 'very, very long time'. Though a veteran of Fort Hare protests, she says that the 1973 unrest was different:

> They beat students up. It was terrible. I returned one day from work and I thought, I thought, what was happening here? And then they said the students just overran the campus. They came into our houses and hid. And then my domestic worker said they hid everywhere, in toilets, and everywhere. And she said, 'I had to lock the doors against the police.' It was terrible. Whoa, they were brutal. You see, now in the 70s, you know after SASO and all that, they really were openly, it was warfare.[106]

Makhenkesi Arnold Stofile receives his honours degree in theology from J.M. de Wet, 1973

Makhenkesi Arnold Stofile (in foreground, back to camera) leads the Fort Hare
rugby team in action, some time between 1969 and 1971

Makhenkesi Arnold Stofile and his future wife, Nambita, win a ballroom dancing
competition, 1975

Stofile, who was lecturing at Fort Hare by 1973, remembers shielding students from the police onslaught:

> The Boers came with their dogs and batons and they beat up everybody. I remember I had to open my office at the commerce block … I opened my office and some kids ran there. I put them in. I had a blackboard there. So when the police came, I was busy teaching Greek. I started writing Greek there. And I said, Yes, can I help, no, sorry. [They said] 'Are you having a class?' 'Yes, I'm having a class.' I was just writing and they left.[107]

Mtintso says that the violence did not achieve De Wet's goal of silencing the students. She believes it had the opposite effect and says that the violence 'completely politicised her'.[108] 'When De Wet began to bring in the police, that hardened the attitude of students. That hardened all of us, even the abaThembus, because when the police came, they didn't say who was amaKaringe and who was abaThembu. They were hitting all of us.' Mtintso recalls the first instance of violence, where the police charged the student meeting on the football field, as a turning point. 'Many of those students who had not been activists, that incident, they had not done anything; they'd only attended a meeting.' She remembers the case of one of her classmates:

> One student arrived at her home and her parents were asking, 'What is the strike about?' She says, 'I don't know. What I do know is that I've been bit by a dog and I'm not going back to Fort Hare.' … She had not internalised what it was all about, but one thing she was sure was there was no reason why she was bitten by a dog. The institution was wrong … So De Wet had helped our cause indirectly.[109]

Selby Baqwa agrees that the batons and dogs created a spirit of resistance:

> Whenever you'd want this or that, you'd want to negotiate. I mean, I don't know how many strikes we had, where we'd be asking for the rector to come and address you on the issues you raised. It's something that you never get. And even as we had sit-ins, boycotts of classes, you knew you'd never get it. You'd stay for a number of days, you could send delegations and so on to see whoever … There were a number of days and then you'd know the next thing that is going to come is the police and dogs and you'd be taken to your rooms and shoved. That's the way it always happened. In this sense, it's always amazing because you look back and say, these are the people who actually promoted the political influences that shaped these fellows into different animals than they would have been.[110]

Selby Baqwa was a key player in the events of 1973. Like his brother Jeff, Selby was forced to leave the university because of his political leanings. For Selby, it wasn't easy:

> When we left, some of us wanted to study. I remember Pumzile Majeke and I talking and saying man, one wishes you were in a normal country where you would study peacefully ... Some of us would have studied to get a PhD. We used to regret it, not in a regretful manner, but in that we wished we were in a normal situation. Not that we shouldn't have done what we did. We accepted the fact that what we did was for a good cause, a good reason. If I could do it all over again, I would do it the same way or even more.[111]

Selby Baqwa's journey that resulted in expulsion from Fort Hare had begun in Natal, where he was born into a family that was middle class by the standards of African society. His father was a school inspector and his mother a nursing sister who later became a matron in a few small hospitals in Natal. Neither of Baqwa's parents was politically active and his maternal grandfather was a minister in Kaiser Matanzima's first cabinet. If Baqwa had any influences growing up, they were conservative ones. 'As a child ... you say, oh yes, my grandfather is a minister, and you are actually proud of it. Matanzima was alleged to have said, "Ask for what you want; take what you get; make use of what you get to get what you want"; and you think, well, great thinking', he says. Baqwa talks of his high school education, at the Catholic high school St Francis College, Mariannhill, as a 'significant growth point' in terms of his political maturation. 'It was only when I got into Mariannhill that I started seeing, no, things can be viewed differently. They are different.'[112]

Selby's brother Jeff says Mariannhill attracted people who were intellectually quite astute. 'They wanted to confront problems and go through analyses of strategies of what should be done,' says Jeff Baqwa. Steve Biko was a classmate of the two Baqwa boys. 'That's the calibre of [student] that went up to that school,' he comments. 'And as a result we engaged the administration in a whole lot of things that we thought were not just or fair.'[113] Selby Baqwa says he and Jeff were able to avoid Bantu Education by studying at Mariannhill:

> Not taking you out of Bantu Education in terms of books ... but in terms of the environment. There were German missionaries who came there ... who were coming directly out of Germany so they didn't treat you like a Bantu or a black person. They had that normal interaction with people which you take it as people who had not been tainted by local politics. They treated us as students and taught us as students. Not

as Bantu or black students. I thought that was very important in terms of making you grow, that there is another way of living … that things can be different.[114]

Selby Baqwa remembers that an African teacher who supervised study used to explain the significance of political events of the time. Baqwa says the teacher, Mr Baldwin, would analyse the system of separate development in South Africa to his charges: 'He would explain about how South Africa was being balkanised in the Bantustans.' Baqwa remembers Baldwin spending evenings talking of the Unilateral Declaration of Independence (UDI) in Rhodesia, harping on the negative effect it would have on blacks in South Africa. He says, 'Politically, I think my eyes got opened in St Francis College, Mariannhill, through interaction with certain personalities there.' Immediately on completing his matriculation in 1968, Baqwa's schoolmate Steve Biko began speaking in terms of the SASO. At that point, Baqwa adds, 'There was never to be any looking back.'[115]

A dangerous neighbour

'If Fedsem[116] had not been there,' says Jeff Baqwa, 'there's a doubt we could have gotten as far as we did.'[117] A multi-racial institution that prepared black students of four denominations for the ministry, Fedsem was established in Alice in 1963. Adjoining the Fort Hare campus, it was opposed to everything that the new Fort Hare stood for. The institution arrived in the wake of the government takeover of the college, reinvigorating the area with the spirit of community trust irrespective of race that had been predominant at the old Fort Hare. Allowed to exist unencumbered during the Ross era, a relationship grew between Fort Hare students and Fedsem. With the chapels at Fort Hare closed after the takeover, students found a place to worship at Fedsem. Staff such as Desmond Tutu and Ronnie Samuel served as both spiritual and political advisors to Fort Hare students. In the mid 1960s, with ANC activity at Fort Hare hampered, Fedsem provided the operational base for religious groups to assert themselves politically. With the inception of SASO, the seminary became one of the most intense centres of black consciousness thinking.[118] It also became a second campus for students who felt their actions were restricted at Fort Hare, providing physical and emotional space for the students to develop their activism. 'Anything you couldn't do at Fort Hare, you could easily do at Fedsem,' says Selby Baqwa.[119]

Once De Wet arrived on campus in the second half of 1968, the Fort Hare administration's previous tolerance of the seminary began to dissipate. 'Fedsem was a second, more liberated campus, which did exactly the opposite of what De Wet wanted to be the case,' says Selby Baqwa. 'It was diluting or undoing anything physically and mentally that Fort Hare was supposed to represent.'[120] Sigqibo Dwane says De Wet 'thought that Fedsem was influencing students to resist authority … that Fedsem was a dangerous neighbour to have. That while he was busy trying to tell his students that government policy was an excellent policy, Fedsem on the other hand was saying the opposite.'[121] As early as September 1968, in the initial days of the De Wet regime, the role of Fedsem preoccupied the authorities. At a Senate meeting, a committee was established to 'investigate and formulate a report on the extent of the influence on, and access to, Fort Hare students exercised by members of the staff of the Fedsem'.[122]

By 1971, De Wet's concern about the influence of Fedsem on Fort Hare students was sufficient to warrant a government investigation into taking control of the seminary. Under the guise of needing to expand the university to accommodate growing student numbers, De Wet wrote to seminary officials, asking whether they would be prepared to sell their land to the university.[123] The minister of Bantu Education told the officials that there was no alternative to address the problem of overcrowding at Fort Hare except to acquire the seminary. But to the Fedsem officials, Fort Hare's desire to purchase their land was politically, not spatially, motivated. In the *Daily Dispatch* of 16 August 1972, the Fedsem council dubbed the Fort Hare move to take over its land as 'a political one to rid the university of a multi-racial community on its doorstep'.[124]

For two years after Fort Hare's initial inquiry into buying Fedsem, De Wet and the government continued to couch their interest in logistical terms. It was said that Fort Hare was expanding its student numbers by 25 per cent each year and that without the seminary land, large numbers of black students would be deprived of a university education.[125] To Fedsem, the government's motives were clearly political. As *South African Outlook* reported,

> The argument about Fort Hare having nowhere else to expand might be valid if the university was situated somewhere like the middle of Manhattan Island … Examination of the area in question shows that not only does Fort Hare have a fair amount of room still left for buildings, but that it is situated on the edge of a tiny town where there is un-built-up land in almost any direction for scores of miles.[126]

Supporters of the seminary wondered why the university had to have the seminary's 94 hectares of land when 1 104 hectares were available in the vicinity of Fort Hare.[127]

Indeed, the university's actions outside the public eye in the early 1970s reveal their real intent. Fort Hare officials expressed concern at the seminary's influence on its students as early as 1968. De Wet was also upset that Fedsem did not encourage its students to take classes at Fort Hare. And as SASO's activism grew, De Wet's ill-will only increased. Jeff Baqwa speaks of Fedsem's role in the 1972 student strike: 'At some point when they were praying and appealing to God, the next thing they were hearing screams and voices of students and they had to run out and basically play the practical role of the church being the protecting saviour.'[128]

Evidence given before the government-appointed commission into the unrest at Fort Hare in 1972 reveals a preoccupation of the authorities with the role of Fedsem. Both student and faculty witnesses were subjected to numerous questions about Fedsem's influence at Fort Hare. At one point, a commissioner called Fedsem's justification for wanting to hold onto its land 'so much nonsense'.[129] A government witness said the university was concerned with the 'the types of sermons preached' by Fedsem staff.[130] One student witness was asked whether students were addressed by seminary representatives 'with the intention of getting them to come to some disturbance?'[131] Professor Coetzee, who was called to testify, was asked, 'Do you think that the theological seminary across the road is exercising such influence that would hurt cooperation with this university?' Worried that the seminary was encouraging Fort Hare students to resist authority, the commission also asked Coetzee, 'Have they [the seminary] accepted the policy as exercised by this university?'[132]

Clearly, the university and government were concerned about the political influence Fedsem had on its students. 'It was regarded as a thorn in the face of Fort Hare,' says Ntombi Dwane. 'And somehow, like all repressive people, they will never think that you are taking this resistance position because of your ideas, but because somebody is instigating you to do it.'[133] The final report of the commission stated: 'Every time there was trouble at Fort Hare the seminary offered shelter to the students who had been "sent down" … the suspicion [arose] that the seminary was aiding those persons who were opposed to, or created trouble at, Fort Hare.'[134] The report pointed to certain preachers who 'delivered themselves of hostile sermons'. Showing that there was a genuine fear of Fedsem on the part of Fort Hare authorities, the report concluded that there 'can never be peace between the two institutions'. It stated:

> The influence of the seminary on the Fort Hare student could not be said, to say the least, to help settle things peacefully at Fort Hare. Certainly

the seminary was not indifferent to what was taking place at Fort Hare: certain individuals … were openly hostile to Fort Hare.'[135]

In 1973, relations between Fort Hare and Fedsem worsened. When protests broke out at the campus, Fedsem played an important, visible role in the disturbances. As the university closed and opened on numerous occasions, and students were shuttled back and forth to the train stations throughout the year, Fedsem officials lent a helping hand. 'We were accompanied by the priests to the station,' says Mtintso. 'They had to take us to the station so that the police didn't arrest us. They literally had to accompany us.'[136]

Mtintso says Fedsem served as a refuge for Fort Hare students during the strike:

> When we were chased by police, we used to run from Fort Hare straight to Fedsem. And police would not get into, they would surround Fedsem, but they would not get into the classrooms or dormitories and take us out. There was still this element that this was a theological institution. And the priests would come out and talk to the police and we would be sitting there hiding.[137]

Sigqibo Dwane, who was a Fedsem staff member in 1973, remembers one instance that year when Fort Hare students descended upon the seminary:

> One morning we were listening to a lecture by Theo Kotze on violence, the whole seminary. And while he was talking, somebody noticed that there was movement from St Peter's College up towards the seminary building. And then all of us became curious and stood up. There were Fort Hare students running towards the seminary building. We had abandoned the lecture. And Grant Brown, who was the president, suggested we should go to the front of the seminary building and just sit there with Fort Hare students. So we walked out, met them there, sat together with them. They were being chased by the police. The police came in a van and said they have come to collect Fort Hare students. And Grant Brown said, no, we can't tell who's a Fort Hare student and who's a seminary student. If you can tell, you can try. Of course they were furious.[138]

Mtintso says that the seminary staff, in addition to playing the role of protector, served in an advisory capacity to Fort Hare students:

> They also had to counsel us. Some students were quite young. It was
> traumatic. It's not like it was just a picnic. It's traumatic for students to
> find that they are kicked out, and suddenly when you are all alone, you
> realise, I'm going to have to go home and face my parents. They would
> provide that. In a very political way.

She says that the Fedsem staff gently nudged Fort Hare students to action
by clarifying issues for them. To Mtintso, the counselling sessions were
invaluable. She came from a poor family that was relying heavily on her
education to provide relief from their poverty. Being expelled from Fort Hare
generated a variety of emotions. Mtintso remembers talking with a Fedsem
lecturer who helped her realise that she was acting with conviction. 'She sat
with me, just talking about how things can't be that bad,' Mtintso recalls. 'You
are standing for what is just. You are standing for justice. Your mother will be
proud of you for standing for justice.'[139]

As 1973 drew to a close, De Wet and the government intensified their efforts
to gain control of Fedsem. For two years following their initial letter, Fort
Hare charged the seminary with employing 'delaying tactics', but did little
to wrest control of the land from Fedsem.[140] The renewed drive by Fort Hare
to take over the seminary coincided with the disturbances of 1972 and 1973,
and shows Fort Hare's politically motivated intentions. Indeed, following the
1973 unrest at Fort Hare, it was apparent that the university was going to make
a move. Sigqibo Dwane notes that the turning point came during the 1973
unrest, when De Wet discovered a list of student grievances had been typed on
a Fedsem typewriter. He says,

> De Wet noticed that this was not typed on a Fort Hare machine and
> came to the conclusion that it was typed at the seminary. And from
> that he deduced that we had actually helped the students to draw up
> the document. And so he wrote a letter to the president of the seminary
> saying, this is what I discovered. You are aiding my students in this
> strike. And then a sinister note at the end: 'This is not the last time that
> you hear of this matter.'[141]

Indeed, the De Wet letter to Grant Brown was not the final word from Fort
Hare. On 26 November 1973, an order of expropriation was served. Fort Hare
was to seize control of Fedsem. Seminary officials fought to keep control of
their land, but much like the Fort Hare attempt to confront government control
in the late 1950s, their efforts were ultimately unsuccessful. They met with
the minister of Bantu Education, who told them there was no going back on

the decision to expropriate.[142] Next, the seminary leaders met with De Wet. According to Sigqibo Dwane, De Wet made it clear he preferred the seminary to leave immediately. He says,

> De Wet had drawn up his terms. The terms were that if we wanted to stay … you will surrender two of the four colleges because I need accommodation when the students return. And Fedsem said, No, you can't do that because it will affect our life. Because your students will live at Fedsem, you're going to have to control us.[143]

Unwilling to surrender control of the seminary campus to De Wet, Fedsem officials decided to pack up and move. Sigqibo Dwane says,

> When the students returned, they didn't want to go. So we persuaded them that we didn't have a choice in the matter. And they were saying, no, we must stay here and protest and let the government get us out … Then the vans started coming in to move us out, and when they came in a group of about 11, students decided they would stop the vans from carrying stuff out of Fedsem. That was another painful thing. Imagine having to go to the students and then ask them to move and then force them to move. And they were taken and locked up in one of the side chapels at St Peter's. That was a very, very painful experience.[144]

Fedsem packed up and moved to Umtata. It was later forced to move out of Umtata to near Pietermaritzburg. The expropriation of Fedsem, important in that it removed a significant organisational and spiritual ally from the students, also had a symbolic meaning. As the traditional Fort Hare began to fade with the government takeover, Fedsem emerged as a reminder of what was possible in South Africa. The vibrant, multi-racial community that mirrored the traditional Fort Hare served to ease the pain caused by the introduction of ethnic higher education. Fedsem's demise marked the last in a string of government blows that succeeded in transforming Fort Hare from a unique institution to just another bush college.

Beyond Fort Hare

The NP's experiment with ethnic universities led indirectly to the formation of SASO. Beale writes that the university colleges 'ended up creating the ideal medium for the evolution of the new, vigorous ideology of black consciousness'.[145] The Fort Hare campus was affected, but, more importantly, SASO was part of a wider stream of resistance that swept across the country in the 1970s. By the end of 1973, scores of leaders had abandoned their efforts to receive an education at Fort Hare and instead, like Mtintso and Jeff and Selby Baqwa, began to organise full time for SASO.

Gerhart writes that one of the results of the expulsion and voluntary withdrawal of large numbers of students from the bush colleges was a transfer of energy to activities outside the campuses. Some 30 students who dropped out of Turfloop after Tiro's expulsion found employment as teachers in Soweto, including Tiro himself, who politicised the student body at Morris Isaacson High School before the Bantu Education Department orchestrated his dismissal.[146] As ex-bush-college students travelled the country, they made an impression on the age group behind them. This led to an upsurge of activity among high school students from the end of 1972, resulting in the formation of a number of new political youth organisations across the country, most notably the South African Students' Movement in Soweto and the National Youth Organisation in Natal.[147] Thus, by the time the government had stepped up repression of SASO in 1973, it was too late. The organisation had already indirectly given birth to a new wave of political activity that would culminate in the 1976 Soweto uprisings.[148]

At the same time that increased government vigilance forced people such as Mtintso and Selby Baqwa out of Fort Hare, the prototype of the Fort Hare student began to change. Indian, coloured and non-Xhosa African students from South Africa and beyond had almost entirely been phased out of the student body after the takeover. With the entrenchment of Bantu Education and the linked nationwide government attack on missionary institutions, another significant change occurred in the type of student that arrived to study at Fort Hare: the pre-university experiences of the Fort Hare student in the late 1960s and more so in the 1970s was very different from previous years. Whereas the pre-1960 Fort Hare student grew up in the missionary tradition, attending such schools as Clarkebury, Healdtown, Lovedale, and St Matthew's, the post-1960 Fort Harian was educated at BC schools, with 'BC standing for Bantu Community'.[149] In earlier decades, students were often introduced to politics through activity at mission schools. They frequently challenged authority, but in the end, limits to their resistance were born out of the very system they confronted in their protest. Indeed, even the most militant of Youth Leaguers in the 1940s were products of missionary education; their worldviews, for the most part, were grounded in a liberal Christian notion that education would lead to assimilation and equal rights. The new Fort Harians did not grow up in the mission environment, but in a world where Bantustans and Bantu Education made notions of assimilation far-fetched at best.

Selby Baqwa was among the last of the mission-educated students to enter Fort Hare. His alma mater, St Francis College in Mariannhill, was one of the few remaining private high schools for blacks in South Africa.[150] Baqwa says that even taking into account the ambiguities of missionary education, the institutions were significant in that they took students 'out of Bantu Education'. Baqwa says the German missionaries were instrumental in opening his eyes and mind to the idea that there were possibilities other than those espoused by the government:

> As opposed to if I went into a government institution where already your teachers are Afrikaners and they treat you [badly] … [Being at St Francis College] … gave you that realisation that things must be different and that they can be different. It was a very formative influence in that sense.[151]

By contrast, Satyo was among the first of the Fort Hare students to know only Bantu Community schools. He attended Mount Arthur Bantu Community School in Lady Frere. He comments:

> The methods that were used in teaching us … we were spoon-fed and … beaten up … It was a common practice not to be allowed to speak your own language. You'd end up being a caricature, speaking a language you understand only imperfectly and yet you've got a language in which you can communicate effectively. So it was another very strange thing at school. You really felt you were there to be changed into some other animal with a new language, because Afrikaans was also introduced.[152]

As Bantu Education took root, more and more students with experiences closer to those of Satyo than Baqwa arrived at Fort Hare. By the middle of the 1970s, Fort Hare students arriving in Alice knew nothing but Bantu Community schools. The lack of mission school experience among new students was exacerbated by government control of Fort Hare. In earlier times, students, given relative freedom to develop, could have caught on to the elements that made Fort Hare special without prior experience in such an environment. But with the government firmly in control, there was no chance for students to immerse themselves in an open intellectual environment and Fort Hare moved further from the place it had been before 1960.

Thus, the confluence of several factors marks 1973 as an appropriate point to end this book. First, the expansion of the third-rate system of black higher education, followed 10 years later by Fort Hare's autonomy, meant that the university no longer occupied a unique position. Second, many student activists left Fort Hare after the tumultuous 1973 school year to work full time for SASO. When put together with the 42 students that had walked out the previous year, it is clear that young political activists found it exceedingly difficult to remain at the bush colleges. As activists left Fort Hare and the other bush colleges, the starting point in the struggle for liberation shifted from the university campus to the nation's high schools. The passing of the last generation of mission-high-school graduates and the loss of Fedsem at this time underscored the new reality that Fort Hare was no longer what it once had been.

Notes

1   'Report of Fort Hare Local Committee to SASO', July 1973, in Karis and Gerhart, volume 5, *Nadir and Resurgence, 1964–1979,* 531.
2   Pityana, interview.
3   Sipho Buthelezi, 'The emergence of black consciousness: An historical appraisal', in N. Barney Pityana, Mampehela Ramphele, Malusi Mpumlwana and Lindy Wilson (eds), *Bounds of Possibility: The Legacy of Steve Biko and Black Consciousness* (Cape Town: David Philip, 1991), 112.
4   Pityana, interview. A segment of the Fort Hare student population that had been steeped in the non-racial tradition of the ANC never joined SASO. This is discussed in further detail later in the chapter.
5   Buthelezi, 'The emergence of black consciousness', 114.
6   Pityana, interview.
7   Selby Baqwa, interview.
8   *Ibid.*
9   Pityana, interview.
10   Quoted in Gerhart, *Black Power*, 269.
11   Selby Baqwa, interview.
12   Buthelezi, 'The emergence of black consciousness', 115.
13   Pityana, interview.
14   *Ibid.*
15   *Ibid.*
16   Stofile, interview.
17   *Ibid.*
18   Deal Party coast is located on the Indian Ocean coast right next to New Brighton in Port Elizabeth. The strange name comes from the group of 1820 settlers who came from Deal, in England.
19   Stofile, interview.
20   *Ibid.*
21   *Ibid.*
22   Pityana, interview.
23   Buthelezi, 'The emergence of black consciousness', 114.

24   Mtintso, interview.
25   See for example, 'Report of Inquiry into Sit-In Protest at Fort Hare,' 1972, Fort Hare Papers, 2.
26   Karis and Gerhart, volume 5, *Nadir and Resurgence, 1964–1979,* 125.
27   'Evidence before Commission of Enquiry on Student Unrest', Student Unrest, Fort Hare Papers, 43.
28   'Notice to Students With Regards to the Position of the Joint House Committee', 21 April 1972, Fort Hare Papers.
29   *Ibid.*
30   'Report of Inquiry into Sit-in Protest at Fort Hare,' May 1972, Fort Hare Papers.
31   Karis and Gerhart, volume 5, *Nadir and Resurgence, 1964–1979,* 125.
32   *Ibid.*
33   *Ibid.*
34   *Ibid.*, 126.
35   Jeff Baqwa, interview.
36   J.M. de Wet, Letter to SASO secretary, 7 November, 1972, SASO File, Fort Hare Papers.
37   'Report of Inquiry into Sit-in Protest at Fort Hare,' May 1972, Fort Hare Papers, 6.
38   Stofile, interview.
39   'Evidence Before the Commission of Enquiry into Unrest at Fort Hare', Student Unrest, Fort Hare Papers, 8.
40   *Ibid.*, 10, 'Mr' in original.
41   'Memorandum of Student Grievances', 22 May 1972, Fort Hare Papers.
42   Leslie Xinwa, 'What's behind the trouble at Fort Hare?', *Daily Dispatch*, 10 June 1972.
43   'Memorandum of Student Grievances,' 22 May 1972, Fort Hare Papers.
44   *Ibid.*
45   'Fort Hare students stand firm on sit-in', *Daily Dispatch*, 25 May 1972.
46   'Report of Inquiry into Sit-in Protest at Fort Hare', May 1972, Fort Hare Papers, 6.
47   SASO Local Committee, Letter to J.M. De Wet, 3 August 1972, Fort Hare Papers.
48   'Students stage sit-in, boycott at Fort Hare', *Daily Dispatch*, 23 May 1972.
49   *Ibid.*
50   Ray ka Msengana, 'Saso "not to blame" for Fort Hare disturbances', *Cape Times*, 9 August 1973.
51   Selby Baqwa, interview.
52   Jeff Baqwa, interview.
53   Jeff Baqwa, letter to author, 12 April 1999.
54   Selby Baqwa, interview.
55   'Report of Inquiry into Sit-in Protest at Fort Hare', May 1972, Fort Hare Papers, 9.
56   Jeff Baqwa, letter to author.
57   'Report of Inquiry into Sit-in Protest at Fort Hare', 8.
58   'Fort Hare Students' Manifesto', Fort Hare Papers.
59   *Ibid.*
60   Jerry Modisane, 'Why I walked off Fort Hare in protest', *SASO Newsletter*, May/June 1972, Fort Hare Papers.
61   Selby Baqwa, interview.
62   *Ibid.*
63   Lindy Wilson, 'Steve Biko', 32.
64   *Ibid.*, 33.
65   Karis and Gerhart, volume 5, *Nadir and Resurgence, 1964–1979,* 125.

66 'Summary of Important Events,' 1972, Fort Hare Papers.
67 J.M. de Wet, Letter to SASO secretary, 7 November 1972, SASO File, Fort Hare Papers.
68 J.M. de Wet, Letter to Selby Baqwa, 21 September 1972, SASO File, Fort Hare Papers.
69 J.M. de Wet, Letter to Selby Baqwa, 29 August1972, Fort Hare Papers.
70 Karis and Gerhart, volume 5, *Nadir and Resurgence, 1964–1979,* 530.
71 Beginning in January 1973, the apartheid regime was challenged by the greatest strike wave in the country's history as an estimated 100 000 workers downed tools in factories and workplaces throughout the country. The strikers advanced economic demands that could not be accommodated without a total transformation of society itself. Strike activity was particularly strong in Durban, where more than 61 000 walked off their jobs in a three-month period.
72 Karis and Gerhart, volume 5, *Nadir and Resurgence, 1964–1979*, 120.
73 Pumsile Majeke, student file, Fort Hare Papers.
74 Selby Baqwa, interview.
75 'Report of Fort Hare Local Committee,' Karis and Gerhart, volume 5, *Nadir and Resurgence, 1964–1979,* 531.
76 Selby Baqwa, interview.
77 Vuyiso Qunta, student file, Fort Hare Papers.
78 Selby Baqwa, interview.
79 Stofile, interview.
80 Tim Clarke and Marianne Gray, 'Fort Hare students issue "ultimatum"', *Sunday Express,* 5 August 1973.
81 'Fort Hare students plan to quit', *Pretoria News*, 4 August 1973.
82 *Ibid.*; 'Fort Hare boycott ends', *Rand Daily Mail*, 15 August 1973.
83 Clarke and Gray, 'Fort Hare students issue "ultimatum"'.
84 'Fort Hare students plan to quit', *Pretoria News*, 4 August 1973.
85 'Students want all, or nothing', *Natal Mercury*, 1 September 1973.
86 *Ibid.*
87 'Students return to Fort Hare', *Rand Daily Mail*, 21 August 1973.
88 Selby Baqwa, interview.
89 *Ibid.*
90 Mtintso, interview.
91 'Police on Fort Hare Campus', *The Evening Post*, 27 August 1973.
92 'Police stop sit-in at Fort Hare', *Eastern Province Herald*, 28 August 1973.
93 '13 students held after campus riot', *Eastern Province Herald*, 29 August 1973.
94 'Violence erupts At Fort Hare', *Daily Dispatch*, 29 August 1973.
95 '400 sent home from Fort Hare', *Eastern Province Herald*, 29 August 1973.
96 'Violence erupts At Fort Hare,' *Daily Dispatch*, 29 August 1973..
97 Mtintso, interview.
98 'Students riot at Fort Hare', *The World,* 28 August 1973.
99 Mtintso, interview.
100 'Violence erupts at Fort Hare', *Daily Dispatch*, 28 August 1973.
101 'Fort Hare students sent home', *Natal Witness*, 29 August 1973.
102 *Ibid.*
103 'Violence brings varsity to a halt', *Cape Argus,* 29 August 1973.
104 Sigqibo Dwane, interview.
105 Mtintso, interview.
106 Ntombi Dwane, interview.

107 Stofile, interview.
108 Goodwin, *Cry Amandla!*, 20.
109 Mtintso, interview.
110 Selby Baqwa, interview.
111 *Ibid.*
112 *Ibid.*
113 Jeff Baqwa, interview.
114 Selby Baqwa, interview.
115 *Ibid.*
116 For more on Fedsem (Federal Theological Seminary), see Khayalethu Gxabalashe's MA thesis, 'Church, state and theological education under apartheid: The relationship between the Federal Theological Seminary, the University of Fort Hare, and the South African government, 1963–1976' (University of Fort Hare, Alice, 2002).
117 Jeff Bawqa, interview.
118 Gerhart, 294.
119 Selby Baqwa, interview.
120 *Ibid.*
121 Sigqipbo Dwane, interview.
122 Senate minutes,10 September 1968, Fort Hare Papers.
123 J.M. de Wet, 'Statement by the Rector to Members of Staff Re: Fedsem', Document File 1, Background to the Fort Hare and Alice Seminary Dispute, Fort Hare Papers.
124 *Ibid.*
125 *Ibid.*
126 'Magazine devotes entire issue to takeover of seminary', Document File 1, Fort Hare Papers.
127 'Alien culture at seminary reason for expropriation', *Natal Daily News*, 26 February 1975.
128 Jeff Baqwa, interview.
129 'Evidence before Commission into 1972 Fort Hare Unrest', Fort Hare Papers, 24.
130 *Ibid.*, 22.
131 *Ibid.*, 42.
132 *Ibid.*, 22.
133 Ntombi Dwane, interview.
134 'Evidence before Commission into 1972 Fort Hare Unrest', Fort Hare Papers, 6.
135 *Ibid.*, 7.
136 Mtintso, interview.
137 *Ibid.*
138 Sigqipbo Dwane, interview.
139 Mtintso, interview.
140 De Wet, 'Statement by the rector to members of staff re: Fedsem'.
141 Sigqipbo Dwane, interview.
142 'Background to the Fort Hare Alice Seminary Debate', Document File 1. Fort Hare Papers.
143 Sigqipbo Dwane, interview.
144 *Ibid.*
145 Beale, 'Apartheid and university education', 4.
146 Karis and Gerhart, volume 5, *Nadir and Resurgence, 1964–1979,* 128.
147 Gerhart, *Black Power in South Africa,* 297.

148 There is some controversy over the precise role the overtly political organisations played in the genesis of the 1976 events. In *The Soweto Uprisings: Counter-memories of June 1976* (Randburg: Ravan, 1998), Sifiso Ndlovu argues that the uprising was completely unexpected to the formal organisations. He writes that it was a product of the young schoolchildren who had Afrikaans forced on them, and that only later did the activists of a more overtly political nature become involved and take credit for the insurrection.

149 Catholic mission schools such as St Francis stayed open after the advent of Bantu Education and a few Fort Harians, like Jeff and Selby Baqwa, attended such schools.

150 Gerhart, *Black Power in South Africa*, 259.

151 Selby Baqwa, interview.

152 Satyo, interview.

6

Conclusion

Who could not have been aware?
Govan Mbeki[1]

Lule for president

In 1938, an unassuming, intelligent Fort Hare student, Yusuf Lule, aspired to become elected to the SRC. His supporters coined the phrase 'Lule for president'.[2] The slogan proved to be prophetic, as Lule went on to serve as the president of Uganda for 69 days in 1979. Other ex-Fort Hare students had even more success than Lule. Nelson Mandela, elected to the Fort Hare SRC in 1940, became South Africa's first black president, and Robert Sobukwe, the SRC president in 1949, became the president of the PAC. Robert Mugabe, of Zimbabwe, was a Fort Hare student in the early 1950s.

Up to the late 1950s, Fort Hare produced a large share of east and southern Africa's black university graduates and many of its early nationalists. In the 1960s and beyond, political leaders continued to emerge from the ranks of the university's student body. Clearly then, the University of Fort Hare played a significant role in African history. Why? What was it about the Fort Hare that made it 'the most historically significant institution for higher education in sub-equatorial Africa'?[3] Asked this question, Joe Matthews answered: 'What if this is all one big historical accident?' His response, though rhetorical in nature, raises legitimate questions. For Fort Hare was not created to be a centre of revolutionary thought. Most people attended Fort Hare because it was their only educational option, even before the 1960 takeover.

241

Fort Hare's most famous student, Nelson Mandela, wears his university blazer, 2006

Yet though the course of Fort Hare's development did not proceed as intended by its missionary founders and apartheid trustees, it is too simplistic to attribute Fort Hare's central role to 'one big historical accident'. Fort Hare clearly influenced South African history, but South African history also affected Fort Hare. That the university turned into a hotbed of nationalism, producing political leaders throughout Southern Africa, was not merely a coincidence.

If Matthews had said that the history of Fort Hare was one long string of unanticipated consequences, he would have been more accurate. Fort Hare was not created to breed revolutionaries, and its role in the production of leaders throughout southern Africa is primarily owing to the circumstances of South African history. Speaking at his inauguration as chancellor of Fort Hare in 1991, Oliver Tambo said:

> The history of Fort Hare cannot be retold as if it were one event. It was, and is, the culmination of a drama of interpenetrating and, at times, contradictory forces. It was moulded by the peculiarities of the history of this region of southern Africa, and the struggles authored by that history.[4]

In the interviews with ex-Fort Hare students, it became clear that their politicisation was not a historical accident, but rather the result of a confluence of factors, both general to South African history and specific to the surroundings in which they grew up. There is no single clear path towards politicisation. For some, such as Jeff Baqwa, experiences at mission boarding schools were instrumental in awakening a sense of political consciousness. Others first encountered politics on arriving at Fort Hare. All interviewees were affected by the entrenched white supremacy that coloured everyday life.

While some of the factors affecting politicisation at Fort Hare are unique to the university and its students, others are common to students all over the world. Students have almost invariably been more responsive to political trends and opportunities for social change than any other group. From revolutionary Russia before 1905 to civil rights and anti-war protest in the US in the 1960s, students have almost always been in the vanguard of political change.[5]

The most general hypothesis explaining student protest suggests that it is the result of a 'generational dissidence', that is, rapid rates of social change creating a sharp discrepancy between the formative experiences of parents and their children.[6] A student culture develops that denounces adult values and behaviours. Other theories suggest that students do things 'excessively and vehemently' because they 'have not yet been humbled by life or learnt its necessary limitations'.[7] Another hypothesis is that students are idealists who demand that the values of their society be implemented in the actions of that society.[8] In the United States, opposition to the Vietnam War placed American actions in Vietnam at odds with core American beliefs such as self-determination.

While there was a generational conflict of sorts between the young militants of the YL and the organisation's older members over tactics and degrees of militancy, at the core the two groups were united in their fight against white supremacy. The theory of students as idealists may come closest to describing the South African context. Though South African society did not purport to be democratic, students were demanding the rights afforded to white citizens of South Africa. Fort Harians frequently felt they were treated badly because they were black. Such issues as the poor quality of food, compulsory attendance at religious services, and lack of control over their education led black students to believe they were not receiving equal treatment to white students at other institutions. More importantly, voicing dissatisfaction with campus conditions often served to express deeper discontent with the wider political climate.

While the root cause of student activism in South Africa is particular to its history of segregation and apartheid, some of the factors that facilitated student protest around the world can be seen at Fort Hare. Students, as compared with other groups, have less responsibility in the form of commitments to families and jobs. Radical staff and the logistics of a university, with large numbers of students in relatively small areas, make mobilisation easy.

Through 34 interviews, distinct patterns of politicisation emerge at Fort Hare. Many students became involved in politics because their parents, relatives or members of their community were active. Mangosuthu Buthelezi learned politics at his 'mother's knee'.[9] Ambrose Makiwane, whose mother was an organiser for the ANC in the Engcobo district of the Transkei, was sent on errands for the movement before he was old enough to understand what he was doing. Thenjiwe Mtintso's sister offered her a vivid analysis of their family's class situation. Marumo Moerane vividly recalls his father, M.T. Moerane, speaking out against the 1949 anti-Indian riots. Andrew Masondo's mother left him stacks of papers of the CPSA. Joe Matthews was constantly engaged in political discussion and debate with his father.

Geography sealed the fate of many Fort Harians. Formative years spent in particularly active areas of the country nudged many towards politics. Many students came from the Eastern Cape, an area that has a complex and often radical political tradition. Students such as Stanley Mabizela, Barney Pityana and Makhenkesi Stofile were all introduced to politics as they grew up in

New Brighton, Port Elizabeth. In the 1950s, New Brighton was a hub of ANC activity and, according to Pityana, those students that grew up in Port Elizabeth could not avoid politics.[10]

Experiences and personalities in mission boarding schools influenced some. Makiwane and Mtintso led protests over skimpy menu offerings. Oliver Tambo mentored Henry Makgothi, indirectly introducing him to politics. Ntombi Dwane's history teacher was 'openly political', and Selby Baqwa's political consciousness was awakened through contact with a teacher who explained the significance of events such as the 1965 unilateral declaration of independence in the then Rhodesia. That they were viewed and treated as students and not 'black students' by their German missionary teachers profoundly influenced both Selby and Jeff Baqwa. A large contingent of Fort Harians, including Isaac Mabindisa and Sigqibo Dwane, received their start in politics at Lovedale, where they attended political meetings led by people such as Makiwane.

Politically astute colleagues influenced many students. Oliver Tambo, the SRC president in Devi Bugwhan's student days, opened her eyes: 'I mean Oliver Tambo was sitting there as a grown man, as president of the SRC when I was a 15 year old. I do remember him and what dynamism he had even then.'[11] Robert Sobukwe, perhaps the most politically astute student of his generation, impressed numerous classmates, including Herby Govinden. Buthelezi drew Frank Mdlalose to his first YL meeting. Ivy Matsepe-Casaburri was both awed and influenced by the debating ability of Makiwane, and V.R. Govender recalls being challenged by the argumentative YL president. From the time they met as high school classmates in Johannesburg and through their years at Fort Hare, Makgothi learned from Joe Matthews.

Aside from learning through debate and discussion with fellow students, many Fort Harians were influenced by their teachers at the university. Though D.D.T. Jabavu did not openly encourage student involvement in politics, Wycliffe Tsotsi and Govan Mbeki took note when their professor convened the AAC. Fort Hare would not have been the same place without the influence of Z.K. Matthews, who engaged his students in debate, always encouraging them to think. To a lesser degree, younger staff members in later years such as Andrew Masondo and Herby Govinden helped students develop politically.

Over the years, Fort Hare's neighbours – Fedsem, Lovedale, and Victoria Hospital – directly and indirectly spurred student activism. Nurses' strikes at Victoria hospital in 1949 and 1958 politicised the student body. The 1949 strike was an especially important event in the development of a nationalistic outlook among the students. The relationship with Lovedale was symbiotic.

Fort Hare students supported Lovedale students in their battles with the high school authorities, particularly in 1946, and Lovedale students joined with Fort Hare students in protest against the university apartheid bills. All the while, a continuum of resistance was being forged as Lovedale students such as Mabindisa moved on to Fort Hare as seasoned activists. In the 1970s, Fedsem had a direct politicising effect on Fort Hare students. In addition to the institution serving as a refuge for students being chased by the police, Fedsem staff helped Fort Hare students such as Thenjiwe Mtintso find a comforting political meaning in their expulsion from university.

The atmosphere at Fort Hare served to politicise the student body. Its diversity was unusual in a racially divided South Africa. As Indians such as Rama Thumbadoo and G.S. Tootla came into contact with blacks as equals for the first time in their lives, stereotypes were put to rest and friendships were formed. Similarly, black students, like Ivy Matsepe-Casaburri, met Indian and coloured students for the first time. In segregated South Africa this interaction was in and of itself political. The rural, residential nature of the college also boosted activism. Students were placed together in a small town, and developed into a tight-knit community, despite political factions that emerged. Terence Beard points out that the lack of contact with white students created a commonality of experience that furthered political mobilisation.[12] With little on the outside to entertain them, the students were forced to turn inwards, resulting in what Beard calls 'a highly integrated society with its own *mores*, its own mutually recognised identity, and a cherished *esprit de corps*'.[13] Politics was an integral component of this shared Fort Hare identity.

Even more than the residential nature of the college, the political *esprit de corps* that developed was owing to the rules of the college and conditions under which students lived. Students' politics were forged in reaction to the very institution that was educating them. Many students felt the strict, conservative nature of college life and the paltry dining hall diet existed because they were black. Wycliffe Tsotsi's first political involvement came in the form of a 1935 protest against the prohibition of a mixed campus dance. Devi Bugwhan was introduced to student politics by agitation against the prohibition of Sunday tennis. Protests against the poor quality of food did not result in a more palatable diet for Logan Naidoo, but he says the agitation served to unite the students. In later years, the administration's complicity with government policy, its heavy-handed approach, and its refusal to communicate with the students spurred protest.

While some of the interviewees were influenced by fellow students, others by staff members and still others by mission school experiences, all interviewees agreed that their politicisation was related to the question, posed by Govan Mbeki in 1996 at the eightieth anniversary celebrations of the university: 'Can you separate the history of South Africa from what took place around Fort Hare?'[14] Indeed, from its founding, which was a conservative reaction to increasing numbers of South Africans going abroad to study, to the SASO period, where the organisation was initially applauded and then brutally repressed by government and university authorities, the experiences of Fort Hare students were largely shaped by the ever-changing South African political scene.

Students brought personal experiences of growing up in a racist society with them to Fort Hare. Most had direct encounters with racism, and, as Beard notes, the entire student body suffered in some degree the effects of legal discrimination.[15] The vicious pass laws he encountered each day aroused Govan Mbeki's consciousness. Wycliffe Tsotsi was upset when forced to ride in the back of a truck on top of mealie sacks. Ivy Matsepe-Casaburri's family were forcibly removed from their homes on two occasions. Her school principal was arrested for not carrying his pass. Marumo Moerane, Isaac Mabindisa and Makhenkesi Stofile remember watching as police arrested respected community elders during the 1952 Defiance Campaign. Thenjiwe Mtintso recalls being poorer than anyone else she knew. As Mbeki says: 'Who could not have been aware?'

On arrival in Alice, students began to contextualise their experiences of growing up in South Africa, giving voice to feelings that had previously been internalised. Before 1960, a great deal of the political mobilisation on campus came about as students began to construct a more nationalistic identity. This often manifested itself in scuffles with college authorities. In the 1930s, reacting to legislation of the Pact government and the assault on the Cape franchise, students began to agitate for change within a conservative, missionary institution. The 1940s witnessed a national ferment in extra-parliamentary politics with Fort Hare at the centre. The founding of the YL in 1944 in Johannesburg and of a branch at Fort Hare in 1948 injected militancy into the national liberation movement and ushered in a golden era of political activity at Fort Hare. In the early 1950s, students played a role in the nationwide Defiance Campaign.

Later in the decade, government efforts to expand the reach of Bantu Education to include universities served to politicise the student body. The fight against university apartheid signified a shift in student politics at Fort Hare as the attack was now focused on concrete government policy. Though Fort Hare's history had always been intricately tied in with the politics of South Africa, the rapid and calculated transformation of Fort Hare into a bush college brought about unprecedented conflict and made it abundantly clear that events outside campus would impact on university life in ways previously unseen. There was no chance of separating the fight at Fort Hare from the national struggle against apartheid as tension between the administration and the students was now centred on the imposition of government policy. After a brief dip in activism in the 1960s with the banning of the ANC and PAC, the arrival of SASO, in large part a response to the government's segregated university system, re-energised the student body, but also brought on a new wave of government repression.

Different directions

Thus, their backgrounds, school experiences and the political climate in South Africa influenced students at Fort Hare. Yet while discernible patterns of politicisation do emerge and many students were influenced by similar factors, students did not join the same political organisations after Fort Hare. How does one account for the diverse political paths to which students gravitated on leaving the university? Govan Mbeki, Nelson Mandela and Oliver Tambo aligned themselves with the ANC, while Wycliffe Tsotsi and Herby Govinden joined the Unity Movement. In later years, Robert Sobukwe founded the PAC. Kaiser Matanzima and Mangosuthu Buthelezi participated in homeland politics. After remaining in the ANC to try to counter what he viewed as communistic influences, Frank Mdlalose eventually joined Buthelezi and Joe Matthews in the IFP. Mbeki, Makiwane and Thenjiwe Mtintso went in an opposite direction, joining the CPSA.

Clearly, because of the location of Fort Hare in the Eastern Cape and the political leanings of many of its graduates, the ANC influence at Fort Hare was strongest. Most Fort Harians remained with the organisation after leaving the university because of ties that had been created during their student days. But aside from students remaining loyal to the ANC, there is little evidence to suggest that Fort Hare experiences impacted the diversity of political paths followed by its students. I asked Wycliffe Tsotsi why he, Govan Mbeki and Kaiser Matanzima, near-contemporaries at Fort Hare, travelled down different political roads. He responded:

> Matanzima grew up in a very conservative traditional way. Traditionally, we were ruled by chiefs. He looked upon himself as a natural, almost divine ruler of his people … When Govan came to Port Elizabeth here and joined the Communist Party … we were strongly against the

Communist Party in South Africa. That is when the difference between us began to arise … I came under the influence of a group which was opposed to the Communist Party; they called it the Trotskyite elements. I was not myself a Trotskyite, but I came under the influence of this. They were in fact the leaders of the AAC and the Unity Movement when it was born. It was that background. So the Mbekis and others were always saying that we were Trotskyites. And we turned back and said that they are Stalinists. Those were the roots of our divergence … They were influences not from the within the college itself, the university, but outside the university.[16]

I asked Henry Makgothi how he remained with the ANC, while classmates Frank Mdlalose and Mangosuthu Buthelezi ended up in the IFP? He replied, 'Isn't that normal?'[17] Makgothi's point was that there are always going to be different views in any group of people. Joe Matthews agreed, saying that any family will consist of members who think differently.[18] Despite the homogeneity of a student group in terms of age and educational attainment, family background, coupled with experiences of students after leaving Fort Hare, often determined an individual's political course. Makgothi says:

Buthelezi, how he went to IFP, initially when he left Fort Hare … he went to assume his duties as a tribal leader. It was with the ANC, he consulted the ANC … He was against it, but they said, no, no, no, no, you must go. You must go and fulfil this role. So he went there and he tried his best … And then a new generation began springing up and there were conflicts and he ended up where he is today. But honestly speaking, I think he's an ANC person … Well, he's an IFP, but his education is ANC, you understand, and I think he can only go so far against the ANC. [Frank] Mdlalose too. Mdlalose was a good chap when we were at Fort Hare … But, well, circumstances were such that he also became IFP. Sobukwe became PAC. But these are people with very strong ANC backgrounds. Very strong.[19]

As for Makgothi himself, after being introduced to politics at St Peter's and Fort Hare, his commitment to the ANC was cemented when he moved to Johannesburg after university. He says:

I met the real guys … I was fortunate. After I left Fort Hare, I went to teach. I taught for only one year. Then I was thrown into the ANC. I met [Walter] Sisulu who made a hell of an impression on me. That is the kind of man who makes a lifelong impression on you … And Duma Nokwe was one of the best. So I was lucky in the sense that I was in the

> company of those people and I had the good fortune to develop in what
> I think is the right way.[20]

Students' backgrounds and the influences they came under on leaving Fort Hare were the most formative factors in determining future political direction.

Despite political differences among graduates, Fort Hare's *esprit de corps* lives on in the governing of the new South Africa. Joe Matthews says that party differences are tempered because so many politicians studied at Fort Hare: 'I think if people have been obviously to the same schools or the same universities, it makes personal relations easier.' He compares the relationships between Fort Harians of different political parties to that of political opponents from the same clan:

> If people belong to the same clan, they are supposed to find it easy to work together. So [former] Minister [Steve] Tshwete who is the same clan as my mother, I can talk to him more easily because of that.[21] And you get that kind of relationship among Africans, especially because they have these totems, their tribal totems which they express when they meet … That makes it easier for people to have easy relations, even between people who are actually politically antagonistic … It cuts across politics.[22]

I asked Buthelezi if the Fort Hare factor makes political debate in South Africa less contentious. He says:

> Of course it does. It does, really. Even some of the senior civil servants here, some of them are from Fort Hare. They are not in politics like us, but they're all graduates of Fort Hare as well and are working with us here. But there's always that sentiment that we are ex-Fort Harians.[23]

Stofile of the ANC told me only half jokingly that whenever he gets into an argument with Buthelezi of the IFP, all he has to do is say the two words 'Fort Hare' and Buthelezi will change from his opponent to his best friend.[24] Zolani Ngwane notes that this spirit of fraternisation dominated the eightieth anniversary celebrations at Fort Hare, writing that 'the past eclipsed the present'. He comments that Professor Francis Wilson, the chairman of the Fort Hare Council, emphasised the 'impressive manner in which the event managed to transcend political differences among the alumni'. Wilson was particularly struck by the warm reception given to Buthelezi by his political opponents.[25]

Ngwane makes the point that the diversity of the alumni was 'underplayed by a constant use of the homogenising pronoun "we"' throughout the festivities. He writes: '[They] talked about themselves as if they were all the same and had believed the same things.'[26] Ivy Matsepe-Casaburri of the ANC offers a partial explanation: 'Fort Hare experiences are unique experiences. Whenever you go anywhere, Fort Harians can find themselves in a group and dominate everybody because you share experiences that only Fort Harians had experienced.'[27] Fort Hare connections also helped ex-students in exile feel a warm and comforting bond. Thenjiwe Mtintso says: 'When I met Chris Hani and told him I had been at Fort Hare," he hugged me like I was his long-lost younger sister. "You're from Fort Hare, yes. That's why you are so good."'[28]

Though Fort Hare's influence on South African politics is wide, the university did not produce only politicians. Fort Harians also became teachers, religious leaders, lawyers and doctors. The university offered a four-year teaching diploma that provided many graduates with a secure form of employment. Many ex-Fort Harian teachers led the fight against Bantu Education. The influence of Fort Hare as a producer of educators was particularly evident in Natal, where the Department of Education offered bursaries to students to study at Fort Hare and return as science teachers. Among the interviewees, V.R. Govender became an official in the Natal Department of Education and Logan Naidoo and a group of Fort Harians worked to desegregate high schools in Natal. Rama Thumbadoo, who went on to teach at Sastri College and Springfield College, both in Natal, says:

> I was doing research for a brochure for Springfield College and I found that no less than 32 members of the staff of Springfield College were ex-Fort Harians. The majority of them were science people ... You must think of Fort Hare educating people who educated others.

In 1991, I.C. Meer, the president of the Natal School Grantees' Association said: 'We who deal with education ... in Natal are forever indebted to Fort Hare for providing community-built schools such as Sastri College and hundreds of others with graduate teachers trained by Fort Hare when all universities were practising outright racism.'[29]

Fort Hare's impact on southern Africa is wide reaching. In this study, I examine the importance of Fort Hare through the eyes of its former students. In the course of looking at the role the university played in politicising students, it quickly became evident that Fort Hare's importance stretches beyond its illustrious alumni. The institutional history of the university can contribute much toward an understanding of the 20th and 21st century African elite, the rise of African nationalism, the policies of the apartheid government, and the advent of various streams of resistance.

Despite the parallels between Fort Hare's history and that of South Africa at large, perhaps the most lasting image of the university over the years can be located where these two histories diverge. Before 1960, Fort Hare was a place where Indians, coloureds, and blacks mixed freely and happily. A vibrant, non-racial society in the heart of apartheid South Africa, the university stood as a living testimony that the nation's people could live and work together. Over the years, as Fort Hare changed from missionary to government hands, this multi-racial community was destroyed. The fight to preserve Fort Hare was really the fight to save democracy. The university apartheid legislation dealt Fort Hare a severe blow, but the institution already showed that a non-racial democracy could flourish in South Africa.

Epilogue

At an orientation to Fort Hare on my first visit to the university in January 1997, I heard the term *toyi toyi* for the first time. The university's director of public affairs told me that it was common for students to abandon their studies in favour of the traditional form of protest that had been the trademark of South African resistance to apartheid. I soon learned that it was customary for students to begin each semester by boycotting classes to protest against the exclusion of those who owed money to the university. One morning, about two weeks later, I woke up to sounds of voices singing in harmony outside my hostel room. I joined my classmates as they sang of the heroism of Oliver Tambo and MK soldiers, imploring the administration to allow all students to register. Over and over again, we sang '*sizo zabalaza*', which I quickly learned means 'we will struggle'. The students knew they had little chance of having their demands met, but they continued to march. The *toyi toyis* were as much a celebration of the past as they were a protest against present financial issues.

The *toyi toyis* also showed how the past can become a part of the living present. Though I did not know it at the time, the tumultuous state of affairs at Fort Hare on my arrival in 1997 could be traced back to legislation of the late 1950s that resulted in the balkanisation of Fort Hare and the expansion of black university education. As I moved about campus trying to familiarise myself with the steps to the *toyi toyi* and the words and meanings of the accompanying songs, I was unaware that I was protesting because Makiwane and his compatriots had been unsuccessful in walking the same route 40 years earlier. Indeed, the financial, academic, and organisational problems confronting Fort Hare on my arrival were, in large part, a result of the 1960 government takeover that systematically tore into the fabric of the university.

Ralph Ellison wrote that 'man cannot simply say "Let us have liberty and justice for all" and have it'. He describes Americans as being afflicted with an illness that he describes as 'historical amnesia'. This disorder results in us 'filing and forgetting' certain parts of our past and thus preventing true progress from taking place. Much of Fort Hare's history is in danger of falling prey to this Ellisonian disorder. In addition, many of those interviewed for this book have, sadly, passed on.[30] The stories I heard from alumni and the documents I sifted through in the archives of the Fort Hare administration building were, literally and figuratively, filed away.

This study is an attempt to comprehend the events that led to the *toyi toyis* I encountered at Fort Hare. Fort Hare has many, often contradictory, pasts. Its founding was intricately tied to policies of segregation and its existence today is intricately bound with the policy of apartheid. In an open letter to alumni on the occasion of Fort Hare's eightieth anniversary celebrations, English lecturer Msimelelo Silinga wrote that the university 'is a monument to both the failure and success of the human race'.[31] Indeed, over the course of its history, Fort Hare has illustrated the depths of humankind's depravity and the height of its humanity. Understanding Fort Hare's history is the only way to grasp its present, and the only way to begin rebuilding the institution that once stood for all that was possible in South Africa.

Notes

1 SABC, 'Fort Hare at 80', 1996, SABC video on Fort Hare's 80th anniversary celebration, lent to author by Mbulelo Mzamane.
2 Thandeka Gqubule, 'The African nursery', *The Saturday News*, 19 October 1991.
3 Fort Hare Division of Marketing and Communication, 'The crucible of African leadership', Alice: Media Relations and Production Office, 2000.
4 *Ibid.*
5 Seymour Lipset, *Rebellion in the University: A History of Student Activism in America* (London: Routledge & Kegan Paul, 1972), 14.
6 Norman Birnbaum, *The Crisis of Industrial Society* (New York: Oxford University Press, 1969), 148.
7 Lipset, *Rebellion*, 16.
8 Gary Weaver and James Weaver (eds), *The University and Revolution* (New Jersey: Prentice-Hall, 1969), 4.
9 Buthelezi, interview.
10 Pityana, interview.

11 Bughwan, interview.
12 Beard, 'Background to student activities', 158.
13 *Ibid.*, 159.
14 SABC, 'Fort Hare at 80'.
15 Beard, 'Background to student activities', 158.
16 Tsotsi, interview.
17 Makgothi, interview.
18 Matthews, interview.
19 Makgothi, interview.
20 *Ibid.*
21 Tshwete died in 2002.
22 Matthews, interview.
23 Buthelezi, interview.
24 Stofile, interview.
25 Zolani Ngwane, 'The 80th anniversary celebrations at Fort Hare: Past as symbol, history and imagination', paper presented at the Govan Mbeki Research Resource Centre Seminar, 25 February 1997, University of Fort Hare Staff Centre.
26 *Ibid.*
27 Matsepe-Casaburri interview.
28 Mtintso, interview.
29 Charmaine Pillay, 'Fort Hare: Decisive role in uplifting blacks', *The Leader*, 25 October 1991.
30 Jeff Baqwa, Ntombi Dwane, Sigqibo Dwane, Stanley Mabizela, Sipo Makalima, Ambrose Makiwane, Andrew Masondo, George Matanzima, Kasier Matanzima, Ivy Matsepe-Casaburri, Govan Mbeki and Wycliffe Tsotsi have all died.
31 Msimelelo Silinga, 'An Open Letter To Fort Hare Alumni', November 1996.

Interviewees

Thelma Appavoo

Selby Baqwa

Terence Beard

Devi Bughwan

Mangosuthu Buthelezi

Ismail Dada

Ntombezinhlanu (Ntombi) Dwane

Sigqibo Dwane

V.R. Govender

Herby Govinden

Isaac Mabindisa

Stanley Mabizela

Sipo Makalima

Henry Makgothi

Ambrose Makiwane

George and Kaiser Matanzima

George Matanzima

Kaiser Matanzima

Ivy Matsepe-Casaburri

Joe Matthews

Govan Mbeki

Marumo Moerane

Thenjiwe Mtintso

G.C. Oosthuizen

R.A. Pillay

Barney Pityana

Sizwe Satyo

Makhenkesi Arnold Stofile

Rama Thumbadoo

G.S. Tootla

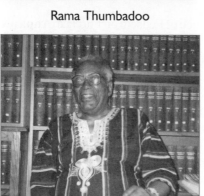

Wycliffe Tsotsi

Postscript

Life after Fort Hare[1]

Immediately after graduating from Fort Hare in 1945, **Thelma Appavoo** was offered a teaching post in Port Elizabeth. She did not accept the offer, explaining, 'I'd already got engaged and those were the days, there wasn't so much women's lib, although I had my degree, my husband said, "no, no, no, don't you start go and teach now." We're getting married.' Appavoo was married in 1946 and had two children. Her East London home was a frequent meeting place for Eastern Cape activists. She says, 'we had a lot of people coming in and out, staying overnight. It wasn't unusual for someone to knock on the door at 12 at night, give them a meal, then before sunrise they're gone.' When we met, Appavoo was in East London in the house she had called home for more than 50 years.

After obtaining a B.Sc. degree in 1971, **Jeff Baqwa** abandoned study towards an honours degree in biochemistry in 1972 when he walked out of Fort Hare along with 41 others. He immediately began to work full-time for SASO as literacy director and community development projects coordinator. Baqwa also served on the SASO Executive Committee. In 1973, the National Party government served him with a banning order restricting him to the village of Mzimkulu in the Transkei. In 1974, following the assassination of Tiro, he was sent to Botswana to begin developing strategies for guerilla training. He was active in the establishment of the black consciousness guerilla camps in Tripoli, Libya and Beirut, Lebanon. Baqwa traveled throughout the United States, Canada, Europe and Africa on in an attempt to spread the message of black consciousness and build solidarity for the black South African cause. He graduated from the University of Saarland Medical School in West Germany in 1988. He then did a diploma in tropical medicine and hygiene and earned an MA in community health at the University of Liverpool in the United Kingdom. He returned to South Africa in 1991, where he did research into community health elements of the country's health system. In 1994, he was the first black South African to be made a professor in the faculty of health sciences at UCT. Baqwa worked on various committees and presented papers at dozens of conferences detailing how South Africa's health system could be improved to serve the majority of its people. When I met him, Baqwa was chair of the Department of Primary Health Care at UCT Medical School and an associate dean. He died suddenly in August 2001.

After receiving his B. Juris. degree from Fort Hare in 1972, **Selby Baqwa** left the university before completing his L.LB. degree. He finally received his L.LB. from UNISA in 1975. Baqwa began his legal career in 1976 as a professional assistant in a Durban firm. In 1978, he opened his own practice, Baqwa & Company, in Durban, specialising in civil and criminal litigation. In 1986, Baqwa became senior partner in another firm: Baqwa, Moloto, Nzimande, Webster and Mbuli. In 1988, he was admitted as an advocate of the Supreme Court of South Africa. In 1993, Baqwa was named assistant general secretary of the National Executive Committee of the National Association of Democratic Lawyers. A year later he was named president of the committee when Pius Langa was named to the Constitutional Court. Baqwa achieved notoriety for his investigation as part of the Browde Commission of irregular promotions and corruption in the Ciskei and Transkei governments prior to the 1994 transition. He taught in the University of Natal Mercantile Law Department and at the university's School for Legal Practice. In 1995, Baqwa was named National Public Protector of South Africa. In that position, he earned praise for his hard-hitting report on the Sarafina 2 disaster in 1996. When we met, Baqwa was still making headlines as the nation's public protector. In 2002, he joined the corporate governance group at Nedcor.

Devi Bughwan graduated from Fort Hare in 1944 and began a long career as an educator. She taught at a grade school, a high school and a teacher training college. In 1952, she was awarded an MA from the non-European section of the University of Natal. Bughwan continued to work and study part time while raising three children and she ultimately obtained a Ph.D. her dissertation was on Indians and the English language. She says, 'I as an Indian learned to speak English. When it came to research, this is what I wanted to do. What are we doing with this language? How come we are saddled with it?' After receiving her Ph.D., Bughwan worked at the University of Durban-Westville, where she was the second woman professor to join the staff. She was the first Indian woman professor of English on the entire continent. Bughwan was professor of English for 11 years and then professor of Drama for 10 years. She also taught at the University of Natal.

After his expulsion from Fort Hare in 1950 following the boycott of the governor-general's campus visit, **Mangosuthu Buthelezi** wrote his examinations at the University of Natal and graduated from Fort Hare. He served as a clerk in the Department of Bantu Administration for a year before resigning to work for a Durban law firm. In 1953, at the urging of Albert Luthuli, among others, he returned to his place of birth, Mahlabathini, to take up the position of chief of the Buthelezis. In 1970, when the KwaZulu Territorial Authority was established, Buthelezi was named its chief executive officer. In 1972, he was made head of the KwaZulu Legislative Assembly and in 1976, he was appointed chief minister of KwaZulu, a position he held until 1994. He emerged as the most outspoken Bantustan leader, arguing that fighting apartheid from within the system was the best way to defeat it. He supported federalism and encouraged foreign investment in South Africa on the grounds that it created jobs for Africans.

In 1975, Buthelezi founded Inkatha yeNkululeko yeSizwe, a black liberation movement that advocated non-violence. During a meeting with the exile leadership of the ANC in London in 1979 he broke all ties with the organisation, refusing to accede to its use of the armed struggle. Though Buthelezi worked for the release of Nelson Mandela from prison, from the 1980s Inkatha was involved in a virtual civil war with the United Democratic Front in KwaZulu-Natal. This developed into a conflict between Inkatha and the ANC in the early 1990s, resulting in the loss of as many as 10,000 lives. In 1991, Inkatha was converted into a political party named the Inkatha Freedom Party. Buthelezi was elected its leader. Having rejected the interim constitution negotiated at the World Trade Centre in 1993 because of its opposition to federalism, Buthelezi threatened to boycott the April 1994 election. At the last minute, he was persuaded to participate and his party won 10 per cent of the vote, including control of KwaZulu-Natal. After the 1994 election, he became minister of Home Affairs in the Government of National Unity, a position he held until a dispute with President Thabo Mbeki boiled over in 2004. He remains a member of Parliament.

Ismail Dada graduated from Fort Hare in 1961 and was immediately accepted into the University of Natal Medical School. He received his medical degree and has a private practice in Durban.

After graduating from Fort Hare in 1964, **Ntombi Dwane** taught in King William's Town and at her alma mater, Cicirha, in the Transkei. She married Sigqibo Dwane in 1967 and they moved to London, where he studied. Upon returning to South Africa, Dwane taught at Lovedale in Alice, and at Jabavu Secondary School, located adjacent to the Fort Hare campus. In 1978, she returned to London, where her husband was studying for his Ph.D., and earned a BA Honours degree from the University of London. Back in South Africa, Dwane became principal of Nombulelo Secondary School in the Grahamstown township Joza. When we met, she was a senior official in the Western Cape Department of Education. She was killed, along with her husband, Sigqibo, in a car accident in July 2006.

After graduating from Fort Hare, **Sigqibo Dwane** remained in Alice to study at Fedsem. After two years at Fedsem, he went to London to study. He returned to South Africa in the middle of 1973 and was appointed lecturer at Fedsem. He also served as Anglican chaplain to the students at Fort Hare and was involved in the fight against the expropriation of the seminary. In 1978, he returned to London to study for his Ph.D. Back in South Africa, he became president of the South African Council of Churches, serving from 1995 to 1998. When we met, he was bishop of the Ethiopian Episcopal Church. Shortly after he retired, he was killed, along with his wife, Ntombi, in a car accident in July 2006.

After graduating from Fort Hare in 1959, **V.R. Govender** went on to lead an almost 40-year career as an educator in Natal. He worked as a teacher, principal and chief inspector of schools before moving on to head Natal's Department of Education. When we met, he was recently retired from his post as regional director of education in KwaZulu-Natal. He died of a heart attack around 2006.

Upon graduating from Fort Hare in 1949, **Herby Govinden** wanted to pursue a career in medicine. He says, 'I finally never did [medicine] because of lack of finances ... I decided to ... get into teaching.' But before beginning his career, Govinden took an historic detour. On the advice of Professor A.S. Galloway, he enrolled at Rhodes University to do an honours degree in chemistry. He says, '[n]ow that was unheard of in that time. We stopped with simply a degree and teaching certificate ... I was quite possibly the first person to go there for post-graduate chemistry.' Govinden, who was not allowed to stay in the hostels, lived with an Indian student in Grahamstown. After completing his honours, he received a scholarship to do an M.Sc. He says, 'I didn't complete my M.Sc. because my supervisor thought I had enough to get a Ph.D., which I did. So I finally got my Ph.D. in physical chemistry.' He was the first Indian student to obtain a Ph.D. in Chemistry at Rhodes. Govinden applied for a job with an oil firm in Durban, but was turned down because there were no toilet facilities for 'non-whites'. He worked in a technical laboratory at Fort Hare for six months before starting a job as a research chemist with a Swedish firm in Durban. He was there for about 21 months when Galloway offered him a junior lectureship in chemistry at Fort Hare. Govinden began teaching at Fort Hare in 1959, after a six-month delay due to permit problems.

While lecturing, he joined the NEUM and played an important role as a staff member sympathetic to students in the wake of the takeover. Govinder was then promoted to senior lecturer. In 1963, he received a post-doctoral fellowship in Canada and left the university. While in Canada, he received a letter from the rector of Fort Hare that said he no longer had a position at the university because an Indian university had opened in Durban. Upon returning to South Africa, with his position at Fort Hare taken away, Govinden began teaching at the University of Durban-Westville. When we met, he was retired and living in Durban.

After receiving his U.E.D. from Fort Hare in 1963, **Isaac Mabindisa** taught English and social studies at Kwazakele Secondary School in Port Elizabeth for two years. While teaching, he was also involved in underground organising for the ANC, which had been banned in 1960. In 1964, he was arrested and charged with membership of a banned organisation. He went into exile in Zambia, where he continued to work as a teacher. Mabindisa then moved to Canada, where he lived for more than 20 years. He obtained an M.Ed. at the University of Manitoba in 1977 and a Ph.D. from the University of Alberta in 1984. He returned to South Africa in 1990, when Mandela was released from prison. When we met, he was the registrar at Fort Hare, a post he relinquished in the face of adversity in 1999. Afterwards, he took a job in his hometown of Port Alfred as community projects executive for the Educational Institute for Service Studies, an outpost of a Dutch hospitality school.

Stanley Mabizela received his U.E.D. from Fort Hare in 1961, but because of Bantu Education, never put his teaching degree to use in South Africa. 'My conscience would not allow me to go and be a teacher where I was going to destroy my own people,' he says. 'So I never taught in South Africa.' Mabizela found work as a lorry driver in Port Elizabeth and later served articles in a law firm. Mabizela's law career was short-lived because early in 1963, he was arrested and charged with membership of a banned organisation. He was sentenced to one year in prison, which he served in East London. Mabizela would have spent more time in prison, but a technical error resulted in his release and he wasted no time in going into exile.

Mabizela was in exile for 24 years and became active in ANC structures abroad. He moved from Swaziland to Tanzania, where he headed the ANC exile operation, to Zimbabwe, and finally to Zambia. During his time in exile, Mabizela was elected to the National Executive Committee of the ANC. He returned to South Africa in 1990 and in 1991 lost his seat in the National Executive. Following the elections in 1994, Mabizela was nominated for Parliament, but he declined to serve. He travelled to the United Kingdom and the United States, where he was trained in diplomacy and administration and was named high commissioner to Namibia by Mandela. He served as spokesman for international affairs for the ANC and worked closely with President Thabo Mbeki, who was then head of International Affairs. When we met, Mabizela was recently retired from his position in Namibia. He died in April 2003.

After receiving his BA from Fort Hare in 1938, **Sipo Makalima** studied towards an MA in history. But, as he explains, 'the committee that was testing me, my dissertation, said the dissertation is alright, but we don't agree with your standpoint … In my thesis I brought in new attitudes which were not accepted by the missionary historians then.' Finding fault with his emphasis on stolen land as the main reason for conflict between white and black people in the Eastern Cape, the committee did not accept Makalima's dissertation. It was not until 1947 that he received credit for the work, but then, he received a BA honours degree and not an MA. Makalima taught briefly in the Transvaal and then returned to Alice, assuming a post at Lovedale. He taught in the secondary school for 33 years. During that period, Makalima studied towards his Bachelor of Education degree, receiving it in 1960. He was also active in the Cape African Teachers' Association and then the Cape African Teachers' Union. In 1973, he left Lovedale for Fort Hare, where he trained teachers and taught history for 19 years. In 1982, he received an honorary doctorate from Fort Hare. I found him at home in Alice, retired, but still a keen observer of events at Fort Hare. He died in 2002.

Henry Makgothi taught for a year after graduating from Fort Hare in 1951. He was dismissed in 1952 for participating in the Defiance Campaign. He briefly took up law, but did not finish his studies. In 1953, Makgothi attended the Bucharest World Youth Festival, and in 1954, he was elected president of the YL in the Transvaal. He was a defendant in the Treason Trial until released due to illness in 1958. With the ANC banned in 1960, he tried to leave South Africa, but was arrested and imprisoned on Robben Island for eight years. He was released in the early 1970s and restricted to Mabopane outside Pretoria for two years. Makgothi fled to Botswana in 1977, where he was co-opted onto the ANC National Executive Committee (NEC). He was elected to the NEC at the Kabwe Conference of 1985. For the majority of the 1980s, Makgothi was secretary of Education of the ANC with oversight of the Solomon Mahlangu Freedom College (SOMAFCO) in Tanzania. In 1987, he attended a three-month course at the Lenin School in Moscow. A year later, he became assistant secretary general of the ANC under fellow Fort Harian Alfred Nzo. Makgothi was also a member of the central committee of the SACP. He returned to South Africa in 1990 and was chief whip of the ANC in the National Council of Provinces from 1994 to 1999. He was a founding director of Chancellor House Holdings, the ANC's investment firm. He also helped start Zonkizizwe Investments, a private investment firm, where he is a director.

After graduating from Fort Hare in 1958, **Ambrose Makiwane** went to Port Elizabeth to serve legal articles. 'The government there expelled me from PE. And I went to East London. The same thing happened.' Hampered by banning, Makiwane could not pursue his legal studies. 'And meantime [Kaiser] Matanzima was attempting to get the government to keep me in my father's farm. But he didn't have any power. He tried to use Chief Sabata, who was then the paramount chief of Thembuland. And Chief Sabata refused. In fact, he quickly sent a letter to my father to tell me that there was this move by Matanzima. So I could hardly work because they were following me everywhere.' Makiwane went into exile, where he was commander of the Kongwa training camp in Tanzania. He then worked for nearly 10 years for the ANC in Cairo.

In 1969, he was suspended from the NEC of the ANC for six months due to dissident activity. He was also expelled from the SACP. Upset by the SACP role in the 1969 Morogoro Conference that opened the ANC membership to non-Africans, Makiwane and a group of seven others moved increasingly towards African nationalism. In 1975, at the unveiling of the tombstone of veteran ANC leader Robert Resha in London, Makiwane made a speech that labeled the Morogoro conference as 'disastrous'. In September 1975, the eight were called 'traitors' and expelled from the ANC by the NEC. Makiwane rejoined the ANC in 1986 after the declaration of an amnesty for those who had been expelled. When we met, he was semi-retired, living in his hometown, Cala. 'I'm very busy,' he repeatedly told me, tending to cows and working for the ANC in places like Elliot and Cala in the Transkei. Makiwane died in 2004.

After graduating from Fort Hare with honours in 1959, **Andrew Masondo** began working as an applied mathematics lecturer at the university the next year. At the same time, he was a rural area organiser for the ANC under the direction of Govan Mbeki. Against Mbeki's wishes, Masondo also became commander of MK in the Eastern Cape when it was founded. In 1963, after sabotaging pylons in the vicinity of Fort Hare, Masondo was arrested and sentenced to 12 years on Robben Island. Another year was added to Masondo's term and he ended up serving 13 years. 'I was among the first 10 MK people on Robben Island,' he says. 'I actually developed the ANC structures on Robben Island.' Masondo was tortured and beaten in prison and was finally released in 1976. He was banished to Umlazi, where he stayed for three months. Masondo left the country following the Soweto uprising. 'The MK chaps came to fetch me. Because the old man Oliver [Tambo] thought that I might, in fact he was right because I was already in touch with the underground and he saw that I was going to be arrested. So they collected me and I went outside.'

Masondo joined the ANC leadership in exile. 'I went to Tanzania. From Tanzania I went to the Soviet Union to do my military training. When I completed my military training, then I went to Angola.' Masondo served as the national political commissar of the ANC from 1977 to 1985 and from 1991 to 1994. It was in this capacity that he was responsible for abuses of suspected informers in ANC camps abroad, notably the Morris Seabelo Rehabilitation Centre in Angola, known also as Quatro. Upon returning to South Africa, he appeared before the Truth and Reconciliation Commission to apply for amnesty. When we met, Masondo was chief of Defence Corporate Communication for the South African Defence Force, in charge of integrating the military. He held the position until retiring in 2001. A traditional healer by training, Masondo also contributed to studies on diseases such as HIV/AIDS and tuberculosis. He died in 2008.

George Matanzima went to Fort Hare with the intention of becoming a doctor. However, he quickly changed courses after watching a doctor perform an autopsy following a fight in a township. 'I was there when I saw a doctor opening up a human being,' he says. 'I said "no, this is not for me".' After graduating from Fort Hare, Matanzima taught geography at Lovedale for one year. He then served articles in Engcobo and, after returning to teaching for two years, began to practise as an attorney in 1952. He interrupted his legal practice in 1959 to 1960 when he acted as chief of the Emigrant Thembus. His brother Kaiser Matanzima says, 'my subjects went to him for advice in everything. He was a leader of his people in everything.' According to Wycliffe Tsotsi, George Matanzima joined the Unity Movement, frequenting meetings in the Umtata area. Matanzima says he was 'only an observer'.

In June 1963, Matanzima was struck from the roll of attorneys for misappropriating trust funds and making a false statement before the Eastern Cape division of the Supreme Court. When Kaiser was named chief minister of the Transkei in 1963, Matanzima entered the assembly as an elected member for Emigrant Thembuland. From 1971 to 1978, he was minister of justice in the Transkei. During the early days of independence, he was hostile towards the ANC and PAC despite his brother's more open stance. In 1977, he was awarded the title of deputy prime minister of the Transkei; a year later he added the title of minister of defence. In 1979, when his brother became president of the Transkei, George Matanzima automatically became prime minister after being elected head of the ruling party.

In May 1987, as a result of a power struggle with his brother, George Matanzima banished Kaiser Matanzima to his home district of Qamata. In September, George Matanzima was ousted from office in a military coup led by Major-General Bantu Holomisa, who installed Stella Sigcau as president. Three months later, Holomisa unsuccessfully conspired with his brother and Charles Sebe in an attempt to oust Lennox Sebe. In August 1988, charging that he had pocketed large sums of money, the Holomisa government issued a warrant of arrest for embezzlement on George Matanzima. Matanzima fled to Port Elizabeth and disappeared. He resurfaced in Austria before returning to South Africa penniless. He was extradited from South Africa to Transkei and in 1989 was convicted on three counts of bribery and sentenced to nine years in prison. He was released in December 1991 and died in 2000.

Kaiser Matanzima graduated from Fort Hare in 1939 and began legal studies in 1940. His articles were interrupted when he was appointed to succeed his father as chief of the AmaHalas. In 1942, the South African government appointed him to the Bunga, the historic Transkei representative council. He resigned from that body in 1944 to resume his articles and in 1948, qualified as an attorney. In 1955, after the Bantu Authorities Act passed, Matanzima returned to the Bunga. He was installed as regional chief of Emigrant Thembuland in 1958, a controversial appointment as it was opposed by Paramount Chief Sabata Dalindyebo. However, Matanzima accepted the government's separate development policies and continued to rise through its structures.

In 1961, he became chairman of the Transkeian Territorial Authority, and in 1963, he was elected chief minister, having received the support of the majority of government-appointed chiefs despite losing the popular vote. In 1966, contrary to tradition, the government named him paramount chief. In March 1974, his party voted to move towards independence. Later that year, he obtained an honorary doctorate from government-controlled Fort Hare. Leading up the pre-independence election, Matanzima increased repression of dissident voices. In 1976, following the death of Chief Botha Sigcau, Matanzima became president of the Transkei. His brother George was prime minister. The Transkei government banned 34 organisations, including the ANC. When we met in 1999, Matanzima, then 83, was at home in Qamata, suffering from an inability to remember many of the details of his life. He died in June 2003.

Ivy Matsepe-Casaburri went into exile shortly after leaving Fort Hare in 1961. After a period in Swaziland, she travelled to the United States, where she received an MA and Ph.D. from Rutgers University in New Jersey. She taught and worked for the United Nations Institute for Namibia in Lusaka, Zambia until her return to South Africa in 1990. She formalised links with the ANC Women's League and participated in defining the ANC's position on gender issues. In 1993, she became the first black person and first woman to head the South African Broadcasting Corporation Board. When we met, Matsepe-Casaburri was serving as the first woman premier of the Free State. In June 1999, she was appointed to Thabo Mbeki's cabinet as minister of Communications. She died in 2009.

After graduating from Fort Hare, **Joe Matthews** taught briefly at Newell High School in Port Elizabeth before moving to Johannesburg to study law at Wits. In 1952, he abandoned his studies and, as national secretary of the YL, returned to the Eastern Cape to participate in the Defiance Campaign. In September 1953, he was served with banning orders and forced to undertake political work underground. While banned from 1954 to 1956, he completed his L.LB. degree via correspondence through the University of London. He then completed articles in 1958 in Port Elizabeth. Matthews joined the SACP in 1957 and served on its central committee from 1962 to 1970. The Treason Trial interrupted his legal career, as he and his father were among the 156 defendants. Matthews practised law in Durban until 1960. Following Sharpeville, he was arrested and imprisoned without trial. He was released and escaped into Basutoland (now Lesotho), where he became involved in local politics and worked as a lawyer until 1965.

He moved to London, where he served as editor of *Sechaba*, completed an MA in History at the University of London in 1968, and was an ANC representative. After 1970, he moved to Botswana and gave up his active involvement in the ANC. He became secretary in the offices of Prime Minister Seretse Khama, an ex-Lovedale student. He was assistant attorney general of Botswana from 1972 to 1976 and then opened a private practice, where he worked until returned to the UK in 1984. He was expelled from the Central Committee of the SACP in 1976 after he rejected the armed struggle and expressed doubts about communism in an interview given to the Johannesburg *Sunday Times*. In the late 1980s, he lived in Canada and the Netherlands, where he wrote articles for journals and engaged in academic work.

Matthews returned to South African in 1991, still an ANC member after 30 years in exile, and settled in Durban. He renewed contact with his Fort Hare classmate and friend of more than 40 years, Mangosuthu Buthelezi, and in 1992 was appointed chief executive officer of the IFP. In the April 1994 general election, he was elected to Parliament. In May of that year, he was named deputy minister of Safety and Security, a position he held until retiring in 2004.

After finishing at Fort Hare in 1937, **Govan Mbeki** taught at various schools, including Clarkebury and Adams College, but was eventually dismissed for his political activity. He then opened a cooperative store in Idutywa. In 1939, he published his first essays in book form, *The Transkei in the Making*. In 1940, he earned a B.Econ. degree in social studies by private study through UNISA. He was editor of *Territorial Magazine*, later renamed *Inkundla yaBantu*, from 1938 to 1944. In 1941, Mbeki became secretary of the Transkei African Voters' Association, and in 1943, he was elected to the Transkei Bunga, representing Idutywa. He was also a director of the *Guardian* newspaper, until it was banned.

Mbeki had a keen ability to transform the harsh realities of apartheid into the written word. In 1954, he joined the editorial board of *New Age*, serving on the 'Eastern desk' of the paper and opening the eyes of South Africans to the bloody struggles in the countryside. In 1962, *New Age* was banned, along with its successor, *Spark*. Mbeki went underground. He joined the SACP in the 1950s, helping it forge links with the ANC.

Mbeki rose through the ANC structures in the Eastern Cape, emerging as one of the key figures of the underground movement. He was arrested at Rivonia and sentenced to life imprisonment. He was released from prison in November 1987 and immediately continued working with the ANC. He was elected deputy president of the Senate after the 1994 elections. Mbeki died in September 2001 in Port Elizabeth.

Upon completing his U.E.D. in 1953, **Frank Mdlalose** studied medicine at the University of Natal, becoming a doctor in 1958. When the Freedom Charter was adopted in 1955, he opposed it, believing it was more socialist than nationalist in character. He toyed with the idea of joining the PAC when it was founded in 1959, but chose instead to remain in the ANC in an attempt to counter its left wing. Mdlalose did a medical internship in Durban and then, in 1960, opened a private practice in Atteridgeville, outside Pretoria. Following time in Ladysmith, he moved to Madadeni, where he reconnected with Buthelezi, whom he had met at Fort Hare. In 1974, he advised Buthelezi on the founding of a new political organisation and, the next year, participated in a meeting at which the organisation's constitution was discussed. Inkatha yeNkululeko yeSizwe was founded and Mdlalose was soon elected its national chairman. He became chairman of the Madadeni Town Council in 1971 and, in 1978, was elected to the KwaZulu legislative assembly and appointed minister of the Interior. In 1983, he became minister of Health and Welfare, and in 1990 became minister of Education and Culture in KwaZulu.

In the early 1990s, Mdlalose worked with the ANC to try to stop the violence between ANC and IFP supporters in the Transvaal and Natal. In March 1991, he was relieved of his portfolios to enable him to focus on his position as national chairman of Inkatha and stopping the violence. In December 1991, Mdlalose headed the IFP delegation at the Convention for a Democratic South Africa. In 1993, he served on the 10-person planning committee of the Concerned South Africans' Group and became co-leader of the IFP's delegation at the constitutional talks at Kempton Park, until the IFP withdrew from the meetings. After Buthelezi decided the IFP would participate in the elections, Mdlalose stood as the leader of the IFP's list for the KwaZulu-Natal Legislative Assembly. In May 1994, he was elected premier of the province. When we met, he was South African ambassador to Egypt. He retired from the IFP in 2005.

After graduating from Fort Hare, **Marumo Moerane** studied at the University of Natal, where he was a member of the underground PAC. He received a Bachelor of Commerce degree in 1967 and a Bachelor of Laws in 1969 before embarking on a successful legal career. He is currently an advocate in Durban and is often mentioned as a prospective member of the South African Constitutional Court. He also serves as deputy chairman of the Competition Commission. Moerane has worked on many high-profile cases, including representing his first cousin, Thabo Mbeki, in the Jacob Zuma corruption probe.

Thenjiwe Mtintso was expelled from Fort Hare following student protest in 1973. She immediately began to travel around the country, meeting with parents to explain the causes of the unrest. Having joined SASO at Fort Hare, she moved to King William's Town and became involved with the Black People's Convention. She worked for a political prisoner support group and helped found the Zimele Trust Fund, a self-employment programme for ex-political prisoners and detainees. In King William's Town, she also came into regular contact with Steve Biko, who had a major influence on her political growth. In 1975, at Biko's suggestion, Donald Woods hired her as a newspaper reporter for the *Daily Dispatch* in East London. Mtintso was arrested in 1976 and following her release, was confined to Orlando East. She spent most of the next two years in detention.

In December 1978, Mtintso left the country with her son, crossing through the Transkei into Lesotho, where she joined the ANC. She became active in the Lesotho Front under the leadership of Chris Hani, editing political publications, leading recruitment drives and handling underground political structures in the Orange Free State and the Cape. She received military training in Angola and East Germany before returning to Lesotho in 1982, where she worked in the political-military structures. After a year of political training in Cuba, Mtintso again returned to Lesotho, where she worked in the ANC military command until 1985.

That same year, she became head of the Regional Political Military Council of the Botswana Front, the first woman to head a front. In 1989, she was transferred to Uganda, where she oversaw the opening of the first ANC mission in Uganda. In Lesotho in 1990, she joined the SACP, before returning to South Africa to participate in an ANC Women's League Conference and to tend to her mother. She enrolled for a BA degree in social work at Wits and was elected in 1991 to the central committee and politburo of the SACP. Mtintso was part of the SACP negotiating team at the Codesa. In 1994, she was elected to Parliament as an ANC member. When we met, she was on the SACP executive committee and was deputy secretary-general of the ANC, a position she held from 1997 to 2002. She was appointed South Africa's ambassador to Cuba in 2003.

Logan Naidoo was an educator and activist in Natal following graduation from Fort Hare.

G.C. Oosthuizen left Fort Hare for a post at the University of Durban-Westville in 1968, where he was appointed dean of the faculty of Divinity. He was instrumental in founding a Department of Comparative Religions. Over the years, the department grew from three students to more than 400. Oosthuizen resigned in 1984 to concentrate on work with the African independent churches. He worked part-time, from home, for the University of Zululand and when we met, he was semi-retired, but still involved with research on the African independent churches.

After graduating in 1954, **R.A. Pillay** remained at Fort Hare as a junior lecturer in chemistry. He was forced to resign in 1955 because, as an Indian, he needed a permit to travel to the Cape and the government would not provide him with the document. Pillay returned to Durban, where he taught for two years to fulfill the teaching requirement of his bursary to Fort Hare and to earn money to pay for medical school. He attended the University of Natal Medical School and taught in the evenings at M.L. Sultan Technikon. Pillay quit his teaching job in the wake of the introduction of university apartheid and started a job as a medical researcher at Natal. After qualifying as a medical doctor, Pillay opened a general practice, which he kept for seven years, before returning to medical school for further study. He then opened a specialty practice and taught medicine.

Barney Pityana never graduated from Fort Hare. He was expelled following the student unrest in 1968. As regional director of the UCM, Pityana spent most of the early months of 1969 traveling around the country meeting students on college campuses. In July 1969, with energy and enthusiasm on bush college campuses growing, SASO was formed. In 1970, Pityana became SASO's second president, replacing Biko. In 1973, Pityana was banned to Port Elizabeth as part of the government's crackdown on SASO. He later completed his BA (English, Political Science and Private Law) and B.Proc. degrees at UNISA in 1975 and 1976 respectively. He served as a candidate attorney in Port Elizabeth, but was barred from legal practice by the apartheid government.

In 1978, after years of bannings and a year in detention, he went into exile with his wife and daughter in Lesotho. Pityana then fled to Botswana. He spent 16 years in exile in the United Kingdom and Geneva, Switzerland. An ordained priest and qualified attorney, Pityana worked in Geneva for the World Council of Churches' Programme to Combat Racism. He returned to South Africa in 1992. In 1995, he received a Ph.D. in Religious Studies from UCT. That same year, he was appointed to chair the Human Rights Commission, a position he held when we met. In 2001, he was named vice-chancellor and principal of UNISA.

Upon graduating from Fort Hare in 1970, **Churchill Sizwe Satyo** began teaching at Lovedale. He then continued to pursue his interest in African languages, writing books on Xhosa grammar such as *Ingrama noncwadi* and *Iwesixhosa*, both of which are widely used in the South African educational system. When we met, he was head of the Department of Linguistics and Southern African Languages at UCT.

After receiving his BA from Fort Hare in 1971, **Makhenkesi Stofile** continued at the university, studying towards a theology degree, which he received in 1974. He completed B.Th. Honours in 1975 and his BA Honours in 1977. From 1975, Stofile served as a minister in the Presbyterian Church of South Africa. In 1977, Fort Hare awarded him an MA in Theology. From 1973 to 1979,

Stofile worked as a senior lecturer in Theology and Philosophy of Religion at Fort Hare. In 1981, he completed his post-graduate Diploma in Philosophy at Tubingen University in Germany, and in 1983, he received an MA from Princeton University in the United States. He then returned to Fort Hare, where he continued to lecture. From 1969, Stofile had been involved in sports administration and he rose to national prominence in 1985 when, as general secretary of the Border region of the UDF, he was sent to New Zealand to campaign against the proposed Kiwi rugby tour of South Africa. In 1968, while lecturing at Fort Hare, he was detained by Ciskei security police during protests surrounding recognition of a trade union on campus. He was again detained by the Ciskei security police in October 1986.

In March 1987, he became the first UDF member to be associated with the armed struggle, and was charged with terrorism, possession of arms and harbouring terrorists. After a controversial trial, Stofile received an 11-year sentence on the main count of promoting the activities of the ANC. He was also served a one-year sentence to run concurrently for possessing a Soviet-made pistol and ammunition. He resigned from Fort Hare, saying: 'It was impossible to be there and in prison.' In December 1989, the Ciskei government released him on humanitarian grounds. A month after his release, he was active in the campaign against an English cricket tour of South Africa.

Following the release of Mandela and the unbanning of the ANC, Stofile helped the ANC set up structures within South Africa. Later that year, he was elected chairman of the Border region of the ANC. He held that post until he became a senior lecturer in the Religious Studies department at the University of Transkei in 1991. From 1992 to 1994, Stofile was director of public relations and development at Fort Hare. In the 1994 election, Stofile was elected as a member of Parliament and was then appointed chief whip of the ANC. Considered a favourite of Mandela, he was late that year elected the organisation's treasurer-general. When we met, Stofile was premier of the Eastern Cape. He was appointed minister of Sport and Recreation in 2004.

After graduating from Fort Hare in 1948, **Rama Thumbadoo** went on to a long career as a teacher in Durban, first at his alma mater, Sastri College, and then at Springfield College, where he was joined on the staff by many Fort Harians. When we met, Thumbadoo was retired and living in Durban, reading and listening to music.

After graduating from Fort Hare, **G.S. Tootla** went to Wits Medical School, where he qualified as a dentist. When we met, he ran a private practice in

Durban. In addition to his practice, he founded an institution for youth in Changa, outside Durban.

After graduating from Fort Hare in 1935, **Wycliffe Tsotsi** worked as a teacher and lawyer in Lady Frere. He became involved with the AAC and was instrumental in bringing the Cape African Teachers' Association into the AAC in the 1940s. In 1948, he was elected to replace D.D.T. Jabavu as president of the AAC. In the early 1960s, he moved his law practice to Basutoland, but left in 1966 when it gained independence. He moved to Zambia, where he worked as a lawyer for the Zambian government. When we met, Tsotsi was a lawyer for the Truth and Reconciliation Commission. He died in 2005.

Note

1   These updates come from the author's interviews and secondary sources listed in the bibliography, including *Who's Who in South Africa, Volume 5* and *From Protest to Challenge, Volume 4.*

Fort Hare/South Africa Chronology

1892: Cape Franchise and Ballot Act raises property qualifications for voting.

1901: H. Isaiah Bud-Mbelle, a leader of Kimberley's Mfengu community, proposes the Queen Victoria Memorial fund-raising campaign to establish a university for Africans.

1903–1905: Following the decision of the Native Affairs Commission to support an African college, the Inter-State Native College Scheme quickly and powerfully overshadows the more radical Queen Victoria Memorial programme.

1905: Planning begins in King William's Town for developing a tertiary education institute for Africans.

1906: The Bambatha Rebellion is brutally crushed in Natal.

1912: South African Native National Congress formed, with J.L. Dube as its first president.

1913: Natives Land Act is passed, making it illegal for Africans to own or rent land outside designated reserves. The act set aside just 7 per cent of the country's land for Africans.

February 1916: Prime Minister General Louis Botha officially opens the South African Native College with Alexander Kerr as its first principal. Kerr and D.D.T. Jabavu are Fort Hare's first lecturers.

1919: Industrial and Commercial Workers' Union formed.

1916–1923: As the South African Native College, Fort Hare is engaged in secondary school work, preparing students for the matriculation examination.

1923: Fort Hare is incorporated as a declared institution for higher education under the Higher Education Act of 1923.

25 January 1924: Z.K. Matthews becomes the first African to qualify for the degree of Bachelor of Arts of the University of South Africa.

1933: Edward Roux arrives at Fort Hare with his donkey and pitches a tent on Sandile's Kop. He subsequently offers political education to the students, influencing such people as Govan Mbeki.

1935: Professor D.D.T. Jabavu founds the All African Convention to protest the attack on the African franchise.

1936: Representation of Natives Act removes Africans from Cape voters' roll.

1936: Z.K. Matthews is appointed lecturer in anthropology and Bantu law and administration.

1939–1945: The Second World War provides the spark for many campus debates and has a powerful effect on politicising the student body.

16 March 1940: Kaiser Matanzima is awarded the degree of Bachelor of Arts in Politics and Roman Law.

1941: Nelson Mandela leaves Fort Hare on principle after a disagreement with Principal Kerr over his serving on the Students' Representative Council. Oliver Tambo is awarded the Bachelor of Science degree.

1942: Residents of the Anglican Hostel, Beda Hall, protest against the university rule of prohibiting sporting activities on Sundays. The Beda Hall Tennis Court Dispute, as it came to be known, resulted in the suspension of future ANC president Oliver Tambo.

3 April 1943: Mandela, who completed his degree externally, is awarded a Bachelor of Arts in Native Administration and Politics.

1944: The ANC Youth League is formed and Anton Lembede is elected its first president.

1948: The National Party comes to power with its apartheid platform.

1948: Alexander Kerr retires and Clifford Dent of the Chemistry Department becomes Fort Hare's second principal.

1948: A.P. Mda and Godfrey Pitje meet, and a branch of the ANC Youth League is established at Fort Hare. It is prohibited by the university authorities, but gains prominence nevertheless as the Victoria East Branch.

1948: Mangosuthu Buthelezi begins his studies at Fort Hare and joins the ANC Youth League.

1948: Robert Sobukwe speaks at the Completer's Social on behalf of continuing students, providing the first glimpse of his political acumen.

1949: Sobukwe is elected Students' Representative Council president.

21 October 1949: Sobukwe's speech at the Completer's Social on behalf of graduating students urges Fort Harians to build a new Africa. 'Only we can build it,' he says.

1950: Z.K. Matthews is elected vice-chairman of Senate, Fort Hare.

1950: Among others, Joseph Matthews and Buthelezi participate in a boycott of the visit of governor-general and his wife to campus, charging that he is 'a living embodiment of British Imperialism'.

1950: Buthelezi is expelled from Fort Hare for pouring water on the bed of W.M. Chirwa, who, despite advocating a student boycott of Governor General van Zyl's visit to campus, attended the meeting anyway. Despite his expulsion, Buthelezi, in a letter to Principal Clifford Dent, refuses to regret his actions.

1951: The constituent colleges of UNISA are granted autonomy and under the Rhodes University (Private) Act of 1949, Fort Hare affiliates to Rhodes and its name changes to the University College of Fort Hare.

1951: Robert Mugabe is awarded a Bachelor of Arts degree.

1952: The Fort Hare student body votes to disaffiliate from the National Union of South African Students.

1952: Fort Hare students, led by ANC Youth League leader Frank Mdlalose, participate in the nationwide Defiance Campaign by ignoring curfew laws and sitting on benches in Alice reserved for Whites. After arrests, Mdlalose leads a delegation to the magistrate's court, singing freedom songs. The group is attacked by police, who had been called in from King William's Town.

1955: Universities Act No 61 includes Fort Hare among the universities of South Africa.

1955: The South African government begins to look into the feasibility of separate university facilities for blacks.

1955: The Freedom Charter is adopted by the Congress of the People.

2 May 1955: The entire Students' Representative Council resigns, charging the university senate with ignoring them.

1955: Fort Hare is temporarily closed down after the students boycott the graduation ceremonies. The Duminy Commission is appointed by the Department of Education to look into the governing of the university.

December 1955: Z.K. Matthews is chosen as acting principal of Fort Hare.

1956: The Treason Trial begins of 156 defendants, including many Fort Harians.

1958: With Matthews on trial for treason, H.R. Burrows is appointed Fort Hare's fourth principal.

1958: Students' Representative Council President Ambrose Makiwane leads a protest against the proposed Extension of University Education Bill. More than 300 staff members, students, and Alice community members march through the streets of Alice.

18 August 1958: The Extension of University Education Bill is passed, providing for the 'establishment, management and control of university colleges for non-white persons; for the admission of students to and their instruction at university colleges; for the limitation of the admission of non-white students to certain university institutions; and for other incidental matters'.

1959: Sobukwe founds the Pan Africanist Congress.

1959: The Fort Hare Transfer Act, Act No 64 of 1959, is passed, providing for the transfer to the apartheid government of the university, once a constituent college of UNISA and subsequently an affiliate of Rhodes University.

1959: Seven staff members resign before 23 September. After that date, Z.K. Matthews resigns his post and forfeits his entire pension three months before his intended retirement, in protest against the assumption of control of the university by the Department of Bantu Education. Others soon follow. By the end of 1959, three out of every four staff members have either resigned or been fired.

28 October 1959: Plaque is unveiled marking the death of Fort Hare, reading: 'The University College of Fort Hare, in deep gratitude to all who between 1905 and 1959 founded, maintained and administered this college at Fort Hare and in remembrance of all who between 1916 and 1959 taught and studied here in association with the University of South Africa and Rhodes University'.

1959: A delegation of academics, who were due to assume control of the university after the transfer, visit Fort Hare. The students unleash a barrage of tomatoes on the incoming registrar.

1 January 1960: The government takes control of Fort Hare after making arrangements to do so from 1955 to 1959, placing it in the hands of the Department of Bantu Education. Fort Hare becomes a government institution with two senates: one made up of whites; and an advisory one constituted of black staff. Professor J.J. Ross is the first government-appointed rector.

1960: Police kill 69 at Sharpeville; Sobukwe is sentenced to three years in prison; Tambo leaves the country to set up an ANC mission in exile; a state of emergency is declared; the ANC and PAC are banned.

1961: Stanley Mabizela is suspended for badmouthing Kaiser Matanzima after Matanzima overhears him saying, '*Kuzele apha ziinyhwagi,*' and '*Nantsi le nyhwagi uMatanzima*'. At the time, Matanizima was a member of the all-black Fort Hare advisory council, which the students felt was useless and made up of sell-outs. Following protests by students and black staff, Mabizela is reinstated. As it turns out, Mabizela was not the student that directed the harsh words towards Matanzima, but he took the rap, refusing to 'sell out' his fellow student.

1961: Chris Hani is involved in protesting against the creation of a republic. The underground ANC calls for a three-day stay-away.

1961: ANC adopts armed struggle and *Umkhonto we Sizwe* is formed, with Mandela as chief of staff.

1968: Professor Johannes Marthinus de Wet, a member of the Broederbond, is appointed principal after Professor J.J. Ross retires. The students boycott his installation ceremony, beginning a rocky relationship with the new rector that culminates in the closure of the university later in the year. Among 23 others, Barney Pityana and Kenneth Rachidi are not allowed to come back.

1969: South African Students' Organisation formed by Bantu Steve Biko.

1970: Fort Hare is granted autonomy, relinquishing its relationship with UNISA. Students now obtain Fort Hare degrees, but are upset over what they perceive as the 'ghettoisation' of black education and vehemently protest this change. Once autonomy is granted, students continue to wear UNISA robes to graduation.

1971: Supporting the principles of the 1959 Students' Representative Council boycott, but believing the students need an effective organisational body, a delegation of 23 students led by, among others, Jeff Baqwa, begins to campaign for the reintroduction of an Students' Representative Council. In early 1972, a mass meeting of students supports the proposition wholeheartedly. However, De Wet refuses to accept the motion, charging that the meeting did not adhere to official regulations.

1972: As students prepare to strike in protest against the university's refusal to recognise a Students' Representative Council, O.R.Tiro is expelled from the University of the North at Turfloop for giving a speech deemed inappropriate by the university. A sympathy strike breaks out at Fort Hare as campus unrest coincides with a 'national revolutionary upsurge' sparked by SASO.

1973: In a continuance of the unrest of 1972, a student strike is sparked after the suspension of a student for breaking the notorious 'Hogsback Rule', which limits contact between men and women. The strike escalates and the police are called onto campus.

1974: Worried that the Federal Theological Seminary, located on Fort Hare's present-day East Campus, is being run by 'communists' and that it is having a negative impact on students, Fort Hare expropriates the seminary's land, resulting in its closure.

1976: Following the Soweto uprising, Fort Hare goes on extended holiday, reopening in October.

21 March 1980: Students stay away from classes to protest the impending 'independence' of the Ciskei. By May, the university closes down.

1982: Confrontation between students and the Ciskei Security Police follows student protest against the intended presence of Lennox Sebe, chief minister of the Ciskei, at graduation. Unrest continues until the university is shut down.

1986: Fort Hare goes from being a 'bush college' to a Bantustan college, as control is transferred to the Ciskei government; Sebe finally attends graduation as the 'guest of honour'.

1990: Bantu Education ends at Fort Hare. Sibusiso Bengu is appointed the first black principal of the university. Oliver Tambo, the new chancellor, accepts his post and remarks that Fort Hare has been, 'since its birth, a site of epic battles between forces of democracy and those opposed to it'.

1992: Following a bloodless coup, Brigadier Gqoza assumes control of the Ciskei government and sends his troops to Fort Hare to thwart student protest.

1994: Professor Mbulelo Mzamane assumes the rectorship as Professor Bengu takes up the post of education minister.

1996: Fort Hare celebrates its 80th anniversary in style as President Mandela and Miriam Makeba arrive on campus for the festivities.

1997: Fort Hare is closed down for two weeks because of student protest over fees.

1999: Independent assessor Stuart Saunders issues a report charging Mbulelo Mzamane with misuse of university funds. Students, staff and workers pledge not to return to work until the '3 Ms' are removed from office. On 25 March, Mzamane, along with his deputy, Professor Maqashalala, and the university registrar, Isaac Mabindisa, are asked by the council to take six months' paid leave. An interim management team is set up, led by acting vice chancellor Professor Derrick Swartz.

2000: The university launches a strategic plan for transformation and repositioning. Underlying the plan is a universal commitment to make the university worthy of its rich inheritance.

2008: Dr Mvuyo Tom, a former student, takes over as vice-chancellor of Fort Hare. In his inaugural address, he says: 'If we forget the history we have been through in this country we are bound to abuse and misuse our freedom.' He lays out a five-year strategic plan to improve curriculum, enhance research, boost student life and ensure financial stability.

Select Bibliography

INTERVIEWS

Thelma Appavoo, 20 May 1999, East London
Jeff Baqwa, 18 April 1999, Cape Town
Selby Baqwa, 15 July 1999, Pretoria
Terence Beard, 30 October 2008, Grahamstown
Devi Bughwan, 27 April 1999, Durban
Mangosuthu Buthelezi, 17 February 1999, Cape Town
Seretse Choabi (conducted by Thomas Karis), 5 April 1989, Lusaka, Zambia
Ismail Dada, 27 April 1999, Durban
Ntombi Dwane, 19 February 1999, Cape Town
Sigqibo Dwane, 20 April 1999, Cape Town
V.R. Govender. 27 April 1999, Durban
Herby Govinden, 27 April 1999, Durban
Isaac Mabindisa, 18 November 1998, Bisho
Stanley Mabizela, 19 April 1999, Cape Town
Sipo Makalima, 26 October 1998, Alice
Sipho Sidney Makana (conducted by Thomas Karis), 13 September 1999, Moscow
Henry Makgothi, 17 February 1999, Cape Town
Ambrose Makiwane, 4 March 1999, Cala
Andrew Masondo, 25 May 1999, Pretoria
George Matanzima, 9 March 1999, Qamata
Kaizer Matanzima, 9 March 1999, Qamata
Ivy Matsepe-Casaburri, 25 February 1999, Bloemfontein
Joe Matthews, 17 February 1999, Cape Town
Govan Mbeki, 19 November 1998, Port Elizabeth
Frank Mdlalose, 25 May 1999, Johannesburg
Marumo Moerane, 28 April 1999, Durban
Thenjiwe Mtintso, 14 July 1999, Johannesburg
Logan Naidoo, 28 April 1999, Durban
William Nkomo (conducted by Thomas Karis), April 1964, Pretoria
G.C. Oosthuizen, 28 April 1999, Durban
R.A. Pillay, 29 April 1999, Durban
Nyameko Barney Pityana, July 1999, Grahamstown
Churchill Sizwe Satyo, 17 February 1999, Cape Town
Makhenkesi Arnold Stofile, 22 March 1999, Bisho

Rama Thumbadoo, 26 April 1999, Durban
G.S. Tootla, 26 April 1999, Durban
Wycliffe Tsotsi, 28 November 1998, Port Elizabeth

ARCHIVAL AND MANUSCRIPT COLLECTIONS

Cory Library, Rhodes University, Grahamstown

- ### Alexander Kerr Papers

PR4123: Thomas Alty: Address to meeting of protest against university bills, 4/4/59
PR4128: Leslie Blackwell: Alice, where art thou? 1/8/58
PR4215: Raymond Burrows: Article on Fort Hare University College, 1959
PR4158: *The College Review* (1st magazine of the South African Native College, April 1916–March 1917
PR4118: Records of the Governing Council, Senate and Committees including minutes, memoranda, financial statements and related papers, 1928–1961
PR4148: Memoranda and notes on the history and development of Fort Hare prepared by Alexander Kerr, H.R. Burrows and others.
PR4145: Records: minutes, memoranda, petitions and related material dealing with the Council and student activities, 1951–1959
PR4119: Letterbooks: letters about the Inter-State Native College Scheme and the establishment of the college
PR4159: Jabavu, Davidson Don Tengo, biographical details
PR4088: Kerr, Alexander, correspondence and related documents generated by Kerr and succeeding principals of Fort Hare: C.P. Dent, Z.K. Matthews and H.R. Burrows
PR4095: Biographical files: curricula vitae, letters of reference, testimonials, press cuttings, obituaries, etc., written or assembled by Kerr
PR4098: Addresses, including opening and graduation addresses delivered by Dr Kerr at Fort Hare University
PR4105: Articles mainly for *South African Outlook* on Fort Hare University, including Kerr's eulogy for Z.K. Matthews.
PR4228: Shingler, John: 'Leave Fort Hare alone – Away with indoctrination.' *Student: The International Student Magazine*, 1959.
PR4204: Teacher's League of South Africa, statement on university apartheid
M(77)g1: Plan of proposed buildings for the Inter State Native College
S(77)g3: United Free Church of Scotland lands
MP1493: Diagrams and explanations of the grant by the United Free Church of Scotland of land to Fort Hare

- ### R.W. Shepherd Papers

- ### Miscellaneous

Cragg, E. Lynn. 'Fort Hare and other memories.' Unpublished memoir.

Howard Pim Library of Rare Books, University of Fort Hare, Alice

Series I

- **Box 10**

Serial 85: South African Students' Organisation (SASO) news, reports, conference communiqué, minutes, correspondence 1969–1971
Serial 86: SASO introduction, newsletters, statement on SASO
Serial 87: SASO 3rd General Council

- **Box 12**

Serial 108: Unity Movement Historical Notes 1987–1989

Series II

- **Box 1**

Serial 9: Committee for Fort Transfer, 1958
Serial 12: Eluk Hostel, 1940–1955

- **Box 2**

Serial 13: Establishment of Interstate Native College, 1908–1912
Serial 14: Extension of University Education Bill, 1958
Serial 17: Fort Hare History, 1957–1960
Serial 18: Fort Hare Lecturer's Association, 1956–1957
Serial 23: Jubileum publication, 1916–1966
Serial 24: Report on Native Education, 1947

- **Box 3**

Serial 27: NUSAS VI, 1948–1953
Serial 28: NUSAS VII, 1954–1959

- **Box 5**

Serial 43: SRC, 1918–1946

- **Box 6**

Serial 47–51: Establishment of Fort Hare 1909–1915

- **Box 12**

Serial 86: SASO and the Black Consciousness Movement towards black theology
Serial 108: Notes on the Non-European Unity Movement

Fort Harian (student publication)

- June 1951
- August 1951
- September 1951
- November 1951
- April 1953

- March 1954
- April 1955
- April 1956
- Graduation Issue 1959
- April 1960
- October 1960

University Calendars, 1916—Present

Newspaper clippings about Fort Hare from the following publications:

The Alice Times
The Cape Argus
The Cape Times
The Christian Recorder
The Citizen
The Daily Dispatch
Diamond Fields Advertiser
Die Burger
Die Oosterlig
Die Transvaler
Die Volksblad
Drum
The Eastern Province Herald
The Friend
Grocott's Daily Mail
India Views
The Leader
The Natal Daily News
The Natal Mercury
The Natal Witness
The New York Herald Tribune
Port Elizabeth Evening Post
The Pretoria News
The Queenstown Daily Representative
The Rand Daily Mail
The Rhodesia Herald
The Rhodesian Review
The Saturday News
South Africa, London
The Star
Sunday Express
The Sunday Times
The Times, London

Torch
The Windhoek Advertiser
The World

Fort Hare Papers, University of Fort Hare Administration Block (uncatalogued), Alice

Student Record Room

Of the approximately 27 000 student files, I consulted the following:
Jeffrey Baqwa
Selby Baqwa
Orton Chirwa
Herbert Chitepo
Seretse Choabi
Ismail Dada
Sigqibo Dwane
Abdool Karrim Essack
Devilliers Zilindie Galada
Vincent Gobodo
Vadival Ramsamy Govender
Herby Govinden
Helenard Joe Hendrickse
Herbert Temba Hleli
Isaac Mabindisa
Stanley Mabizela
Pumzile Majeke
Sipo Makalima
Henry Makgothi
Andrew Masondo*
Ambrose Makiwane
Kaizer Matanzima
Ivy Matsepe
Joe Matthews
Zachariah Koederling Matthews*
Frank Mdlalose
Dennis Merckel
Jerry Modisane
Billy Modise
Marumo Moerane
Clement Ntsu Mokhehle
Justice Moloto
Nthato Motlana
Thenjiwe Mtintso

Robert Mugabe
C.G. Muhoya
Loganathan Naidoo
Rosette Ndziba
Duma Nokwe
Ratinasabapathy Arumugam Pillay
Godfrey Pitje
Barney Pityana
Kenneth Rachidi
Sizwe Satyo
Kelly Seseane
Fred Simon
George Singh
Dennis Siwisa
Robert Mangaliso Sobukwe
Pelem Galazi Stamper
Makenkesi Stofile
Rama Thumbadoo
Goolan Hoosen Suleman Tootla
Wycliffe Tsotsi
Picton Vernett
Peter Vundla

*Matthews and Masondo were also on staff at Fort Hare and their student files are
   contained within their staff records in the staff room.

Fort Hare History Shelf
- Student statistics, 1916–1958
- Student statistics, 1959
- The high commissioner for India, 1942–1959
- SRC and other committees: volume I, 1945–1950; volume II, 1951–1953;
   volume III, 1954–1959
- Student societies, 1958–1961
- Student matters, 1917–1951
- University land

Other Shelves
- University calendars, 1916–Present
- Student unrest: Fort Hare, 1960–1972
- Document file 1, newspaper clippings re: seminary
- Prof. J.J. Ross, 1963–1967

Staff Record Room
- Staff files
   D.D.T. Jabavu

A.C. Jordan
Andrew Masondo
Z.K. Matthews

- Senate, 1941–1949
- Senate, 1949–1951
- Senate, 1952–1957
- Senate November 1957–1959
- Senate volume 1, 15 February 1960–12 May 1964
- Senate volume 2, 26 May 1964–6November 1967
- Senate volume 5, 16 November 1972–25 May 1976
- Senate minutes volume 3, 27 November 1967–31 August 1970
- Agendas and minutes of Senate meetings, 1960–1973 (33 Binders)
- Council minutes volume 1, 1960–1969–18 June 1975 (Binders 1–19)
- Minutes of Council meetings, 2 March 1928

PRIVATE PAPERS

Thelma Appavoo
Herby Govinden
Mbulelo Mzamane
Rama Thumbadoo
G.S. Tootla
University of Fort Hare offices of Public Affairs and Alumni Relations
Msimelelo Silinga, 'An Open Letter to Fort Hare Alumni', November 1996

LETTERS TO THE AUTHOR

Jeff Baqwa, 'The Role of Jeffrey Dumo Baqwa in the struggle for liberation', 12
    April 1999
Selby Baqwa, 12 May 1999
Mangosuthu Buthelezi, 11 February 1999
Frank Mdlalose, 6 April 1999
Thenjiwe Mtintso, 9 April 1999

BOOKS AND PAMPHLETS

Anthony, David H., III. 'Max Yergan in South Africa: From evangelical Pan-
    Africanist to revolutionary socialist'. *African Studies Review* 34, 2 (September
    1991): 27–55.
Balintulo, M. 'The black universities in South Africa'. In J. Rex (ed.). *Apartheid and
    Social Research.* Paris: Unesco Press, 1981.
Barron, Chris. 'Academic helped pioneer health reform'. *Sunday Times* (12 August
    2001).

Beale, M. 'The task of Fort Hare in terms of the Transkei and Ciskei: Educational policy at Fort Hare in the 1960s'. *Perspectives in Education* 12, 1 (1990): 41–54.

Beard, Terrence. 'Background to student activities at the University College of Fort Hare'. In H.W. van der Merwe and D. Walshe (eds). *Student Perspectives on South Africa.* Cape Town: David Philip, 1972.

Behr, A.L. *Education in South Africa: Origins, Issues and Trends: 1652–1988.* Pretoria: Academica, 1988.

Birnbaum, Norman. *The Crisis of Industrial Society.* New York: Oxford University Press, 1969.

Bradford, Helen. *A Taste of Freedom: The ICU in Rural South Africa: 1924–1930.* New Haven: Yale University Press, 1987.

Brookes, Edward H. *A History of the University of Natal.* Pietermaritzburg: University of Natal Press, 1966.

Brooks, Alan and Jeremy Brickhill. *Whirlwind before the Storm.* London: IDAFSA, 1980.

Burchell, D.E. 'African higher education and the establishment of the South African Native College, Fort Hare'. *South African Historical Journal* 8 (November 1976): 60–83.

Burchell, D.E. 'Alexander Kerr of the University College of Fort Hare: South African liberalism and the domestication of an African intelligentsia'. *Acta Academica,* 23, 2(1991): 1–33.

Burchell, D.E. 'The emergence and growth of student militancy at the University College of Fort Hare in the 1940s and 1950s'. *Journal of the University of Durban-Westville* 3 (1986): 149–167.

Burchell, D.E. 'The pursuit of relevance within a conservative context: The University College of Fort Hare to 1960'. *CON-TEXT* 1 (1988): 45–67.

Burrows, H.R. and Z.K. Matthews. *A Short Pictorial History of the University College of Fort Hare, 1916–1959.* Alice: Lovedale Press, 1961.

Callinicos, Luli. *Oliver Tambo: Beyond the Engeli Mountains.* Claremont: David Philip, 2004.

Calvocoressi, Peter. *South Africa and World Opinion.* London: Oxford University Press, 1961.

Carter, Gwendolyn M., Thomas Karis and Newell M. Stultz. *South Africa's Transkei: The Politics of Domestic Colonialism.* Evanston: Northwestern University Press, 1967.

Cobett, W. and R. Cohen (eds). *Popular Struggles in South Africa.* London: Africa World Press, 1988.

Comaroff, Jean and John. *Of Revelation and Revolution: Christianity, Colonialism, and Consciousness in South Africa,* Volume 1. Chicago: University of Chicago Press, 1991.

De Wet, J.M. *Fort Hare Autonomy, 1970.* Alice: Fort Hare University Press, 1970.

Dreijmanis, J. *The Role of the South African Government in Tertiary Education.* Johannesburg: SAIRR, 1988.

Dunaway, David K. and Willa K. Baum. *Oral History: An Interdisciplinary Anthology.* Nashville: American Association for State and Local History, 1984.

Edgar, Robert (ed.). *An African-American in South Africa: The Travel Notes of Ralph J. Bunche.* Athens, Ohio: Ohio University Press, 1992.

Ellison, Ralph. *Invisible Man.* New York: Vintage, 1995.

Feuer, Lewis. *The Conflict of Generations: The Character and Significance of Student Movements.* New York: Basic, 1969.

Fort Hare Division of Marketing and Communication. 'The Crucible of African Leadership'. Alice: Media Relations and Production Office, 2000.

Frisch, Michael. 'Oral history and the presentation of class consciousness: *The New York Times v. The Buffalo Unemployed*'. In Michael Frisch (ed.). *A Shared Authority: Essays on the Craft and Meaning of Oral and Public History.* Albany: State University of New York Press, 1990: 59–80.

Gastrow, Shelagh. *Who's Who in South African Politics, 5.* Johannesburg: Ravan, 1995.

Gerhart, Gail M. *Black Power in South Africa: The Evolution of an Ideology.* Berkeley: University of California Press, 1978.

Gish, Steven D. *Alfred B. Xuma: African, American, South African.* New York: NYU Press, 2000.

Goodwin, June. *Cry Amandla! South African Women and the Question of Power.* New York: Africana, 1984.

Grele, Ronald (ed.). *Envelopes of Sound: Six Practitioners Discuss the Method, Theory, and Practice of Oral History and Oral Testimony.* Chicago: Precedent, 1975.

Higgs, Catherine. *The Ghost of Equality: The Public Lives of D.D.T. Jabavu of South Africa, 1885–1959.* Athens, Ohio: Ohio University Press, 1997.

Hoffman, Alice. 'Reliability and validity in oral history'. In David K. Dunaway and Willa K. Baum (eds).*Oral History: An Interdisciplinary Anthology.* Nashville: American Association for State and Local History, 1984: 68–73.

Hyslop, Jonathan. *The Classroom Struggle: Policy and Resistance in South Africa, 1940–1990.* Pietermaritzburg: University of Natal Press, 1999.

Jabavu, Noni. *Drawn in Colour.* London: John Murray, 1968.

Jabavu, Noni. *The Ochre People.* Johannesburg: Ravan, 1982.

Jordan, A.C. *The Wrath of the Ancestors.* Alice: Lovedale Press, 1980.

Kallaway, Peter (ed.). *Apartheid and Education: The Education of Black South Africans.* Johannesburg: Ravan, 1984.

Karis, Thomas and Gail Gerhart (eds). *From Protest to Challenge: A Documentary History of African Politics in South Africa, 1882–1990.* Volume 5, *Nadir and Resurgence, 1964–1979.* Bloomington: University of Indiana Press, 1997.

Karis, Thomas and Gwendolyn M. Carter (eds). *From Protest to Challenge: A Documentary History of African Politics in South Africa 1882–1964.* Stanford: Hoover Institution Press. Volume 1, *Protest and Hope, 1882–1934,* by Sheridan Johns III (1972). Volume 2, *Hope and Challenge, 1935–1952,* by Thomas Karis (1973). Volume 3, *Challenge and Violence, 1953–1964,* by Thomas Karis and

Gail Gerhart (1977). Volume 4, *Political Profiles, 1882–1964,* by Gail Gerhart and Thomas Karis (1977).

Kennedy, Elizabeth Lapovsky and Madeline D. Davis. *Boots of Leather, Slippers of Gold: The History of a Lesbian Community.* New York: Penguin, 1994.

Kerr, Alexander. 'University apartheid'. *South African Outlook,* 87 (1957).

Kerr, Alexander. *Fort Hare, 1915–1948: The Evolution of an African College.* Pietermaritzburg: Shuter & Shooter, 1968.

Kros, Cynthia. 'Deep Rumblings': Z.K. Matthews and African Education before 1955'. *Perspectives in Education* 12, 1 (1990): 21–40.

Lipset, Seymour. *Rebellion in the University: A History of Student Activism in America.* London: Routledge & Kegan Paul, 1972.

Lodge, Tom. *Black Politics in South Africa since 1945.* Johannesburg: Ravan, 1997.

Lummis, Trevor. 'Structure and Validity in Oral Evidence'. In Robert Perks and Alistair Thomson (eds). *The Oral History Reader.* London: Routledge, 1998: 273–283.

Luthuli, Albert. *Let My People Go: An Autobiography.* Johannesburg: Collins, 1962.

Mager, Anne Kelk. *Gender and the Making of a South African Bantustan: A Social History of the Ciskei 1945–1959.* Cape Town: David Philip, 1999.

Mandela, Nelson. *The Struggle is my Life.* London: IDAFSA, 1986.

Mandela, Nelson. *Long Walk to Freedom.* Boston: Little, Brown and Co, 1994.

Marks, Shula. *Reluctant Rebellion: The 1906–08 Disturbances in Natal.* Oxford: Oxford University Press, 1970.

Matthews, Frieda. *Remembrances.* Cape Town: Mayibuye, 1995.

Matthews, Z.K. 'Ethnic universities'. *Africa South* 4 (1957).

Matthews, Z.K. *Freedom for My People.* Cape Town: David Philip, 1986.

Matthews, Z.K. 'The University College of Fort Hare'. *South African Outlook* (1 April 1957): 57–78.

Mbeki, Govan. *South Africa: The Peasants' Revolt.* London: IDAFSA, 1984.

Mbeki, Govan. *Learning from Robben Island: The Prison Writings of Govan Mbeki.* Cape Town: David Philip, 1991.

Mbeki, Govan. *The Struggle for Liberation in South Africa: A Short History.* Cape Town: David Philip, 1992.

Meli, Francis. *South Africa Belongs to Us.* Harare: Zimbabwe Publishing House, 1988.

Moodley, K.A. 'The politicization of ethnic universities: Experiences within South Africa's "college brews"'. In P.L. van den Berghe (ed.). *The Liberal Dilemma in South Africa.*
London: Croom Helm, 1979.

Moon, Elaine Latzman. *Untold Tales, Unsung Heroes: An Oral History of Detroit's African-American Community 1918–1967.* Detroit: Wayne State University Press, 1994.

Morrow, S. and K. Gxabalashe. 'Records of the University of Fort Hare'. *History in Africa* 27 (2000): 481–497.

Morrow, Sean and Nwabisa Vokwana. "'Shaping in dull, dead earth their dreams of riches and beauty": Clay modelling at e-Hala and Hogsback in the Eastern Cape, South Africa'. *Journal of South African Studies* 27, 1 (March 2001): 137–161.

Murray, Bruce K. *Wits: The Early Years.* Johannesburg: Witswatersrand University Press, 1982.

Nagel, Julian. *Student Power.* London: Merlin, 1969.

Ndlovu, Sifiso. *The Soweto Uprisings: Counter-Memories of June 1976.* Randburg: Ravan, 1998.

Nkomo, Mokubung. *Student Culture and Activism in Black South African Universities: The Roots of Resistance.* Westport, Connecticut: Greenwood, 1984.

Ntantala, Phyllis. *A Life's Mosaic.* Berkeley: University of California Press, 1993.

Ntloedibe, Elias L. *Here Is A Tree: Political Biography Of Robert Mangaliso Sobukwe.* Mogoditshane, Botswana: Century-Turn, 1995.

Nwauwa, Apollos. *Imperialism, Academe and Nationalism: Britain and University Education for Africans.* London: F. Cass, 1997.

Odendaal, Andre. *Vukani Bantu! The Beginnings of Black Protest Politics in South Africa to 1912.* Cape Town: David Philip, 1984.

Patai, Daphne. *Brazilian Women Speak.* New Brunswick: Rutgers University Press, 1988.

Peires, J.B. *The House of Phalo: A History of the Xhosa People in the Days of their Independence.* Johannesburg: Ravan, 1981.

Perks, Robert and Alistair Thomson (eds). *The Oral History Reader.* London: Routledge, 1998.

Phillips, Howard. *The University Of Cape Town, 1918–1948: The Formative Years.* Cape Town: UCT , 1993.

Pityana, N. Barney, Mamphela Ramphele, Malusi Mpumlwana and Lindy Wilson (eds). *Bounds of Possibility: The Legacy of Steve Biko and Black Consciousness.* Cape Town: David Philip, 1991.

Pogrund, Benjamin. *How Can Man Die Better.* Johannesburg: Jonathan Ball, 1990.

Portelli, Allesandro. 'What makes oral history different'. In Robert Perks and Alistair Thomson (eds). *The Oral History Reader.* London: Routledge, 1998: 63–74.

Roux, Edward. *Time Longer Than Rope: The Black Man's Struggle for Freedom in South Africa.* Madison: University of Wisconsin Press, 1948, repr. 1964.

Sampson, Anthony. *Mandela.* New York: Alfred Knopf, 1999.

Saunders, Christopher and Nicholas Southey (eds). *A Dictionary of South African History.* Cape Town: David Philip, 1998.

Schraeger, Samuel. 'What is social in oral history'. In Robert Perks and Alistair Thomson (eds). *The Oral History Reader.* London: Routledge, 1998: 284–299.

Shepherd, R.H.W. *Lovedale, South Africa: The Story of a Century, 1841–1941.* Alice: Lovedale Press, 1941.

Sobukwe, Mangaliso. *Speeches of Mangaliso Sobukwe, 1949–59.* South Africa: PAC Department of Publicity, 1993.

Sparks, Allister. *The Mind of South Africa.* New York: Alfred A. Knopf, 1990.

Streek, Barry, and Richard Wicksteed. *Render Unto Kaiser: A Transkei Dossier.* Johannesburg: Ravan, 1981.

Switzer, Les. *Power and Resistance in an African Society: The Ciskei Xhosa and the Making of South Africa.* Madison: University of Wisconsin Press, 1993.

Tambo, Adelaide. *Preparing for Power: Oliver Tambo Speaks.* London: Heinemann, 1987.

Temkin, Ben. *Gatsha Buthelezi: Zulu Statesman.* Cape Town: Purnell, 1976.

Thompson, Paul. *The Voice of the Past: Oral History.* Oxford: Oxford University Press, 1978.

Thomson, Alistair. 'Anzac memories: Putting popular memory into practice in Australia'. In Robert Perks and Alistair Thomson (eds). *The Oral History Reader* (London: Routledge, 1998): 300–310.

Tonkin, Elizabeth. *Narrating our Pasts: The Social Construction of Oral History.* Cambridge: Cambridge University Press, 1992.

Walshe, A.P. 'The origins of African political consciousness in South Africa'. *Journal of Modern African Studies* 7, 4 (1969): 583–610.

Walshe, Peter. *The Rise of African Nationalism in South Africa: The African National Congress, 1912–1952.* Berkeley: University of California Press, 1970.

Weaver, Gary and James Weaver (eds). *The University and Revolution.* New Jersey: Prentice-Hall, 1969.

White, T.H.R. 'Z.K. Matthews and the formation of the ANC Youth League at the University College of Fort Hare'. *Kleio* XXVII (1995): 124–144.

White, T.H.R. 'Student Disturbances at Fort Hare in 1955'. *Kleio* XXIX (1997): 115–138.

Williams, Donovan. *A History of the University College of Fort Hare, South Africa, the 1950s: The Waiting Years.* Lewiston, New York: Edward Mellen, 2001.

Willis, Justin. 'Two lives of Mpamizo: Understanding dissonance in oral history'. *History in Africa* 23 (1996): 320–330.

Wilson, Lindy. 'Steve Biko: A life'. In N. Barney Pityana, Mamphela Ramphele, Malusi Mpumlwana and Lindy Wilson (eds). *Bounds of Possibility: The Legacy of Steve Biko and Black Consciousness.* Cape Town: David Philip, 1991.

UNPUBLISHED THESES AND PAPERS

Beale, Mary Alice. 'Apartheid and university education, 1948–1959'. MA thesis, University of the Witwatersrand, 1996.

Bundy, Colin. 'Schooled for life?' The early years and education of Govan Mbeki. Paper presented at the UCT Africa Seminar, 30 March 1994.

Dick, Mary. 'The higher education of a minority group as exemplified by the group at the South African Native College, Fort Hare'. BEd dissertation, UCT, 1934.

Gxabalashe, Khayalethu. 'Church, state and theological education under apartheid: The relationship between the Federal Theological Seminary, the University of Fort Hare, and the South African Government, 1963–1976'. Forthcoming MA thesis, University of Fort Hare.

Ngqongqo, Songezo. 'Mpilo Walter Benson Rubusana 1858–1910: The making of the new African elite in the Eastern Cape'. MA thesis, University of Fort Hare, 1996.

Ngwane, Zolani. 'The 80th anniversary celebrations at Fort Hare: Past as symbol, history as imagination'. Paper presented at the University of Fort Hare Govan Mbeki Research Resource Centre Seminar, 25 February, 1997.

Ngwane, Zolani. 'The politics of campus and community in South Africa: An historical ethnography of the University of Fort Hare'. PhD thesis, University of Chicago, 2001.

Seboni, M.O.M. 'The South African Native College, Fort Hare, 1903–1954: An historical critical survey of its development and an assessment of its influence on the education of the non-European races of South Africa in general, but on the Southern Bantu in particular, together with suggestions for future development'. DEd thesis, UNISA, 1959.

White, T.R.H. 'Lovedale 1930–1955: The study of a missionary institution in its social, educational, and political context'. MA thesis, Rhodes University, 1987.

AUDIO-VISUAL

SABC. 'Fort Hare at 80'. 1996.

Index

Entries in **bold** refer to images.